"This is a learned yet readable journey through some newer frontiers of theology. One hopes that Halton's summons to an imaginative, embodied, active form of theology will get a hearing, especially in the ecclesial spaces where it will be most challenging. It has the potential to transform hearts and minds."
—Christopher B. Hays, D. Wilson Moore Professor of Old Testament and Ancient Near Eastern Studies, Fuller Theological Seminary

"When we reimagine God through the terms of embodiment, our theologies and ethics can then stem from fleshly materiality. When we achieve that kind of embodied theology, we might better be able to see folds of salvation among our communities."
—Robyn Henderson-Espinoza, founder of the Activist Theology Project, transqueer activist, Latinx scholar, public theologian, and author of *Body Becoming: A Path to Our Liberation*

"Bold and challenging, learned and instructive, this book is a must-read for scholars of theology and biblical studies, yet it is readable for laypeople as well. At every step, Halton makes his surprising ideas lucid and accessible, and he constantly keeps their theological and ethical import at the forefront of his discussion. He synthesizes multiple fields of scholarship as wide-ranging as philosophy of cognition and biblical criticism, and he does so constructively and with aplomb."
—Benjamin D. Sommer, Professor of Bible and Ancient Semitic Languages, The Jewish Theological Seminary

"Traditional Christian theology has long maintained that God's identity involves both divine and human dimensions, especially in regard to Jesus of Nazareth. One could in fact say that the humanity of God has been regarded as the proverbial 'key' to universal hope and healing. An interesting paradox of Christian theology is that, having admitted and accentuated the humanity of Jesus, it has nearly always leaned in a docetic direction that denies this humanity in its descriptions of Jesus and in its applications of his life to practical theology. Moreover—and this brings us to Halton's work—traditional theology has for the same reason routinely ignored the scores of biblical texts that depict not only Jesus of Nazareth but also God as utterly human.

Whether one seeks to be a responsible historian or theologian, or a responsible citizen of faith and tradition, Halton's work can help us recover these much-neglected biblical portraits of a God who is at once remote and yet, very often, so much like us."

—Kenton L. Sparks, Provost and Vice President for Academic Affairs, Eastern University

"Halton's bold and innovative approach to understanding the nature of God builds on recent advancements in science, philosophy, theology, and biblical studies. In clear and succinct prose, Halton begins the constructive, synthetic work of reimagining God with a twenty-first-century perspective. This book will surely be a touchstone for those looking for new ways to think about God in the midst of a rapidly changing world."

—Brennan W. Breed, Associate Professor of Old Testament, Columbia Theological Seminary

"A wonderful, engaging, and timely exposition of the Old Testament's humanlike depiction of God and a call to take up the theological responsibility of reimagining the Christian doctrine of God as a result—and in so doing to support the continued vitality of the Christian faith. A marvelous book, which I cannot wait to get into the hands of students and pilgrims."

—Peter Enns, Abram S. Clemens Professor of Biblical Studies, Eastern University, and author of *How the Bible Actually Works*

"Is God like us or profoundly not like us? The Bible suggests the answer to this question is yes, which leaves most readers shaking their heads. Halton cuts incisively through the thickets surrounding our biblical understandings of God, frees them from our misconceptions, and puts them in service to serious, intelligible, and compelling theology. *A Human-Shaped God* is a gift to those who care about what kind of a God the Bible offers us."

—Jacqueline E. Lapsley, Dean and Vice President of Academic Affairs and Professor of Old Testament, Princeton Theological Seminary

"Lifting up questions and challenges surrounding God's embodiment in Jewish and Christian religious traditions, Charles Halton presents a thoughtful account of humanity's wrestling with shape, form, and divine presence. *A Human-Shaped God* is fascinating—a critical meeting point of Hebrew Bible scholasticism, constructive theology, and interpretive imagination!"

—Oluwatomisin Oredein, Assistant Professor in Black Religious Traditions and Constructive Theology and Ethics and Director of the Black Church Studies Program, Brite Divinity School

"Halton provides a fresh look at the theology of the Old Testament by focusing on anthropological aspects of God's nature and character that are often overlooked. He opens conventional exegetical practices to a generative cross-disciplinary conversation with philosophy, science, and the humanities in general, and in so doing, he demonstrates how much we have to gain by adding a 'human-shaped imagination of God' to the work of theological interpretation. This book deserves and rewards close attention by specialists and nonspecialists alike."

—Samuel E. Balentine, Professor Emeritus of Old Testament, Union Presbyterian Seminary

"Charles Halton has written a bold, wide-ranging exposition concerning the imaginative, constructive dynamics of doing theology. His general argument concerns the interface of theology and language, so that the God we get is the God we speak. Language matters! His more specific, granular analysis concerns the way of language in the rendering of God in the Old Testament. This exposition moves in two riffs concerning, in turn, the 'body parts' of Israel's humanly rendered God and the emotive practices attributed to God. Halton's work is open-ended in a way that invites the reader into the ongoing work of theological imagination. The sustained insistence of the biblical text, fully appreciated by Halton, is that God is rendered to be jarringly and winsomely 'humanlike'!"

—Walter Brueggemann, William Marcellus McPheeters Professor Emeritus of Old Testament, Columbia Theological Seminary

A Human-Shaped God

A Human-Shaped God

Theology of an Embodied God

Charles Halton

© 2021 Charles Halton

First edition
Published by Westminster John Knox Press
Louisville, Kentucky

21 22 23 24 25 26 27 28 29—10 9 8 7 6 5 4 3 2 1

All rights reserved. No part of this book may be reproduced or transmitted in any form or by any means, electronic or mechanical, including photocopying, recording, or by any information storage or retrieval system, without permission in writing from the publisher. For information, address Westminster John Knox Press, 100 Witherspoon Street, Louisville, Kentucky 40202-1396. Or contact us online at www.wjkbooks.com.

Unless otherwise indicated, Scripture quotations are from the New Revised Standard Version of the Bible, copyright © 1989 by the Division of Christian Education of the National Council of the Churches of Christ in the U.S.A., and are used by permission. Scripture quotations marked NIV are from *The Holy Bible, New International Version.* Copyright © 1973, 1978, 1984, 2011 by Biblica, Inc.® Used by permission. All rights reserved worldwide. In this book, Scripture may be paraphrased or summarized.

Terry Veling, "Incarnation," in L. Callid Keefe-Perry, *Way to Water: A Theopoetics Primer,* used by permission of Wipf and Stock Publishers, www.wipfandstock.com.

BWHEBB, BWHEBL, BWTRANSH [Hebrew]; BWGRKL, BWGRKN, and BWGRKI [Greek] PostScript® Type 1 and TrueType fonts Copyright ©1994–2015 BibleWorks, LLC. All rights reserved. These Biblical Greek and Hebrew fonts are used with permission and are from BibleWorks (www.bibleworks.com).

Book design by Sharon Adams
Cover design by Marc Whitaker / MTWdesign.net

Library of Congress Cataloging-in-Publication Data

Names: Halton, Charles, 1978– author.
Title: A human-shaped God : theology of an embodied God / Charles Halton.
Description: First edition. | Louisville, Kentucky : Westminster John Knox Press, 2021. | Includes index. | Summary: "Approaches the humanlike accounts of God in the Old Testament as the starting places for theology and uses them to build a picture of the divine"—Provided by publisher.
Identifiers: LCCN 2021037020 (print) | LCCN 2021037021 (ebook) |
   ISBN 9780664265007 (paperback) | ISBN 9781646982219 (ebook)
Subjects: LCSH: God—Biblical teaching. | God—Corporeality. | Bible. Old Testament—Criticism, interpretation, etc. | Anthropomorphism. | Image of God. | God (Christianity)
Classification: LCC BS1192.6 .H35 2021 (print) | LCC BS1192.6 (ebook) | DDC 231.042—dc23
LC record available at https://lccn.loc.gov/2021037020
LC ebook record available at https://lccn.loc.gov/2021037021

Most Westminster John Knox Press books are available at special quantity discounts when purchased in bulk by corporations, organizations, and special-interest groups. For more information, please email SpecialSales@wjkbooks.com.

To Andrew

Contents

Acknowledgments	ix
A Short Note to the Reader	xi

1. Imagining a Human-Shaped God — 1
   The Real God vs. the God of Our Imagination — 2
   Shaping God with Our Words — 11
   An Accurate Understanding of God Is Not of Utmost Importance — 18
   Choosing to Imagine a Full-Orbed God — 23

2. God, Humanlike and Not — 27
   The Chronicler's Kids — 28
   Who's Afraid of Contradiction? — 35
   Metaphor — 39
   God as Hyperobject — 44
   Anthropomorphisms — 46
   But Are They Metaphors? — 48

3. God's Body — 53
   What Is a Body? — 54
   Localized Presence — 57
   God in a Land — 60
   God and the Temple — 62
   God in Wood and Stone — 66
   Temporary Theophanies — 72
   Embodiment — 74
   Gender and Sex — 81

4. God's Mind — 93
- What Is a Mind? — 94
- Mind-Body Connection — 100
- Things God Doesn't Know — 102
- The Goings-On of Earth — 107
- The Ways God Learns — 110
- Changes in God's Mind — 115

5. God's Emotions — 121
- What Is Emotion? — 122
- Love — 128
- Sadness — 135
- Hate — 139
- Anger — 143
- What Does God Do for God's Affects? — 153

6. God's Character — 157
- What Is Character? — 157
- Just — 158
- Patient — 162
- Vengeful — 165
- Jealous — 171
- Forgiving — 177
- Forgetting — 183

7. Embracing a Humanlike God — 189
- A Theology of Hermeneutic Activity — 193
- From Monster to Mystery — 195
- A Basis for Relationship — 201
- A Humanlike God and the Incarnation — 204

Index of Biblical References — 207

Index of Subjects — 210

Acknowledgments

I've worked on this book for at least ten years, from the initial idea to outlining the chapters, to compiling a proposal, to landing a publisher, and, finally, to writing the thing.

The idea began when I read Benjamin D. Sommer's incredible monograph, *The Bodies of God and the World of Ancient Israel* (Cambridge: Cambridge University Press, 2009). Sommer introduced me to a new way of imagining God. In many ways, this book is my attempt to apply Sommer's insights to Christian theology.

Along the way so many people have encouraged, critiqued, read, and asked questions that have made this book what it is.

Saint Matthew's Episcopal Church in Louisville, Kentucky, provided me space to write as their writer-in-residence. The entire community was supportive. Almost each week congregants asked for updates on my progress. The parish's two priests, The Revs. Kelly Kirby and Benjamin Hart, were endless sources of encouragement, prayers, and suggestions when my writing was bogged down and stuck. We shared the Eucharist each Wednesday and stuffed our bellies with tacos biweekly. My other office mates there, Joanne Coleman, Betsy Coomes, Charles Frank, Callie Hausman, Daniel Horton, and Harvey Roberts, provided me with daily fun, camaraderie, and tasty snacks.

Jim Kinney at Baker Publishing helped me form the idea and outline of the book. I am most grateful for all of the wisdom and support he gave me. This book would never have come together without him. While Kinney's associates declined to extend me a contract, Daniel Braden at Westminster John Knox stepped in and acquired the book. Dan has likewise shaped the book in innumerable and incredibly helpful ways. He lent his support to it at a crucial time and, again, without him this project would have withered on the vine.

Many friends and colleagues offered critique on versions of the manuscript: Benjamin Blackwell, Ryan A. Brandt, Brennan Breed, Pete Enns, Christopher B. Hays, Christopher M. Hays, Kathryn House, Tremper Longman,

Oluwatomisin Oredein, Faimon Roberts, and Tyler Witman. I'm sure I'm forgetting some folks, but I appreciate you all so much.

Jonathan Wilson-Hartgrove has given me his friendship and encouragement to continue in the writing life. I might have given it up if it were not for him. Dave Harrity offered me his incredible poetry, which fed my heart and mind as I wrote this book. Dave also introduced me to the field of theopoetics, which has helped me greatly in thinking about the doctrine of God. Brother Paul Quenon, OCSO, also offered me his poetry and his unpublished translations of the Psalms. We discussed many of my ideas in this book as we walked to Thomas Merton's hermitage together. Rob Gibson helped me break through a couple of conceptual logjams. My conversations with Joseph Kelly and Wesley Crouser helped me in earth-moving and unquantifiable ways.

The Collegeville Institute supports, encourages, and helps form hundreds of authors, including me. The Institute is one of my very favorite places in this glorious earth.

My dear friends, Angela Roskop Erisman and T. Michael Law, daily support me in all areas of life, including my work on this book.

My parents underwrote my education, encouraged me to follow my dreams, and give me support even when my ideas cause them discomfort.

My incredible daughter, Grey, was born about the time I had the idea for this book. She has given me so much joy as I have written it. One of the reasons I wrote this book is because I am convinced that for the dominant streams of North American Christianity to have any appeal and meaning for my daughter's generation, they must radically change the ways they view God. This book is a very small contribution to that effort, but hopefully for at least a few people it is a meaningful one.

My wife, Lori, is unflagging in her love and support of all of my life, including this book. She encouraged me to share my ideas with the world even when it meant that sharing my ideas forced me to resign from my dream job as an Old Testament professor at a seminary. Speaking the truth as I see it out of my love for the church has made me have to reimagine my professional life as well as my ideas about God. The process has been difficult but worth it. I would not have been able to make this journey without her, and my life would have far less joy as well.

Finally, I dedicate this book to my brother, Andrew. A few years ago he was lying on his bed resting after we returned from one of his chemo treatments. He turned to me and asked about my book. He wanted to know all about it, what it was about, how far along I was, if I had landed a publisher yet. After I explained the general idea, he told me, "The world needs this book." He did not live to see it published, but I like to think that he is glad this book is now in your hands.

A Short Note to the Reader

Back in the early aughts a group of activists fought plans to build Europe's largest wind farm in the Brindled Moor on Lewis and Harris, the largest island of Scotland's Outer Hebrides.[1] The energy company behind this plan, along with most of Britain's urban population, viewed the moor as a wasteland, a wilderness, a *terra nullius*. They assumed it was empty of life, a barren space of nothing. Those supporting the wind farm wanted to turn this nothing into something, convert its barrenness into electrons. Doing so would obliterate the ecosystems and topography of the moor. But the activists opposing the wind farm had a difficult task. It's hard to save something that people believe is nothing.

The protesters found encouragement in the observation of American geographer Yi Fu Tuan, "It is precisely what is invisible in the land that makes what is merely empty space to one person, a place to another."[2] This was the dilemma the protesters faced. The land wasn't invisible to them, but it was to outsiders. The opponents of the wind farm were mostly locals who knew the moor intimately. They understood that it teems with life, that it is filled with intricate plant and animal systems. In their minds it is anything but barren.

The protesters realized the reason the moor was alive to them and dead to city folks was because urban dwellers lack the vocabulary to understand it. Even people who visited the moor and walked through it for the first time would exclaim, "It's nothing but heather!" They had no idea what bog myrtle was, much less tormentil, milkworts, and sphagnum mosses. It was right under their feet but they couldn't see it. They had no words for what was in front of their eyes. The only terms they could associate with the moor were "vast," "dark," and "empty." Paucity of words made them blind.

One of the leaders of the task force working to prevent the development wrote, "What is required is a new nomenclature of landscape and how we

---

1. This story is taken from Robert Macfarlane, *Landmarks* (London: Hamish Hamilton, 2015), 27–32.
2. This is Barry Lopez's summary of Yi-Fu Tuan's thoughts, as cited by Macfarlane, *Landmarks*, 29.

relate to it, so that conservation becomes a natural form of human awareness, and so that it ceases to be under-written and under-appreciated and thus readily vulnerable to desecration."[3] And so he compiled what he called a counter-desecration phrasebook. It was a list of words with definitions that provide the vocabulary one needs to understand the moor in its fullness and beauty.

Deficient vocabulary affects other relationships in addition to our interaction with the natural world. Painter and writer John Berger observes, "Much of what happens to us in life is nameless because our vocabulary is too poor."[4] And as we've seen, if something is nameless it is often invisible. I have come to believe that our theological discourse suffers from this. The lexicons we use to describe God have many gaps and, accordingly, much of who God is is invisible to us. We might be tempted to believe, however, that our theologies already have rich and deep sets of terms at their disposal. This is partially true.

Theological vocabularies serve a great purpose in giving us "swift, non-laborious, and non-repetitive access" to the content of the Bible.[5] The messages of Scripture are easier to remember when we have specific terms to explain them. We can more easily understand who and what God is when we have a list of adjectives at the ready.[6] But none of our vocabularies comprehensively describe the divine. For instance, theologies that describe a god who knows everything that happens, is at every place at the same time, is constant and unchanging, and does not ultimately have material form describe a god that is very different from the kind of god who inhabits many parts of the Old Testament. On the other hand, theologies that picture a god who is constantly changing and developing don't seem to match the vision of Hebrews 13:8, which pictures Christ as the same "yesterday and today and forever."

As beneficial as theological vocabularies are, they also hem us in and constrain our capacity for imaginative thought.[7] The act of defining God necessarily states what God isn't. It draws a boundary around the ideas that are permissible for us to have about the divine. This was one of the reasons early theologians compiled lists of attributes for God: to prevent the pious from

---

3. Alec Findley, cited by Macfarlane, *Landmarks*, 31.
4. *Confabulations* (London: Penguin, 2016), 107.
5. John Webster, "Biblical Reasoning," *Anglican Theological Review* 90:4 (2008): 750.
6. However, see Kwame Bediako's valuable observation that the desire to produce a detailed, literary theology runs the risk of underappreciating or even denigrating oral and grassroots theologies. *Jesus and the Gospel in Africa: History and Experience* (Maryknoll, NY: Orbis Books, 2004), 17–18.
7. Part of this constraint is purposeful. If theological reflection remains abstract and ethereal instead of concrete and embodied, the systems of power have a far greater chance of staying in place. Eleazar S. Fernandez, *Reimagining the Human: Theological Anthropology in Response to Systematic Evil* (St. Louis: Chalice, 2004), 11–30.

becoming heretics.[8] Theological terms form protective walls that keep our thoughts within prescribed limits.[9] Perhaps in some ways this is good, but an unintended consequence is that our theological constructs often prevent us from reading Scripture well. Theological vocabularies can become thin and ill-fitting when they meet certain passages. The Bible becomes for us a dead space like the Brindled Moor to outsiders. We mine the Old Testament for principles and truths but fail to wrestle with its stories. We eschew its complicated and multitextured presentation of God in favor of more uniform understandings. Ancient authors embedded certain ideas about God in the pages of the Old Testament that we are not able to see. We have been blinded and blinkered by the theologies that were intended to be our aids.[10] Those of us who wish to think about the God of the Old Testament need a counter-desecration phrasebook of our own.

Perhaps this isn't true for all of us. It's a general pattern I've observed and judged to be common. You might see yourself as like the locals of the Brindled Moor, able to clearly understand the God of the Old Testament because you already possess a thick vocabulary. But in the course of compiling a dictionary for their home, the locals of Brindled Moor discovered the ways in which people from other places described *their* geographies. The lexicons of Devon and the Lake District, Gaelic phrases and expressions from Cornwall helped the residents of the Brindled Moor more deeply understand their environment. As expansive as our dictionaries might be, there are always more words to learn.

I am not capable of providing anywhere near a complete vocabulary for theological life. What I hope to do with this book is open space in our imaginations so that we can more fully appreciate the discussions of God within the Old Testament. This book is not a glossary per se. It is, rather, a reflection upon some of the Old Testament passages that are typically regarded as anthropomorphic. In the course of reading these reflections I hope your vocabulary for God expands, becomes wider and richer.

---

8. We should note the power dynamics inherent in labeling some position as heretical and the people who hold them heretics. Marcella Althaus-Reid terms this practice colonial theology, in *The Queer God* (London: Routledge, 2003), 133–71. Colonial theology is a type of theological reflection that tries to conquer other viewpoints and make them submit to one's hegemony. Like Althaus-Reid, I think we need to find new pathways to think about God and revisit those which colonial theologians have cast aside. And, as Althaus-Reid observes, hegemony and conquest always work to keep money and power deeply stratified. *Indecent Theology: Theological Perversions in Sex, Gender and Politics* (London: Routledge, 2000), 16–17. For far too long theology has served this purpose.

9. Of course, it doesn't have to be this way. Timothy Radcliffe suggests that theological formations which were originally intended as boundaries could be reframed as icons "which invite us to carry on our pilgrimage towards the mystery, pushing us beyond too easy answers." *Why Go to Church? The Drama of the Eucharist* (London: Continuum, 2008), 67.

10. Kelly Brown Douglas, *Stand Your Ground: Black Bodies and the Justice of God* (Maryknoll, NY: Orbis Books, 2015), 138–39.

I've tried to read the anthropomorphic passages in the Bible straightforwardly, taking their depictions of God at face value, suppressing the urge to explain them away or harmonize them with other portions of Scripture that seem to say something different. I do this as an experiment. I want to see what our picture of God would look like if we took the anthropomorphic passages as a starting point from which to construct our ideas of God.

Over the years many have objected to this kind of approach. They assert that the humanlike pictures of God in the Old Testament are metaphors and should not be taken literally.[11] They narcotize the anthropomorphic language in the Bible or pretend it isn't there. They scorn the contemporary use of it by claiming that it diminishes the grandeur of the divine. Instead of giving us real insight into the reality of God, they say, it pulls deity out of heaven and reduces God to the status of us dirty mortals.[12] Martin Heidegger did not accept this line of thinking. When people use anthropomorphic language, Heidegger said, "God is not debased to the level of man, but on the contrary, man is experienced in what drives him beyond himself."[13] For Heidegger, anthropomorphic language brings God near, or alternatively, it helps us rise above our situation and imagine God more fully.

I think it is crucially important for our time that we expand our understanding of who God is instead of vigilantly patrolling the theological boundaries we've inherited. This involves listening to religious communities that are different from us, but it also includes listening again to the sacred texts we already hold dear. This act of listening should be done with an eagerness to learn something new, to hear a new voice within familiar stories, to embrace biblical accounts that have been ignored or actively suppressed, and to use these texts to embrace and include folks who are often excluded from religious communities.[14] In the religious tradition I was raised in, the

---

11. For instance, H. H. Rowley sees within the Eden narratives of Genesis a "cruder anthropomorphism" when God asks Adam what he has been doing. About this Rowley asserts, "It should not be overlooked that in the story of the Garden of Eden we can hardly presume that when God asks Adam what he has been doing, he is ignorant of the answer until Adam confesses." *The Faith of Israel: Aspects of Old Testament Thought* (Philadelphia: Westminster, 1956), 60. And Maimonides (1138–1204), perhaps Judaism's greatest philosopher, believed that all biblical language that speaks of God having hands or feet, resting or moving should be regarded as figurative. Warren Zev Harvey, "Notions of the Divine and Human Love in Jewish Thought: An Interview with Warren Zev Harvey," *Journal of Jewish Thought* 3 (2012): 2. In spite of Rowley and Maimonides's assertions, for the purposes of this book I presume that the authors of the Bible mean what they say.

12. William C. Placher describes some aspects of this tendency in the first chapter of *Narratives of a Vulnerable God: Christ, Theology, and Scripture* (Louisville: Westminster John Knox, 1994), 3–26.

13. Martin Heidegger, *Schelling's Treatise on the Essence of Human Freedom* (Athens: Ohio University Press, 1985), 163.

14. The Bible can be used for whatever purpose a person has in mind. Someone can quote it to shame or ostracize folks, or Scripture can be "the most important source for the articulation

so-called anthropomorphic descriptions of God in the Bible were sidelined the most often (along with depictions of powerful women in the Bible, as well as instructions to release people from debt and transfer the wealth of the powerful to the poor).

In this book I offer what I think are some of the Old Testament's underappreciated conceptions of God that depict God as a humanlike being. I do not harmonize them with other passages. In this, I am following the model of most biblical authors. Even the few times harmonizations are included in the Bible, as I argue in chapter 2, their presence further reinforces the desire of the Bible's compilers to preserve differences instead of editing them out. They did not see the need to arbitrate every interscriptural disagreement and make the Bible's witness consistent. So I let tensions remain in flex. I do not attempt to reduce or mitigate the conflict between them.

In the last chapter I offer some implications of imagining a god with humanlike features. I use the insights of the eminent Jewish biblical scholar Benjamin Sommer to show how the humanlike God of the Old Testament lays a pathway for the New Testament understanding of the incarnation. Not only will this help Christians better understand Jesus, but I hope it will help deepen Christian appreciation of and dependence upon the Jewish Scriptures and Jewish interpretations.

In this book I do not attempt to construct a comprehensive treatment of the anthropomorphic Old Testament God. The passages I discuss are representative but not exhaustive. I want to leave room for the reader's imagination. Oftentimes we think of theology as a CliffsNotes version of the Bible—a short summation of the entirety of what the Bible communicates. We want to boil Scripture down to its essence so we can know exactly what it says. There is a danger to this approach. It is the same danger that Andre Dubus describes in relation to short stories:

> Wanting to know absolutely what a story is about, and to be able to say it in a few sentences, is dangerous: it can lead us to wanting to possess a story as we possess a cup. We know the function of a cup and we drink from it, wash it, put it on a shelf, and it remains a thing we own and control, unless it slips from our hands into the control of gravity; or unless someone else breaks it, or uses it to give us poisoned tea. A story can always break into pieces while it sits inside a book on a shelf; and, decades after we have read it even twenty times, it can open us up, by cut or caress, to a new truth.[15]

---

of liberation in the experience of [a community of] people." Demetrius K. Williams, "The Bible and Models of Liberation in the African American Experience," in *Yet with a Steady Beat: Contemporary U.S. Afrocentric Biblical Interpretation*, ed. Randall C. Bailey (Leiden: Brill, 2003), 33–60.

15. *Meditations from a Movable Chair* (New York: Vintage, 1999), 49.

We can, I believe, discern the outline of the God of the Old Testament, God's basic shape, but the features of the divine face—the color of his eyes, the shape of her nose, the thickness of their lips—remain in the shadows. God's shadowy appearance reinforces the idea that we can never distill God into a bullet-pointed list of theological observations. The divine resists domestication, refuses to be owned.

As I discuss in chapter 1, it is difficult to predict what it will look like when we integrate a humanlike God into existing theological understandings. Our picture of God is complicated. It's a three-dimensional web. Add a new feature or take one out and the entire structure shifts. Some will regard this as an unacceptable risk and choose to stay within the confines of the theological houses they've already built. I can understand that fear, and sometimes I feel it too. But I also see this as an exciting journey. The great Trappist mystic Thomas Merton believed that the most vibrant and life-giving approach to God is through the imagination.[16] In these pages I use the Hebrew Bible's humanlike portrayals of the divine as fuel for my reimagination of the doctrine of God.

I think these types of reimagination are journeys we *must* take in order for theological reflection to have continued relevance in our age. One of my favorite quotes is from the German theologian Ernst Käsemann, "Christianity does not live on canned goods, especially not from such as are no longer edible and digestible."[17] We can learn much from the theologies of the past, but each generation must reassess what they have received from their forebears and learn to speak in new ways that better fit the contexts they find themselves in. Clayton Crockett captures this well when he defines theology as "an open-ended discourse about value and meaning in an ultimate sense."[18] Theology is an ongoing process. It is not merely the recollection of answers previously decreed in the dusty past.[19]

---

16. Merton wrote, "Why would one suppose that God can be approached dully, without imagination?" This quote is from Frederick Smock in his discussion of Merton in *Pax Intrantibus: A Meditation on the Poetry of Thomas Merton* (Frankfort, KY: Broadstone Books, 2007), 47.

17. "What 'To Believe' Means in the Evangelical Sense," in *On Being a Disciple of the Crucified Nazarene*, ed. Rudolf Landau, trans. Roy A. Harrisville (Grand Rapids: Eerdmans, 2010), 162. For more sustained reflection on the need to think differently about God in order for religion to remain vital and alive in our time, see Sallie McFague, *Models of God* (Minneapolis: Fortress, 1987), 34. Elizabeth A. Johnson put it this way: "To be plausible to any generation, Christian faith must express itself in ways consistent with the understanding of the world at the time." *Ask the Beasts: Darwin and the God of Love* (London: Bloomsbury, 2014), 9.

18. *Radical Political Theology: Religion and Politics after Liberalism* (New York: Columbia University Press, 2013), 50.

19. See the excellent discussions of this topic in James H. Cone, *For My People: Black Theology and the Black Church* (Maryknoll, NY: Orbis Books, 1984), 28–30; John F. Haught, *God after Darwin: A Theology of Evolution* (Boulder, CO: Westview, 2000), 185–91; and Sarah Coakley, *God, Sexuality, and the Self: An Essay "On the Trinity"* (Cambridge: Cambridge University Press, 2013), 40–41.

Consider this book an opportunity to begin a new way of thinking about God. It is an opportunity to imagine God as a being who is very similar to humanity instead of totally other. The idea came to me when I was reading Augustine's comments on Psalm 130. Augustine was troubled by the descriptions of God in this psalm that are profoundly human. He dismissed them whole-cloth in a rather patronizing way:

> If you think of God in carnal terms you go seriously astray. And you are being very childish even if you think of God in terms appropriate for the human soul: if, for instance, you think that God forgets, or has the wrong idea about something and changes his mind, or does something and then regrets it. All of these things are indeed said of him in scripture, but only to make us milk-nourished infants feel at home with God, not to encourage us to take them literally.[20]

I started to wonder: What if Augustine is wrong? What if God speaks to us not as milk-nourished infants but as full-grown human beings? What if all those Old Testament passages that depict God in very humanlike ways communicate something profoundly true that many Christians underappreciate? What if we take the authors of Scripture at their word when they say that God has a body? What if, rather than pushing these thoughts away, we add them to our theological lexicons?

I invite you to imagine yourself as a resident of the Brindled Moor who, in the course of trying to better understand how to communicate their understanding of their beloved home to other people, discovered that the vocabularies of folks from other places deepened their knowledge of the place in which they lived. Some Jewish and Christian communities have long embraced a theology of God that emphasizes God's immanence, and many religious communities have understood God in anthropomorphic ways.[21] Those of you who, like me, were taught to focus on God's transcendence have much to learn from these communities. But we will also discover how recent insights within the humanities and sciences can reframe all of our readings of Scripture and change the ways in which every tradition imagines God.

---

20. *Expositions of the Psalms 121–150*, trans. Maria Boulding (Hyde Park, NY: New City, 2004), 150.

21. For instance, many Eastern Orthodox theologians emphasize the anthropomorphic aspects of theology (John Behr, *Becoming Human: Meditations on Christian Anthropology in Word and Image* [Crestwood, NY: St. Vladimir's Seminary Press, 2013]), and many African American and Latinx communities stress God's immanence. See, for instance, M. Shawn Copeland, *Knowing Christ Crucified: The Witness of African American Religious Experience* (Maryknoll, NY: Orbis Books, 2019); Barbara A. Holmes, *Joy Unspeakable: Contemplative Practices of the Black Church*, 2nd ed. (Minneapolis: Fortress, 2017); Noel Leo Erskine, *Plantation Church: How African American Religion Was Born in Caribbean Slavery* (Oxford: Oxford University Press, 2014); and Miguel A. De La Torre, *Latina/o Social Ethics: Moving beyond Eurocentric Moral Thinking* (Waco, TX: Baylor University Press, 2010).

Studying the accounts of the humanlike god of the Old Testament should not merely be an exercise in knowledge acquisition. As biblical scholar Carolyn Sharp puts it, "Reading is potentially transformative for readers and for reading communities."[22] The way we read matters. It can profoundly change the way we move through the world. I hope you find that the biblical accounts of a human-shaped God are fertile material for this process of transformation.

And, finally, an explanation regarding my use of the word *Yahweh* to refer to the personal name of God that appears in the Hebrew Bible. It is common for translations to use the title Lord in all caps to indicate God's name since within Jewish tradition the name of God was not pronounced out of respect for the divine and to avoid the possibility of using God's name in a less than reverent manner. However, within the biblical period, the name was pronounced.

It appears in shortened form within personal names such as Jeremiah. Hebrew personal names were often sentences that contained significant theological meaning. The name Jeremiah is composed of two parts: a verb from the root *rmh*, which means "to place, give, or establish" and a shortened form of the divine personal name. Jeremiah's name means "Yahweh has given (the child)."

At some point, likely the intertestamental period, scribes within the Jewish community began using various conventions to indicate that readers should avoid pronouncing God's personal name. They used star-shaped symbols in place of the divine name or kept the consonants of the divine name in place but noted that the reader should say the title "the Lord" instead of vocalizing the name itself. With every good intention, these scribes put a "fence around the Torah" (Pirkei Avot 1:1) or a guardrail to keep people from misusing the divine name. If one never used the divine name, the thinking went, one could never misuse it.

This benefit came at a price. When the personal name of God is swapped for a title or a jumble of symbols, God seems more distant, less humanlike. I have the utmost respect for my Jewish and Christian friends who continue the reverent practice of not pronouncing God's name, and I have no desire at all to change their practice. However, for the purposes of this book, a book which aims to highlight the humanlike features of God, that practice does not fit. Therefore, I will use the reconstructed name of God while at the same time respecting the fact that others do not share this approach.[23]

Ascension Day, May 2021

---

22. *Wrestling the Word: The Hebrew Scriptures and the Christian Believer* (Louisville: Westminster John Knox, 2010), 2.

23. Some scholars assert that the vocalization, Yahweh, is a hypothetical reconstruction and that we do not know for certain that this was the way the divine name was originally pronounced. While this is technically true, the reconstruction has a high enough probability of being correct that I feel comfortable using it.

1

Imagining a Human-Shaped God

Say you enter your friend's office. The first thing you notice is the mess. There are papers everywhere, and stacks of books line the walls. As you stand in the doorway, surprised at the disarray, you notice a brown table by the window. You comment on its beautiful construction and remark that its chestnut color is particularly striking.

"Chestnut?" your friend replies. "It's not chestnut, it's tobacco brown."[1]

A debate about the precise color of a desk might seem trivial, but the question of whether two people see the same thing when they perceive an object has preoccupied philosophers from antiquity to today. What we think about this topic has far-reaching implications. If two people see different colors when they look at the same object, can we say that they actually see the same things? And if people see different things when they look at objects in the world they can touch, what happens when we contemplate a god who exists beyond the material plane?

It turns out, I hope to show, that no two people imagine God in the same way. Our understandings of God might agree at substantial points, but they will never be identical. Our perceptions of the divine come to us through our bodies and are interpreted in light of the total experience of our inner lives. Since everyone's inner life is unique, our picture of God will be unique as well.

This is not the way people have traditionally understood their thoughts, religious and otherwise. Most people in European-influenced cultures assumed the idea of God they held in their heads matched the God of the reality outside their bodies. When they interpreted the Bible they assumed

---

1. This is a creative retelling of a passage from the first chapter of Bertrand Russell's *The Problems of Philosophy* (Oxford: Oxford University Press, 1997), 7–16.

they understood its correct meaning. And when they looked out at the world they assumed that what they saw was identical to what the objects really were. Most philosophers and scientists no longer have this confidence.

Scholars now know that each person sees something slightly different when they look at the world. Instead of looking at our friend's desk and assuming they see the same chestnut brown that we do, we must assume that our friend perceives something similar but by no means exactly the same as what we see. If this is true, and from what follows I think you will agree it is, the ways we think about God and engage with Scripture must radically change. The humanlike portrayals of God in the Old Testament can help us with this. But before we turn to biblical accounts of God, we should examine more closely a long-running debate regarding the colors humans see. Unless we understand how humans see the world with their eyes, we will not understand how we apprehend God in our minds.

THE REAL GOD VS. THE GOD OF OUR IMAGINATION

The Greek philosopher Democritus (born ca. 460 BCE) observed that there is only one reality. However, Democritus believed that this one reality is present in at least two places at the same time—in outer space and inside an individual's mind.[2] When we look at a star in the night sky we know the star exists millions of miles away, but an image of that star also appears inside our minds as our brains reconstruct its appearance from the sensations our minds receive through our eyes.

Later philosophers noticed there was slippage between these two iterations of reality. They discovered that the world we perceive in our heads never fully matches up with the reality that is outside of our skin. At the most obvious level, our eyes occasionally trick us. We think we see a pool of water in the desert, then discover it is only a mirage. This is an exceptional situation, but in some ways our eyes trick us all the time. For instance, we take an apple in our hands and believe it to be solid when, on an atomic level, it is almost entirely empty space. And, as we saw above, different people see different things when they look at the same object. One person sees a greenish apple while another considers it pale yellow. What explains the difference between the one reality out there and the many images of reality inside our heads?

---

2. William James, "Does Consciousness Exist?," *Journal of Philosophy, Psychology and Scientific Methods* 1:18 (1904): 481.

Mediated Sensations

The eighteenth-century philosopher Immanuel Kant said that when humans interact with something, they do not experience the object in itself. Instead, we perceive things through the sensations of our bodies and then our minds reconstruct inside our heads the objects we experience out in the world.[3] Nerves in my hand send signals to my brain that the apple I am holding is exerting pressure on my skin, but my mind itself never comes in contact with the apple. Every experience, in Kant's line of thought, is a mediated one. That is to say, we do not directly experience anything, including the feeling I get when I hold an apple. My brain receives signals sent by nerves in my skin and my eyes receive the light refracted by the apple's surface, but my brain does not directly apprehend it. Every sensation my brain uses to construct an understanding of the apple is a *derivative and secondary* sensation.

We do not even have direct experience of the status of our own bodies. If we are hungry, nerves in our stomach send impulses to our brain that signal unease. Our brain then interprets this signal in light of the totality of our experience. Perhaps we recall the times when our discomfort dissipated after we ate. Our mind then assumes that our present state of unease signals hunger. Through all of this our frontal cortex does not split off from the rest of our brain, travel down our spinal column, and meet up with our stomach for a direct encounter. Information is relayed between the nerves in our stomach and our head. Our brain takes this information and creates a thought or an image out of it.[4] But our brain never directly encounters anything.

In any case, we need to return to the analogy of the table in our friend's office. The twentieth-century philosopher Bertrand Russell was the first person to use this analogy. Russell imagined that if someone visited his office and looked at his table, his guest would see a slightly different color than he would:

---

3. Immanuel Kant, *Prolegomena to Any Future Metaphysic*, ed. Paul Carus (Chicago: Open Court, 1912), §32.

4. As an intriguing aside, some physicists believe that information—a series of binary yes-or-no answers—came before matter and provided the structure for the physical universe. John Archibald Wheeler memorably phrases this theory as "it from bit," that is, the material substance of the universe (it) came out of a series of information (bit), in "Information, Physics, Quantum: The Search for Links," in *Foundations of Quantum Mechanics in the Light of New Technology: Proceedings of the 3rd International Symposium, Central Research Laboratory, Hitachi, Ltd., Kokubunji, Tokyo, Japan, August 28–31, 1989*, ed. Shun-ichi Kobayashi and Nihon Butsuri Gakkai (Tokyo: Physical Society of Japan, 1989), 354–68. A form of this idea also appears in Hernan Diaz's novel, *In the Distance* (Minneapolis: Coffee House Press, 2017), where a naturalist discovers that humans "progressed from a shapeless intelligent being that was our remote but direct ancestor. A bodiless brain . . . The inescapable and stunning conclusion of this was that human intelligence, in some form, must have preceded all organic matter on earth" (64–65).

> Although I believe that the table is "really" of the same colour all over, the parts that reflect the light look much brighter than the other parts, and some parts look white because of reflected light. I know that, if I move, the parts that reflect the light will be different, so that the apparent distribution of colours on the table will change. It follows that if several people are looking at the table at the same moment, no two of them will see exactly the same distribution of colours, because no two can see it from exactly the same point of view, and any change in the point of view makes some change in the way the light is reflected.[5]

Russell's point is that each person will see something slightly different when they look at the same object. Again, this is because people do not see objects themselves; our brains create images of what they see based on the sensations they receive as light enters the eye.

The standard human eye contains three types of cone receptors. Each type of receptor is able to detect different wavelengths of light that correspond to the colors we perceive as blue, green, and red. When light hits the eye, the receptors transmit to the brain the intensity of the light they detect, and the brain interprets these signals in various ways. Some of these interpretations are physiological. For instance, the brain tries to correct for variations in light so that colors appear fairly uniform to us even when viewed under different circumstances, such as dim or bright light. The brain makes other interpretations based upon our life experience. For example, we classify the colors we see based upon delineations we are taught. We see a color and might label it green. Classifications of color are a product of one's culture. Delineations of color are, for the most part, learned instead of being intrinsic to the strict physiology of the eye and brain (remember, human receptors detect only three different wavelengths). Different societies interpret colors differently. Ancient Mesopotamians thought that grass and gold were the same color—the color we call green.[6] And even within our own society there is no consensus as to which wavelength corresponds to real green, a green without tinge of yellow or blue.[7] From the eye's physiological capabilities and a person's cultural experience, the mind constructs a composite mental picture of what is before a person's eyes.[8] I should note that this is the

---

5. *The Problems of Philosophy* (Oxford: Oxford University Press, 1997), 2.
6. Benno Landsberger, "Über Farben im Sumerisch-Akkadischen," *Journal of Cuneiform Studies* 21 (1967): 139–73.
7. C. L. Hardin, "Byrne and Hilbert's Chromatic Ether," *Behavioral and Brain Sciences* 26:1 (2003): 32–33.
8. Guy Deutscher, *Through the Language Glass: Why the World Looks Different in Other Languages* (New York: Metropolitan Books, 2010), 241–50.

current *theory* of how humans see. As with every theory, it may change or become more refined in the future.

In Bertrand Russell's example, he and his guest are standing in different parts of the room and so their eyes receive different qualities of light reflecting from the table's surface. Light enters their eyes at different angles and one person may see a shady refraction while the other receives the full force of the sun coming through the open window. This creates a different perception of color within each of their minds. Furthermore, the foreground and background in a person's field of vision will also change their perception of the table's color. If one person sees the table against a white wall their perception of brown will be quite different from that of someone who views the table against a dark gray or checkered backdrop. This is because our brains interpret the color of a particular object within the entire environment the object is in. We do not perceive the color of one specific object in isolation from all the other things in our field of view.[9] Every single variation in our immediate environment contributes to the way colors appear to us.

God is similar to Bertrand Russell's table, in that each person contemplates God from a different point of view. We don't see God directly with our eyes, but we think about God in various ways and from particular stances. We might read about God in sacred texts, we could observe the works of God in the natural world, and we may feel the presence of God during a meditation sit. It is crucially important to understand that all of these ways of apprehending God are mediated. That is, none of the ways we perceive God are direct. Like Russell's guest who saw the light bouncing off the table's surface, our bodies mediate our experiences of God.

Even the experiences we think are the most direct are, nonetheless, mediated. This is always true even in practices like contemplative prayer that try to silence the mind so that the body may experience full union with God.[10] But even in this act, humans are never able to escape their bodies. As Thomas Aquinas observed when he often quoted Aristotle, "Nothing in the mind if not first in the senses." Even when a person empties themselves of conscious

---

9. Adhémar Gelb, "Colour Constancy," in *A Source Book of Gestalt Psychology*, ed. W. D. Ellis (London: Kegan Paul, Trench, Trubner, 1938), 196–209.

10. For instance, the author of a medieval work of Christian mysticism, *The Cloud of Unknowing*, describes a form of prayer in which a person sets aside their logical mind and seeks to unite their consciousness directly with that of God. As Simon Tugwell describes it, "The contemplative does not 'see God'; he enters God's seeing. The abolition of any clear notion of God in the cloud of unknowing thus goes with the abolition of any clear awareness of the knowing subject. Our being must approach God in such nakedness that it is clothed not even in itself." Preface to *The Cloud of Unknowing* (Classics of Western Spirituality; Mahwah, NJ: Paulist, 1981), xxii.

thought and has what they interpret as sensations of the divine presence, these feelings come to that person through their sensory systems and are interpreted by their brain. The experience of emptiness is a product of this. How does human emptiness feel? Maybe we read about this in a book or heard someone talk about it. We then took this cultural information and meshed it with how our particular meditation sit felt to our sensory system. This is a constructed reality. Part of it arises from the set of expectations we bring to meditation, and another part from the state of our bodies, and another part from the processing of our mind. If we experience God's mystical presence, we sense it through these channels. There simply is no other way for us to be. Every apprehension is interpreted from our particular point of view and from the life experience we have had.

Interpreted Ideas

Some might object to this by asserting that God is more of an idea than an object. That is, God is *not* like Bertrand Russell's desk because Russell's guest could walk across the room and touch the desk if she wanted. It is not like this with God, some might argue. Rather, humans create ideas about God from teachings they hear, religious texts they read, and rituals they perform. God resides in our heads as a concept and within our emotions as a feeling, but since God is not a physical object to us, it could be argued, our ideas of God are not open to the same interpretive dimensions as Russell's table. We read a religious text that was authored by someone who had a direct experience of God, and in doing so we imagine that we share in their direct experience. In this way, our perception of God is immediate and direct even if it is simultaneously borrowed.

This proposal may be attractive on some level, but if the apprehension of God is so free of interpretation, why are there so many different religions, sects, and denominations? What we find, I believe, is that ideas are just as mediated and interpreted as objects, maybe even more so. Philosopher Slavoj Žižek asserts this in his magnum opus, *The Parallax View*. He says that *all* human perception is mediated, both tangible and intangible. There is no way for a person to attain a Godlike point of view of anything. We see and understand things within particular contexts and with specific constraints.[11] This means that everything we see and think is always changing because our points of view constantly shift and we continually have new experiences that shape

---

11. This is even more true for theological discourse that is set within historical traditions. As much as we would like to think we are above or outside of these traditions, it is impossible to fully extricate ourselves from them. Rubén Rosario Rodríguez, *Racism and God-Talk: A Latino/a Perspective* (New York: New York University Press, 2008), 6.

how we interpret our sensations. It is important to underscore that not only do our perceptions of *objects* change depending upon the place from which we look at them but so do *ideas*.[12]

One of the constraints that shape our apprehension of the world is the sensory system our body uses to convey information to our brains. These systems develop and become more precise as we grow up, but once we reach a certain age they slowly degrade. A person may hate the taste of stinky cheese in their youth, love it in middle age, and no longer be able to taste much of it in their nineties. Even if the quality of our bodily senses is somewhat stable, the reservoir of our life experience against which our minds interpret the body's sensations is continually expanding. We experience new events and have more thoughts.[13] Our minds constantly reformulate and reposition ideas based upon the new information and experience they receive. For instance, I work through lunch and by midafternoon my stomach hurts. I eat a snack and the aching stops. After several days of this pattern, I correlate an aching stomach with hunger. Every time my stomach is upset I reach for something to eat. One day I see an advertisement for a pill that kills stomach parasites. I never knew such a thing existed. When my stomach hurts the following day, I cannot shake the idea that maybe there is a worm in my belly. My life experience now interprets the *same bodily sensations* in a new and very different way.

Our understandings of God are similarly reinterpreted in light of our changing life experiences.[14] Elizabeth Johnson frames this memorably:

> A human person is a dynamic unity of matter and spirit, an embodied spirit in the world. Far from the body being a dispensable container for the soul, corporal and spiritual dimensions form one unified being. Humans experience themselves as a unity in the way they know and question, with their physical senses interacting with their mind, and the way they desire and love which likewise engages bodily and spiritual dimensions.[15]

Say we imagine God to be a kind and benevolent deity who actively controls everything that takes place. This picture of God may shift after a loved one dies unexpectedly. Perhaps we no longer believe God to be kind, or perhaps we now believe that God's involvement with the world is less direct than we

---

12. Slavoj Žižek, *The Parallax View* (Cambridge: MIT Press, 2006), 17–18.
13. Keith Ward, *The Christian Idea of God: A Philosophical Foundation for Faith* (Cambridge: Cambridge University Press, 2017), 28.
14. We will explore this point more deeply later in this book. A fantastic discussion of the intersection of one's personal experience and theology can be found in Pamela R. Lightsey, *Our Lives Matter: A Womanist Queer Theology* (Eugene, OR: Pickwick, 2015), 1–14.
15. *Ask the Beasts: Darwin and the God of Love* (London: Bloomsbury, 2014), 175.

previously thought. Whatever is the case, it is unlikely that a major life event will leave our understanding of God unchanged.[16]

Let's consider once again the act of physical sight and by analogy theological sight. What if we imagine how Bertrand Russell's table would appear to an animal? Compared to many nocturnal animals who have only one type of photoreceptor in their eyes, the human eye with its three receptors is very advanced. When an animal with one receptor looks at Russell's desk it might see a dark monochromatic outline instead of a shiny and textured brown desk. However, compared to the mantis shrimp, which has sixteen types of receptors, human vision is downright neolithic.[17] What would a mantis shrimp see when it looked at Russell's table? Perhaps it would see a complex rainbow of browns.

If some animals are able to apprehend colors better than humans, are some animals able to sense God more precisely? This may seem like a bizarre question. Most people assume that animals do not sense God because animals are not able to communicate abstract thought. But one can have thoughts and not have the ability to communicate them. Think of paralyzed individuals who cannot move their vocal cords but can still think. Furthermore, abstract thought is not needed to apprehend God, at least according to prominent philosopher Charles Hartshorne. Hartshorne says that in classical religious understanding God influences everything that is. If this is true, since many animals have highly sensitive systems that they use to understand their surroundings, when animals experience the world they necessarily sense the God that influenced it.[18] What exactly animals feel and think about their perceptions of the divine is not known, but from a theological perspective it is undeniable that they do at least sense the influences of God.

What, then, does a mantis shrimp think when it looks out at the world? Does it sense a different kind of God than we do because it sees the world more precisely and in richer color than we are able to? I am not able to answer any of this and I doubt anyone else can either. In this book I'll set aside the question of religion and animals and limit my discussion to human understandings of God, which are diverse enough already. But these questions

---

16. It is certainly possible, and for many people it is the case, that their understanding of God seems to remains static no matter what life experiences they have or what new information they learn. In these situations it may be that this person has purposely closed off the possibility of new interpretations and consciously resists change. Change is likely taking place, however, even if it is minor. Other people may be unaware of the changes taking place in their mental lives because they are inattentive. Ellen J. Langer, *Mindfulness*, 25th anniv. ed. (Boston: Da Capo, 2014), 116 and 96, respectively.

17. Mazviita Chirimuuta, *Outside Color: Perceptual Science and the Puzzle of Color in Philosophy* (Cambridge: MIT Press, 2015), 4–5.

18. Daniel A. Dombrowski, *Hartshorne and the Metaphysics of Animal Rights* (Albany: State University of New York Press, 1998), 64.

should begin to open our imaginations to the possibility that God is quite different in reality from the images of God we have in our individual heads.

It can be disconcerting to learn that the reality we hold in our minds is different from reality-as-it-is.[19] This might lead some of us to conclude that we cannot know anything, that knowledge itself is beyond our grasp, including knowledge of God. While it is true that we do not have the capacity to know things directly and that we cannot apprehend things as they really are, this should not leave us in despair. A Christian way of moving through the world should already assume that our perceptions are murky at best. Paul puts it this way in 1 Corinthians 13:12: "For now, we can only see a dim and blurry picture of things, as when we stare into polished metal."[20] The apostle Paul took it for granted that he could not understand reality as it fully is.

Our sensory systems convey to our minds limited and partial apprehensions of reality. This includes experiences of the divine. And our mental perceptions are somewhat fluid, since they are interpreted in light of new and changing experiences. In spite of this, we are able to use our bodily senses to navigate the world fairly well. The human species has existed and replicated for at least six million years. Our sensory and interpretive systems have been remarkably effective at helping us survive on earth. That is how they are designed.

Our vision is not meant to identify absolute true green. Our eyes are not built to detect the platonic ideal of red. Sight is meant to guide our activity through the world, to help us survive by avoiding dangers and locating food.[21] Our eyes might not be able to differentiate slight shades of turquoise, but we can easily spot a red apple against green foliage. For the purpose of locating food, it does not matter if I see true red when I see an apple in a tree. My ability to see color helps me find a ripe piece of fruit. And if I am able to do that, my sensory systems have accomplished their purpose.

Instead of understanding human sight as a process by which the human eye discovers the true color of an object-as-it-is, Mazviita Chirimuuta, one of the leading philosophers of color theory, provides a different understanding of sight:

---

19. Every single utterance a person can possibly make is debated in academic circles so, naturally, there are folks who take issue with the idea that external reality really exists. I do not believe it makes much sense to debate whether external reality is there because if it is not, everything we experience is a false projection, including the debate of whether reality is a projection, and if one believes this then at the end of the day one is merely arguing with oneself because the self is all that exists and everything else is a projection. Arguing with myself does not seem very productive so I'll refrain from doing it any longer here. Not everyone is like me, though. Those interested in pursuing this debate could do worse than starting with David Chalmers, *The Character of Consciousness* (Oxford: Oxford University Press, 2010). Then again, does Chalmers exist or is he a figment of my imagination . . . ?

20. This translation is from *The Voice* (Nashville: Nelson, 2012).

21. Chirimuuta, *Outside Color*, 110.

What and how we see depends on us—our retinal sensitivities to ambient light, our other neural equipment, and our habitual ways of looking around. Ultimately, of course, visual experience is shaped by all the things around us. Color vision is a joint product of the perceiver and perceived.[22]

We see the world not as it is, but as we idiosyncratically receive and interpret it.[23] Nevertheless, we are not automatically led astray by our inability to see things-in-themselves. In normal conditions when our sensory systems are functioning properly, they are dependable guides that help us live in the world.

I have outlined how human vision functions to show that what we see of the world is highly dependent upon the condition of our physical sensory systems as well as the experiential background of our lives and the assumptions we make about the universe. Our minds create what we see; they do not merely receive the world as it is. We might be tempted to dismiss the relevance of this analogy to the way we form our ideas about God because for many of us the primary way we believe we construct our understanding of God is by reading the Bible. We might assume that the act of reading is different from looking out at the world. After all, various authors of Scripture give us the meaning of the events they witness. They do not merely report what happened when they claimed to hear or see God. They provide a description of an event as well as their interpretation of it. Yet a similar process occurs when our eyes scan a page as when our eyes look out at the world.

When we read, our brains construct meaning by decoding a series of symbols. The ideas of God we get from reading a book are just as dependent upon our individual sensory systems as is our apprehension of color. We rely on sight or (in the case of a blind person) touch or sound to apprehend linguistic symbols. We then decode and interpret these symbols in light of the grammatical rules we have learned, our life experiences, and our assumptions. Giosuè Baggio, a professor of psycholinguistics, describes it this way:

> The processing speed of the human sensory apparatus contributes to producing the impression that, in reading text or listening to speech, information uptake is nearly instantaneous and that the meanings of words and sentences are *given* to us as though they were part of the input. However, this impression is mistaken, as one can realize when reading a text or listening to a conversation in a foreign language. . . . This suggests that language comprehension is rather a *process* that

---

22. Chirimuuta, *Outside Color*, 17.
23. As Karl Ove Knausgaard said, "But the visible world is not objective reality, it appears to each individual as seen by them." *So Much Longing in So Little Space: The Art of Edvard Munch*, trans. Ingvild Burkey (New York: Penguin, 2019), 2.

unfolds in time and what we are given as inputs are just visual or auditory signals. Meaning is *internally generated* in the brain.[24]

When our minds and bodies are functioning well, our sensory systems will not detect the world-as-it-is-in-reality. Our senses will, however, help us navigate through the world successfully. Similarly, when our minds and bodies are functioning well, we are not able to understand God-as-God-is, but we will be able to know enough of God to navigate our relationship with the divine successfully. I will explore this further, but before I do we need to consider how language shapes our understandings of God.

SHAPING GOD WITH OUR WORDS

At the beginning of a semester, Stanford psychologist Lera Boroditsky asks her students to name the cognitive ability they would most hate to lose. The most common answer is sight. A few of the students pick hearing, and on occasion a jokester will mention their fashion sense. Almost never does anyone say they would most hate to lose their facility with language. Boroditsky points out that even if a person is born without their sense of sight or hearing, or they lose this ability later in life, they can still have a very rich social existence. You can have fun with friends, receive an education, and hold down a job without being able to see or hear. Without language, though, it is hard to imagine any of this would be possible in contemporary society.

Boroditsky implies that we would be fundamentally different people if we did not have the use of language. Language shapes the way we think about space, time, color, and objects. Language forms the way people interpret events, think about causation, perceive emotion, vote in elections, and even go about choosing a profession and spouse.[25] Language also informs the way we think about God.[26]

The Purpose of Language

It is common to assume that language exists to facilitate communication. This assumption underlies one of the world's first explanations of the origin of

---

24. Giosuè Baggio, *Meaning in the Brain* (Cambridge: MIT Press, 2018), xiii, emphasis in the original.
25. Lera Boroditsky, "How Does Our Language Shape the Way We Think?," in *What's Next: Dispatches on the Future of Science*, ed. Max Brockman (New York: Vintage, 2009), 116–29.
26. Unfortunately, language is also used for detrimental purposes, such as humiliation, deception, and colonization. David Treuer, *The Heartbeat of Wounded Knee: Native America from 1890 to the Present* (New York: Riverhead, 2019), 27.

writing. A tale from the second millennium BCE tells of a Mesopotamian king named Enmerkar who sent a messenger to do business with the king of another land. Before the other king would trade with Enmerkar, he gave Enmerkar's messenger a series of riddles to take back to Enmerkar. Enmerkar would have to solve the riddles correctly before the other king would permit trade between the countries. The riddles were long and fairly complicated, and the messenger doubted he could remember them, so he wrote them down on a clay tablet. This tale is fictional, but it does reflect the idea that written language exists in order to communicate.[27] Certainly, communication is one of the primary functions of all language, written or unwritten, but language does far more than merely pass information from one human to another. Language also helps us make our way through the world.

Early humans were social creatures, living together and accomplishing tasks for millions of years before language is thought to have arisen around forty thousand years ago. We should note in passing that these early humans communicated with one another for millions of years *before* the invention of language. Facial expressions and gesturing convey information. Language certainly aids communication by making it more precise, but communication can take place in the absence of language.

For much of the twentieth century, scholars believed that language determines how we think. This idea was put forward in the 1930s and spread like wildfire. Researchers conducted many studies trying to prove that Native American speakers saw a completely different universe than folks using English. For instance, some linguists asserted that the Hopi people had no sense of time because they had no tense markers in their language and they lacked words that mark sequence, such as "later" or "before." Prominent journals said that the past, present, and future were collapsed together inside the Hopi mind. All of this was shown to be completely false (the Hopi language does, in fact, have tense markers and words like "already" and "afterward"); nevertheless, linguists agree that language *influences* and *shapes* our thoughts even though it does not *determine* them.[28] Many scholars then asserted that language is necessary for advanced thought. This was also shown to be false.

If language was necessary for and determined thought, then we would have a hard time explaining many things we encounter in the world. Pigeons can distinguish and categorize objects, including leaves, fish, and people. This means that pigeons can identify particular humans by their appearance. This

---

27. Charles Halton and Saana Svärd, *Women's Writing of Ancient Mesopotamia: An Anthology of the Earliest Female Authors* (Cambridge: Cambridge University Press, 2018), 5–6.

28. John H. McWhorter, *The Language Hoax: Why the World Looks the Same in Any Language* (Oxford: Oxford University Press, 2014), ix–xx.

is something that is often very difficult for humans to do for pigeons. As far as we know, pigeons do not have a facility with language, yet they are able to make very precise identifications.[29]

Many of the most important aspects of the human experience can be communicated without language. It does not take language to share emotion. Emotions can be understood and communicated through body expression without the use of grammatical symbols. Sometimes more is communicated with a frown than with an entire monologue of words. And, as children learn to speak, they grasp for new words to express what they think. In these instances, children know what they want to say—the ideas are in their heads—but they do not have a word at hand to represent it. This example, all by itself, should dispel the idea that one needs language in order to have thought. So what, then, does language do for us, and what is its main purpose?

According to psychiatrist Iain McGilchrist, language brings a certain fixity to our thoughts. It provides more definite shape to our perceptions by putting what we see and think into rigid categories. McGilchrist gives an analogy. Say you look over a landscape from a high vantage point. Language does not bring that landscape into being—you see it whether you use words or not. But once we start parceling out that landscape into different political areas like "counties," or we label topographic features as "forests" and "grasslands," we have divided our field of vision into clear sections. From then on we associate particular words with particular patches of land, whether the words be "Hazard County" or "peat bog."[30]

One benefit of a linguistic description of a landscape is that we can take this landscape with us wherever we go. Our eyes do not need to be in front of a particular scene for us to know how it appears. The categorizations that language facilitates enable us to compare one landscape to another and study them both in depth. We can then explain our perceptions of the world to someone else. We could tell someone that Abbot Farm is a rolling meadow of wildflowers and grass, or a friend could describe to us his hike through a dense forest of sixty-foot-tall trees and billowing ferns. With language we can picture a place without ever seeing it with our eyes. Through language we are able to represent something consistently through time and space, too. Even if a bulldozer wipes away a landscape, if we have a description of it, we can remember it.

---

29. Pigeons are able to perceive and represent numbers, along with other animals, including salamanders, raccoons, dolphins, and parrots. Jim Holt, *When Einstein Walked with Gödel: Excursions to the Edge of Thought* (New York: Farrar, Straus & Giroux, 2018), 30–31.

30. Iain McGilchrist, "The Origins of Emotion and Language from the Perspective of Developmental Neuropsychology," in *Emotion in Language*, ed. Ulrike M. Lüdtke (Amsterdam: Benjamins, 2015), 78.

Language also helps us analyze problems and enables other people to test solutions they did not invent. This is, likely, the more fundamental reason language was developed. As Rowan Williams observes:

> It is a mistake to think of speech originating in the (practical) need to communicate information: it has roots in simply articulating and testing mutual recognition, inviting response of an ever more differentiated kind. . . . Communication is not, in this context, passing on information but establishing a world in common, where someone who is radically unsure as to whether their own response to the environment is recognizable and viable can find assurance that they are not isolated. The vicious circle of anxiety and inward-turning strategies can be broken.[31]

Williams says that language probably arose to give humans comfort and a sense of belonging. Language is a bridge that more intimately connects two minds. This bridge helps us understand if another person sees the world in a similar way as we do. If this theory is correct, language exists to help humans cope in a difficult and frightening world. It is a way we can connect with each other and break through the paralysis of fear and unknowing.[32] Two minds can compare their perceptions and see if these perceptions are similar. If they are, there is more likelihood that an individual has a reliable understanding of their environment.

There are downsides to language, though. While sharing our thoughts with others can make our understandings more precise, there are times we can be led astray. As Tim Maudlin observes, "It is only because we reason and think and use language that we can be hoodwinked."[33] Furthermore, since language categorizes and gives shapes to our thoughts, it can close off new ways of thinking and prevent us from considering different and perhaps more useful perceptions.[34] Once we put words around a landscape, it becomes hard to see anything new in it. If we label something a desert, we might not notice the ecosystems of life within it. We can become like the urbanites who visited the Brindled Moor and saw only *emptiness* and *void*. There are other pitfalls with language, too, including confirmation bias and groupthink.

---

31. Rowan Williams, *The Edge of Words: God and the Habits of Language* (London: Bloomsbury, 2014), 99.

32. It is crucially important that humans develop ways of mitigating fear since fear and self-doubt are behind some of society's most destructive tendencies. Martha C. Nussbaum, *The Monarchy of Fear: A Philosopher Looks at Our Political Crisis* (New York: Simon & Schuster, 2018).

33. "The Defeat of Reason," *Boston Review*, June 1, 2018, http://bostonreview.net/science-nature-philosophy-religion/tim-maudlin-defeat-reason.

34. Iain McGilchrist, *The Master and His Emissary: The Divided Brain and the Making of the Western World* (New Haven: Yale University Press, 2009), 110.

Sharing our perception of the world with others can alert us to errors in our apprehension. It can also make our interpretation of the world more precise. And yet, humans are inclined to more readily embrace information that confirms our preexisting views of the world and devalue information that challenges our perceptions. This danger, I have found, is particularly pronounced in religious discussions. Our thoughts concerning God can be deeply entrenched, and when we hear perceptions of the divine that are different from ours, it can make us hold on to our assumptions even tighter. If we are not careful, we can divide humanity into two groups of people: those who agree with me and those who do not. Entire religious communities have been formed around this impulse. Everything that supports the ideology of the group is accepted and everything that challenges it is disregarded out of hand.

Language is a powerful tool that helps human society grow and flourish, but it can also be used to close off productive ways of thinking and can facilitate tribalism.[35] It is very important that we are aware of these dangers because even though language does not determine our thoughts, it does have the potential to radically shape them. And the ways in which we speak and think have physical repercussions. The ideas we hold in our heads can make us more loving people or embitter us in hatred. Thoughts can also cause us to die early or extend our lives. The ways in which we image God and the world are matters of life and death. Before we explore the ways in which our thoughts impact our physical lives, we should look a bit more closely at how language works to influence the ways we think.

The Influence of Language

Most of us believe we make decisions based upon facts. If we are presented with a scenario, we are confident that we have the ability to make an unbiased assessment. Cognitive linguists have shown that the concepts and metaphors we use to think about the world have far more impact on the decisions we make than most of us are willing to admit. Our concepts—the ways in which we linguistically categorize our environment—structure our thoughts and shape how we interact with ourselves and others. As I discussed above, language does not necessarily determine how we think and act, but it does greatly influence it.

For example, take the way we think of arguments. We often frame arguments with the terminology of war.

---

35. Ephraim Radner describes specific situations in which language for God can fuel tribalism and even violence between Christian communities. *A Brutal Unity: The Spiritual Politics of the Christian Church* (Waco, TX: Baylor University Press, 2012).

My arguments were *shot down*.
I *won* him over to *my side*.
His criticism was right *on target*.[36]

One flip through cable news shows will prove how genuinely combative argumentation has become in our society. Linguists George Lakoff and Mark Johnson imagine how a culture might behave if, instead of using metaphors of war to describe argumentation, we thought of argument as a dance. The people involved would be seen as performers whose goal is to act in a balanced and beautiful way instead of trying to obliterate their opponent. They would work together to accomplish something greater than what they could produce on their own—an agreed-upon conclusion. Their tone of voice might soften, they may give their conversation partner more uninterrupted time to speak, they might accept differing points of view more readily. Maybe there would be fewer fistfights and shootings? Lakoff and Johnson's point is that the categorizations we make can shape the way we engage with those around us.

Lakoff and Johnson's example was hypothetical. They tried to imagine how the world would change if we used different words to think about argumentation. Maybe this is just fanciful thinking? How do we know that changing the linguistic frame of a situation would alter the way people act? Two clinical psychologists tested this very thing. They asked a group of people to select the best solution to a variety of problems relating to social issues like climate change, the economy, and crime.[37] The researchers divided their subjects into several groups and gave everyone in the groups a paragraph-long description of a particular problem. The paragraphs contained a narrative and a set of statistics. Each group received the same description of the problem except for the first sentence. One group received a description without an explicit metaphorical frame. The description began with this sentence: "Crime is ravaging the city of Addison."[38] Another group was given a first sentence with a frame that portrayed crime as a monster intent on destruction: "Crime is a beast ravaging the city of Addison." The last group was given a first sentence with a frame that cast crime as a societal symptom: "Crime is a virus ravaging the city of Addison." After the description, the

---

36. This example is from George Lakoff and Mark Johnson, *Metaphors We Live By* (Chicago: University of Chicago Press, 1980), 5–7.
37. Paul H. Thibodeau and Lera Boroditsky, "Natural Language Metaphors Covertly Influence Reasoning," *PLOS ONE* 8:1 (2013): e52961, https://doi.org/10.1371/journal.pone.0052961.
38. The researchers assert that this formula lacks a frame, but I think it does. The verb "ravage" animates the concept of crime and makes it a tangible thing with intention and purpose separate from the people who decide to engage in criminal acts.

subjects were given an identical list of solutions and asked to pick the best option from the list.

The researchers discovered that the frames dramatically influenced the choices the subjects made. Eighty-seven percent of the subjects who received the "crime is a beast" frame selected law-enforcement solutions, while the group that read the "crime is a virus" frame picked law-enforcement choices only 40 percent of the time. Remember, the only difference between the materials the subjects were given was the frame within the first sentence of the paragraph-long narrative that portrayed crime as either a "virus" or a "beast." In other words, the way the subjects were prompted to linguistically categorize crime radically affected the response they selected. More intriguing still, the subjects had no idea they were swayed by this metaphorical frame. The subjects were asked to identify the part of the description that most influenced their thinking, and only 5 percent pointed to the framing metaphor.

Language did not absolutely determine how these subjects reacted. However, the categorizations the researchers suggested to their subjects drastically shaped the way the subjects thought about social problems. The label they attached to crime—either as a beast or a virus—changed the way the subjects identified a solution by a factor of two. It is important for us to remember that the terms we use to describe God influence us much as the frames influenced the subjects of this study. The categorizations we make and the words we use to describe God change the ways in which we go about our lives.

It is very likely that you will act differently if you think of God as a disciplinarian rather than endlessly forgiving. Whether you believe God to be an immaterial spirit or an embodied person will probably affect the way you live. And if you think these concepts do not influence you—if you think that you are able to rationally assimilate various data points and come up with an unbiased understanding of who God is apart from these framing concepts—remember that 95 percent of the subjects in the crime study were unaware that the framing metaphor was the primary influencer in how they approached a solution to an important problem.

The Physical Effects of Mental Ideas

Ideas are not extraneous. They are not curious novelties that academics tinker with in universities. Ideas are not disconnected from the rest of the world. The concepts we have make a real difference in time and space. The ideas a society has about God can produce decades of war—the medieval Crusades, for instance. Theologies can motivate racist genocides such as the *Endlösung* in Nazi Germany. But ideas about God can also bring about healing, as with the Truth and Reconciliation Commission of South Africa. Theologies of God can lead to good or bad results, but they are rarely inert.[39]

Changes in our ideas can affect our bodies, too. Psychologists discovered this in an experiment with women who worked as housekeepers in hotels. When the researchers asked the women whether they exercised, the women claimed they did not. To half the housekeepers the psychologists suggested they view their work as exercise, equivalent to going to the gym. They told the housekeepers to think of changing the sheets on a bed as similar to using an elliptical machine. They did not give any direction to the other group, and no other prompts were introduced to either group. Both sets of women returned to the same work they had been doing. The group that was prompted to frame their work as exercise lost weight, showed a decrease in their waist-to-hip ratio, decreased their body mass, and lowered their blood pressure. The control group experienced none of these changes.[40] If housekeepers can change the shape of their bodies by altering the ways they think about their occupation, what benefits could come to us if we changed how we thought of God?

AN ACCURATE UNDERSTANDING OF GOD IS NOT OF UTMOST IMPORTANCE

The point of studying Scripture is not to arrive at the correct interpretation of it (if there is, in fact, a correct one). Nor is it to gain an accurate picture of God, however helpful a true understanding of the divine might be. Rather, the point of scriptural engagement is for us to become more loving and charitable people.

This might seem like an audacious claim. The idea that theology is not primarily concerned with getting its answers right cuts against the grain of many contemporary religious communities that frame the spiritual life as a journey toward truth. It also undercuts the academic discipline of theology in which scholars argue with each other about who is correct. This perspective is also at odds with the current and all-pervasive science-and-technology-infused ethos that is locked in a frenetic search for confirmable hypotheses and marketable inventions. Ideas that do not produce something

---

39. As James Baldwin said: "Though we do not wholly believe it yet, the interior life is a real life, and the intangible dreams of people have a tangible effect on the world." "What It Means to Be an American," in *James Baldwin: Collected Essays*, ed. Toni Morrison (New York: Library of America, 1998), 142.

40. Langer, *Mindfulness*, xv.

immediately useful or monetizable are regarded as a waste of time.[41] I imagine many would respond to my claim by saying that if a person is not studying the Bible to get an accurate theology they might as well close the book and do something else.

My claim that the primary goal of biblical study is charity instead of truth is not as controversial as it may sound. In fact, it is not my claim at all. I am merely repeating the sentiment originally put forward by Augustine, possibly the most influential theologian in the history of Western Christianity.[42] Augustine believed that what God most wants is for humans to increase their capacity for charity, not that we have correct metaphysical beliefs. If someone has an incorrect interpretation of the Bible, Augustine thought, so be it, as long as that interpretation makes them a more loving and welcoming person. In his own words, "[If a person] is deceived in an interpretation that builds up charity, which is the end of the commandment, he is deceived in the same way as a man who leaves a road by mistake but passes through a field to the same place toward which the road itself leads."[43]

Augustine was not unconcerned about the rightness of theological ideas. He certainly was. He vigorously debated interpretations with his contemporaries. Some of these debates were over topics that today seem incredibly trivial and completely without consequence.[44] Yet Augustine believed that God did not have one purpose in inspiring the Bible—such as fostering correct beliefs about the divine—but many. God has a hierarchy of purposes for Scripture in which charity is at the top and fostering correct belief is somewhere farther down.

At this point Augustine merely reflects what many portions of Scripture say. How else can we understand statements like, "You believe that God is one; you do well. Even the demons believe—and shudder" (Jas. 2:19)? In this passage James commends monotheism but asserts that it will only get a believer so far. According to James, a correct cognitive understanding of who God is puts a person on an equal plane with the malevolent forces of the universe. What separates the people of God from demons? It is not the rightness of their beliefs. According to Augustine, what characterizes the people of

---

41. I should note that many contemplative and monastic Christians believe that the most significant marks of deep and authentic spiritual lives appear to be useless to the modern world. See, for instance, Paul Quenon, *In Praise of a Useless Life* (Notre Dame, IN: Ave Maria Press, 2018).

42. Alan Jacobs, *A Theology of Reading: A Hermeneutics of Love* (Boulder, CO: Westview, 2001), 14–17.

43. *On Christian Doctrine*, trans. D. W. Robertson Jr. (Indianapolis: Bobbs-Merrill, 1958), 31.

44. For instance, Augustine argued with Jerome that the plant which shaded Jonah should be translated as a gourd, an ivy, or a Syrian variety called *cucurbita*. See Joseph A. Fitzmyer, *The Interpretation of Scripture: In Defense of the Historical-Critical Method* (New York: Paulist, 2008), 17–18.

God is embodied charity. In a sermon on 1 John, Augustine said, "But there is nothing to distinguish the sons of God from the sons of the devil, save charity. They that have charity, are born of God: they that have not charity are not. There is the great token, the great dividing mark."[45] This is why Augustine believed that if a person misinterpreted the Bible but that mistake caused them to be more charitable, nothing crucial was lost. The ultimate point of biblical study is fostering charity, not discovering correct beliefs.

At this point it is worth reflecting on what charity is. In English the word "love" refers to a wide array of actions that were distinct within the minds of ancient people. For instance, in ancient Greek there are many words for love, such as *eros* (sexual passion), *philia* (deep but platonic friendship), *storge* (parents' care for their children), *ludus* (flirtatious and playful affection), *pragma* (long-standing commitment), *philauta* (self-acceptance), and *agape* (selfless care for all of humanity, family and stranger alike).[46] This last word, *agape*, was translated into Latin as *caritas*, and then became "charity" in English. In a passage that may have influenced Augustine's idea of charity more than any other, Paul employs the same kind of hierarchical understanding of love and knowledge that we saw with Augustine and the book of James: "If I have prophetic powers, and understand all mysteries and all knowledge, and if I have all faith, so as to remove mountains, but do not have love [*agape*], I am nothing" (1 Cor. 13:2). Without love, Paul says, a person is nothing even if they have all the knowledge one could hope to have. The love that Paul speaks of here is *agape*, which was, as we saw, later rendered as "charity." But what is this love? What does it do?

A couple of verses later, Paul begins to sketch some of the characteristics of *agape*. "Love is patient; love is kind; love is not envious or boastful or arrogant or rude. It does not insist on its own way; it is not irritable or resentful; it does not rejoice in wrongdoing, but rejoices in the truth. It bears all things, believes all things, hopes all things, endures all things" (1 Cor. 13:4–7). It is important to note that one thing *agape*/charity is not, as Wittgenstein said, is a feeling.[47] It is not that feelings are unimportant nor that we should not work to cultivate positive sentiments toward others, but as philosopher Terry Eagleton observes, "One is not required to feel tender

---

45. Augustine, "Fifth Homily on 1 John," in *Augustine: Later Works*, ed. and trans. John Burnaby (Philadelphia: Westminster, 1955), 298.

46. Some of these definitions are explained in David Konstan, *The Emotions of the Ancient Greeks: Studies in Aristotle and Classical Literature* (Toronto: University of Toronto Press, 2006), chap. 8.

47. Ludwig Wittgenstein, *Zettel*, ed. and trans. G. E. M. Anscombe and G. H. von Wright (Oxford: Blackwell, 1967), sec. 504.

sentiments towards those one rescues from white slave traffickers or sherry party bores. This is why the paradigm of love for the New Testament is love of strangers and enemies rather than of friends. Charity is a social practice, not a state of mind."[48]

Charity is not having a warm feeling inside one's chest when you hear the name of the person who bullied you as a child. Charity is not having tender thoughts for the boss who unfairly fired you from a job that you loved. Charity *is* wanting the best for all people, including the people who have hurt us. We put our lives on the line for these folks if need be. Eagleton says that charity expects you "to take another's place in the queue for the gas chambers, but whether the two of you are on intimate terms is neither here nor there."[49] Charity is the kind of love that would move a god to become human and die a gruesome death so that the people who rejected and despised this god could better understand what charity is and come to act more humanely with one another. Charity is the kind of love that embraces the strange-smelling immigrant just as readily as one would embrace a beloved cousin. It is a radical love that breaks through the barriers human society puts around relationships. Charity is also dangerous to practice because acting in charity may cause those around us to reposition how they regard us. As Toni Morrison said, "The danger of sympathizing with the stranger is the possibility of becoming a stranger."[50] According to the biblical narrative, this is precisely what happened when God embodied charity in Jesus.

I think it is good for us, as far as we are able, to have accurate understandings of God. Studying the Bible in order to cultivate more creative or precise ideas about God is a good thing, but it is far less important than living a charity-filled life. It is for this reason that, for the purposes of this book, I will not try to separate fact from fiction within the biblical stories we survey. I am not interested in whether the pictures of God they convey are what God is like in reality. The writers of the Bible depicted God in certain ways, and they encouraged us to think about God in these patterns. I do not care to investigate whether or not these pictures of God are true in and of themselves or whether they point toward a different kind of metaphorical truth. The depictions of God we will study have the potential to make us more charitable people. That, I believe, is their ultimate aim.

Irish poet and theologian Pádraig Ó Tuama reflects this sentiment well when he asks, "Is it a good question to ask whether something happened or

---

48. *Radical Sacrifice* (New Haven: Yale University Press, 2018), 98.
49. Eagleton, *Radical Sacrifice*, 98.
50. *The Origin of Others* (Cambridge: Harvard University Press, 2017), 30.

not? Is information-recovery enough to mine this story for meaning? Is it true that the Blessed Virgin Mary visited my mother? Or is it true that it helped? If it's true that it helped, does it finally matter how it happened?"[51] I ultimately do not care if God has legs or not. It is an interesting theoretical question that I would have a good time discussing over beer, but what I am most concerned about is how this idea may have the potential to help us better understand what charity is and enable us to act more lovingly toward our neighbors.

There is another reason why I shy away from asking whether or not the stories in the Bible happened or whether the ways in which God is described reflect God in actuality. Most of the accounts we will study could be described as mythological. That is, they are narratives that include divine beings as major characters. For the most part, ancient readers never wondered whether the myths they read were true or not. This was not a question they asked. They accepted the stories as they were written and pondered how these stories shaped and influenced their lives. Myths are stories that occupy a special place in our lives.[52] In most cases they are not verifiable. They operate on a different plane of reality and therefore offer a different kind of meaning than scientific description or flat indicative statements. Richard Holloway, the former primus of the Scottish Episcopal Church, describes it this way:

> The Greeks employed an interesting distinction in their use of language. They used the word *logos* for factual discourse about things you could verify through the senses. But they used the word *muthos* to describe another kind of meaning. The most characteristic use of this word was to classify stories about gods, which is why it is easily misunderstood today. The word "myth" has become synonymous with something false or untrue, like the existence of those old Greek gods. Yet the question we should ask of a myth is not whether it is true or false, but whether it is living or dead, and whether it still carries meaning for us today.[53]

This is not to say that the understandings we have about God do not matter. Even if they are not demonstrably verifiable from a scientific point of view, the ways we think about God have tremendous consequence. They shape how we think about ourselves and they influence the manner in which we move about the world. For these reasons our theologies of God are very important, and we should be conscious of the ways in which our understandings of God affect us.

---

51. *In the Shelter: Finding a Home in the World* (London: Hodder & Stoughton, 2015), 36.
52. Simon Critchley, *Tragedy, The Greeks, and Us* (New York: Pantheon, 2019), 40.
53. *How to Read the Bible* (New York: Norton, 2006), 4.

CHOOSING TO IMAGINE A FULL-ORBED GOD

Richard Holloway provides an example of how our ideas about God can radically shape our emotional health as well as the outside world.[54] Many of us grow up thinking that we build ourselves into the people we are. God gives each person the ability to make free choices. In each situation we can choose to respond with cowardice or bravery, love or hate, goodness or evil. Whatever choice we make in a particular situation, we make out of our free and unfettered will. If we yelled something unkind at a friend, we had the capability to respond with love but chose not to. The decision was entirely our own.

This belief in free will can shape the way we view ourselves and other people. If our lives have been successful compared to those around us, we might imagine that our good choices made us who we are and that if our friends and family had made better ones they too would have flourished. On the other hand, many of us struggle with guilt and self-hatred when we recall decisions we made that caused others hardship or that brought us shame. We can carry tremendous pain because we think our choices have caused harm. This has tremendous societal repercussions. We might vote to remove social services that aid people who experience poverty because we conclude they are undeserving because their poor decisions caused their plight. We build a myriad of prisons to separate and punish people who have made bad choices when they had the ability to make good ones.

What if, instead of thinking about the abstract idea of free will, we imagined our decision making in light of a metaphor? What if we thought of the world as a loom and pictured a weaver slowly creating a bolt of cloth, which is our life? We are no longer the sole agent of our creation. We begin to recognize that our genetic code, the upbringings we have had, the societies in which we were born, the languages we speak, and the people who surround us reveal our character like a shuttle ferrying threads back and forth that eventually produces a pattern within a textile. Maybe we are only partially responsible for the decisions we make. Perhaps the circumstances around us have as much influence on our choices as our own wills? If we thought this way, the guilt we feel at the harm we have caused might be less pronounced. Maybe we would be more forgiving of the faults we see in others because we realize that if we occupied their position in life it is likely we would have made the same choices as they did. This, in turn, may lead us to do away with punitive punishment

---

54. I have summarized the story Holloway tells in *Waiting for the Last Bus: Reflections on Life and Death* (Edinburgh: Canongate, 2018), 40–42.

and, as Angela Davis eloquently argues, we might be moved to abolish prisons altogether.[55] One little metaphor could change the entire world.

If the only way we think of God is by using abstract ideas, it is very likely that we will not develop into the charitable people that Augustine envisioned. Right beliefs by themselves do not make us more loving. For one thing, the impulses that tempt us to be selfish, unkind, and destructive do not go away when we realign our mental landscape. We cannot reason them away with an esoteric theology. A pair of coauthors, a psychotherapist and psychologist, explain it this way: "Thinking doesn't help you control your impulses; in fact, you'll find that the more you try to think your way out of an impulse, the more [your tendency to mess things up] will flood you with rationalizations for why you should get what you want."[56] These authors recommend that instead of trying to discipline ourselves by recalling abstract belief systems when we are tempted to act in uncharitable ways, we should recall pictures and metaphors that enable us to not only understand a concept mentally but also *experience* an aspect of reality with the entirety of our person.[57] They recommend we change our behavior by telling ourselves a different *story*. Instead of reminding ourselves that we are intelligent when we feel dumb, we should imagine a situation in the past when we were successful. This technique does not merely engage our abstract thought, it also triggers the emotions connected to the feelings we have when we remember we achieved something great.

Abstract concepts tickle our analytical minds. Pictures, metaphors, and stories connect our emotional and cognitive selves. This is why the anthropomorphic representations of God within the Bible are so important and also why it is such a scandal they have been underappreciated and actively suppressed within many religious communities for so long. The scriptural portrayals of God in human form are tools that can help us become more charitable people. They are far more effective in this regard than abstract descriptions of the divine. And make no mistake—pictures, metaphors, and concrete descriptions of God are equally part of the act of theology as representing God with philosophical categories or analytical terminology. As the former archbishop of Canterbury, Rowan Williams, said: "Theology is what

---

55. *Are Prisons Obsolete?* (New York: Seven Stories Press, 2003).

56. Barry Michels and Phil Stutz, *Coming Alive* (New York: Spiegel & Grau, 2017), 82. Michels and Stutz refer to what theologians call the sin nature as Part X. I do not gravitate to either term. The word *sin* has been used so much in so many different contexts and with so many different referents that it is practically without meaning; in some cases it even carries a misleading connotation. Part X is similarly nebulous. I prefer Francis Spufford's definition of sin: "the human propensity to fuck *things* up," in *Unapologetic: Why, Despite Everything, Christianity Can Still Make Surprising Emotional Sense* (New York: HarperOne, 2013), 27. I have sanitized this description for the main body of the text but I thought that readers attentive enough to read the notes would appreciate Spufford's original formulation.

57. Michels and Stutz, *Coming Alive*, 78–79.

we call any serious attempt to represent and explore the meanings of the word 'God.'"⁵⁸ Using anthropomorphic language to represent God is just as serious an attempt to explore the meaning of the word "God" as any other. I will revisit in detail the ways anthropomorphic language can facilitate a deeper embodiment of charity after we have studied some of the ways the biblical authors used anthropomorphic language to describe God. But before we examine the human shape of God, we must be able to discern the various ways in which the biblical authors go about speaking about the divine and also more deeply understand what metaphor is and why it is used.

---

58. "Theology as a Way of Life," in *The Practice of the Presence of God: Theology as a Way of Life*, ed. Martin Laird and Sheelah Treflé Hidden (London: Routledge, 2017), 11.

2

God, Humanlike and Not

Light is an odd thing. It defies neat definition. It exhibits features of two things normally thought to be mutually exclusive. When a beam of light passes through a transparent object its path alters course. Light acts as a wave. In science-speak: it oscillates along a mathematical curve with a smooth and repetitive motion. Particles are not like this. If a particle meets an object it will bounce off or stick to the thing it hit or perhaps one of these bodies will splinter apart. What a particle will not do is bend its curve through space in calm oscillation. And since particles, like photons, are not in perpetual twitter, their locations are specific and can be determined with precision. This is not true of waves.

How is it that light exhibits properties that in theory cannot coexist? I don't know and neither did Albert Einstein. Yet Einstein thought it was crucial that we understand light as both a wave and a particle even though our brains are not able to reconcile it. This is a bit disorienting to my mind, but Einstein explained how contradictory understandings explain light in a way that each of them on their own cannot:

> But what is light really? Is it a wave or a shower of photons? There seems no likelihood for forming a consistent description of the phenomena of light by a choice of only one of the two languages. It seems as though we must use sometimes the one theory and sometimes the other, while at times we may use either. We are faced with a new kind of difficulty. We have two contradictory pictures of reality; separately neither of them fully explains the phenomena of light, but together they do.[1]

---

1. Albert Einstein and Leopold Infeld, *The Evolution of Physics: From Early Concepts to Relativity and Quanta* (New York: Touchstone, 1966), 262–63.

Einstein says that we must use two languages when we speak of light. We must employ two different lines of discourse that contradict each other. If we describe light with only one of these languages, we fail to accurately represent it. An entire way in which light is—one of its states of being—is left out of the equation. This is also true when speaking of the God of the Old Testament.

THE CHRONICLER'S KIDS

Sometimes the Bible makes God seem very human. God is gendered, God becomes angry, God undergoes a change of mind, and God travels from heaven in order to witness the goings-on in Eden.[2] Yet theologians have often argued that since God is spirit, God is neither male nor female. They have also often asserted that God does not have emotions because God is unchanging at the core.[3] There are also times when Scripture seems to present two radically different perceptions about the nature of God. For instance, Numbers 23 clearly states that God's mind does not waver but, as we will see below, in the book of Genesis God's mind wavers. Proverbs 15:3 seems to imply that God knows everything because God's sight extends everywhere: "The eyes of the LORD are in every place, keeping watch on the evil and the good." But if we read Genesis 3 in a straightforward manner, God did not know where Adam and Eve were because they hid in the bushes (3:8). God also chose a temperate time of day to visit Eden, after the heat waned. This detail only makes sense if we imagine that God did not want to sweat or be uncomfortable beneath the hot sun. This, in turn, is only coherent if we assume that God has a body. Would a disembodied spirit care about the temperature?

Even when we grant poetic license, the Old Testament presents a confusing and contradictory portrait of God. Does God change his mind or not? Is God emotionless or does he get angry? Is God even *he*? The dominant stream of European-influenced Christian theology regards this conflicted state as a problem to be solved.[4] One of the main goals of many theologies is to repre-

---

2. Old Testament authors use predominantly masculine pronouns to refer to God; God is angry quite often—just start reading the Bible after Gen. 3; God changes his mind in Exod. 32:14; and God travels from heaven to Eden and walks in the garden in Gen. 3:8.

3. For example, the fourth-century church theologian Gregory of Nyssa argued that God was neither male nor female. Rosemary Radford Ruether, *Goddesses and the Divine Feminine: A Western Religious History* (Berkeley: University of California Press, 2005), 135.

4. This reality is changing, and many theologies now assume the Bible contains at least several different theologies. You can see this, for instance, in the title of Erhard Gerstenberger's book *Theologies in the Old Testament*, trans. John Bowden (Minneapolis: Fortress, 2002). Scholars like John Rogerson believe that the most interesting parts of the Old Testament are those that seemingly contradict other portions of Scripture. *A Theology of the Old Testament: Cultural Memory, Communication and Being Human* (Minneapolis: Fortress, 2010), 184. (Rogerson uses the word

sent the biblical picture of God as a unified message. They want to show that this contradictory presentation is contradictory only on the surface, if at all. If we properly interpret the Bible, they claim, we see that all of its passages view God in the same way.[5] Biblical authors emphasize particular aspects of the divine and they sometimes describe God from different angles, but at the end of the day all of their definitions are in harmony and revolve around the same central understanding.[6] This is a very difficult idea to put into practice. Interpretations of individual verses often become unmoored from their grammatical meaning. Interpreters bend them out of shape so that they will cohere with the singular picture of the divine person that a theologian has.

For instance, throughout the Christian era many commentators regarded Genesis 6:6 as problematic.[7] Most English translations read: "And the LORD was grieved [*wayyinnāḥem*] that he had made humankind on the earth." Even though many English translations render the first verb "grieved," it is more properly translated "changed his mind." In almost every other instance in which this word appears in the Bible these translators gloss it as "change his mind." Why don't they do the same in Genesis 6:6? The reason for this discrepancy is purely ideological. These translators want to avoid giving Bible readers the impression that the divine mind can change, because this would conflict with their conception of God as unchanging.

"seemingly" in connection to contradictory biblical passages but, personally, I am happy to leave it out.)

5. For instance, Trent Hunter and Stephen Wellum contrast two metaphors for the Bible, a mosaic and a puzzle. They reject the idea of the Bible as mosaic (a compilation of pieces from various pictures) and assert that it is a puzzle, that is, all its pieces fit together to present one, unified picture of God: "A puzzle, on the other hand, is designed for a single purpose. It is intended to fit together, and if put together correctly, it results in the same picture every time." *Christ from Beginning to End: How the Full Story of Scripture Reveals the Full Glory of Christ* (Grand Rapids: Zondervan, 2018), 33. Hunter and Wellum's metaphors for the Bible are not the only ones, however, even though they present them as our only two options. John Kessler, for example, offers a third: "In a sense it is helpful to picture the content of the OT as resembling an apple, sliced down the center. At the center we find a smaller circle, consisting of core beliefs for which there is no theological counterpoint or diversity.... Next we have a large mass of material concerning which the OT canon contains a *diversity of perspectives*." *Old Testament Theology: Divine Call and Human Response* (Waco, TX: Baylor University Press, 2013), 88, emphasis in the original. Kessler's analogy may be helpful but I'm not as optimistic as he is concerning the "core" of beliefs the OT canon has in common. It does not get much more central to the nature of God than to debate whether God has a body.

6. Walter C. Kaiser Jr., *Toward an Old Testament Theology* (Grand Rapids: Zondervan, 1978), 20–40. One of the problems with asserting the Old Testament has a singular theological center is that theologians are unable to agree on what that center is, as Gerhard F. Hasel points out in *Old Testament Theology: Basic Issues in the Current Debate*, 4th ed. (Grand Rapids: Eerdmans, 1991), 139–71.

7. We should stress that while postbiblical interpreters had a problem with humanlike descriptions of God, the biblical authors did not. Andreas Wagner, *God's Body: The Anthropomorphic God in the Old Testament*, trans. Marion Salzmann (London: T&T Clark, 2019), 30.

The Protestant reformer John Calvin also had a difficult time with Genesis 6:6. He noticed that it conflicts quite sharply with Numbers 23:19: "God is not a human being, that he should lie, or a mortal, that he should change his mind [wĕyitneḥem]." The author of Genesis 6 says that God changes his mind while the author of Numbers flatly asserts God does not.

Calvin determined he had to make a choice. He didn't believe this contradiction could stand. He was convinced he had to select one passage as normative and the other as aberrant. The anomaly needed tending. It needed to be interpreted so that it came in line with his singular picture of the divine. Calvin thought that Numbers was clear: "God is not a human being . . . that he should change his mind." There is nothing ambiguous about that statement. It is a straightforward indicative assertion of fact. In Calvin's mind, the Genesis passage is the one that should give way, and so he claimed that its interpretation is different from its surface meaning. Calvin explains with characteristic skill how this realignment should be performed:

> The grief that is here ascribed to God does not properly belong to him but refers to our understanding of him. Since we cannot comprehend him as he is, he has to, in a certain sense, accommodate himself for our sake. God is not sorrowful or sad but remains forever like himself in his heavenly and happy repose.[8]

With breathtaking sleight of hand Calvin argues that Genesis 6:6 means precisely the opposite of what it actually says. Even though the verse unambiguously states that God's mind changed, Calvin assumes this is incorrect. Calvin says that when the author of Genesis 6 says that God grieves, the author is using a fictional metaphor. The plain meaning of the phrase is not intended. The phrase communicates something different from what it means on the surface. Calvin asserts that the human mind does not have the ability to understand what God is really like, so the writer of Genesis 6 presents God in a humanlike manner because that is the only way that his reader can comprehend the divine. According to Calvin, God does not grieve in God's actual being. This passage has a rhetorical function that is different from its literal meaning.[9] To human observers it looks *as if* God is grieving, but in reality God remains the same. It is humanity that undergoes change, not God. In other words, at this point Scripture lies to tell the truth. Its author relays a falsehood—God is grieved—to convey to his readers a small glimpse of God's character in the only way humans are able to receive it. The description of God in Numbers is true, the Genesis passage is accommodation. And thus,

---

8. John Calvin, *Genesis*, ed. Alister McGrath and J. I. Packer (Crossway Classic Commentaries; Wheaton, IL: Crossway, 2001), 70.
9. Rogerson, *Theology of the Old Testament*, 3.

the contradiction is solved. Our understanding of God remains uniform and consistent. And more than that, God remains uniform and consistent.

At this point we should note a couple things. First, what led Calvin to conclude that the Numbers passage was normative and the Genesis passage was accommodation? They are both indicative statements. There is nothing within the narrative of Genesis 6 itself to suggest that its description of God is non-literal. If we did not have the book of Numbers there would be no way of discerning that Genesis 6 is accommodation. We could just as easily say that the Genesis passage is normative and regard the Numbers passage as accommodation. When Calvin identified this tension and determined he had to adjudicate these verses, he relied upon his *assumed* understanding of God to make his choice. That is, he brought to his act of interpretation the extrabiblical idea circulating in philosophical circles that God is impassible. There are many definitions that ancient and modern scholars give for the concept of divine impassibility, but what Calvin seemed most concerned about was avoiding the appearance that God undergoes a change of state. Calvin did not want to believe that outside forces could affect God.[10] God's mind, in his view, must always remain static and unchanging. Calvin thought he understood God's nature, and he chose the passage that affirmed his point of view. He labeled Genesis 6 as accommodation and applied a brand-new meaning to the words in it.

Second, there is nothing within the texts of Genesis and Numbers themselves that would lead an interpreter to a harmonious reading. These verses are diametrically opposed. Calvin's desire to dismiss this opposition came from within himself and not, ultimately, from the Bible. Neither Genesis nor Numbers, or any other portion of Scripture, explicitly advocates the premise of logical consistency. Calvin again brings an extrabiblical assumption to his interpretive act. This is not in and of itself a bad thing. We necessarily and unavoidably bring many extrabiblical assumptions to the act of deciphering and interpreting any text, including the Bible. For example, we apply our emotional temperament, life experience, and theory of history.[11] We also bring our knowledge of vocabulary, syntax, genres, and cultural repertoire.[12] All of this directly affects how we interpret.

We also should note that when it comes to theology, Christianity doesn't require logical consistency.[13] This should be immediately obvious to anyone

---

10. Richard E. Creel lists eight distinct definitions for "impassible" in *Divine Impassibility: An Essay in Philosophical Theology* (Cambridge: Cambridge University Press, 1986), 9.

11. Carolyn J. Sharp, *Wrestling the Word: The Hebrew Scriptures and the Christian Believer* (Louisville: Westminster John Knox, 2010), 10–12.

12. Wolfgang Iser, *The Act of Reading: A Theory of Aesthetic Response* (Baltimore: Johns Hopkins University Press, 1978), 53–85.

13. Peter J. Gomes, *The Good Book: Reading the Bible with Mind and Heart* (New York: Morrow, 1996), 74–75.

who is familiar with Trinitarian thought. To say that God is both three and one does violence to the law of noncontradiction. This hasn't prevented Christians from believing it. And yet, once we move out to other theological concepts or read biblical passages side by side, the argument for logical consistency surfaces. Passages like Genesis 6:6 pay the price.

It is true that a degree of consistency is necessary to avoid chaos and absurdity. I do not mean to argue that theological discourse is a free-for-all of completely illogical and contradictory assertions. Communication requires a degree of coherence. Furthermore, some biblical authors display a desire to harmonize the contradictory assertions of earlier writers. The Chronicler does this often. In his book on the historiographic methods that the Chronicler employs, Isaac Kalimi spends an entire chapter—forty-two pages—detailing the various harmonizations the author of Chronicles attempts.[14]

For example, the Pentateuch contains two contradictory instructions concerning the manner in which the Passover sacrifice should be prepared. Exodus 12:8–9 says in no uncertain terms that the meat should be roasted over fire (*ṣalî ʾēš*) and *not* boiled (*bāšēl*):

> They shall eat the lamb that same night; they shall eat it roasted over the fire [*ṣĕlî ʾēš*] with unleavened bread and bitter herbs. Do not eat any of it raw or boiled in water [*ûbāšēl mabuššāl bammāyim*], but roasted over the fire, with its head, legs, and inner organs.

Deuteronomy 16:7 says precisely the opposite, "You shall boil [*ûbiššaltā*] it and eat it" (my trans.). This is quite a quandary for someone like the Chronicler who desires consistency. He was repulsed by contradiction. Like Calvin, the Chronicler needed a work-around. He merely conflated the verses and obliterated the contradiction: "They boiled [*waybaššlû*] the passover lamb with fire [*bāʾēš*] according to the ordinance" (2 Chr. 35:13). The Chronicler combined two mutually exclusive forms of cooking—roasting and boiling—into the same process! This isn't the same method that John Calvin used with Genesis 6:6 and Numbers 23:19 but it accomplished the same thing: a harmonious reading.[15] In both cases, the authors drained one passage of its

---

14. *The Reshaping of Israelite History in Chronicles* (Winona Lake, IN: Eisenbrauns, 2005), 123–65; for his discussion of this particular instance see 157–58.

15. There are several well-meaning but tendentious attempts to prove that the Chronicler did not forcibly harmonize two contradictory passages but rather rightly discerned that these passages are inherently in concord. These attempts are not persuasive on their own terms (they merely assert that *bšl* is a general word for "cook") and even less so when considered in light of the Chronicler's thoroughgoing tendency of harmonization documented with many and diverse examples in Kalimi, *Reshaping of Israelite History*, 123–65. See also Marc Zvi Brettler's helpful and concise discussion of 2 Chr. 35:13 in *How to Read the Bible* (Philadelphia: Jewish Publication Society, 2005), 135, or for a more expansive treatment see Ehud Ben Zvi, "Revisiting 'Boiling

meaning and applied an entirely new understanding to it. Calvin obliterated the idea that God undergoes a change of mind in Genesis, and the Chronicler papered over the stipulation that the Passover sacrifice should be cooked without water in the Exodus passage.

Not all biblical authors share the Chronicler's disposition. Many are quite comfortable with contradiction. Whoever compiled the early chapters of Genesis saw no problem with putting two conflicting creation accounts right next to each other. Some contemporary translations hide the discrepancies between Genesis 1 and 2 (they must be the Chronicler's progeny) but the venerable King James Version preserves the most obvious contradiction quite clearly. According to Genesis 1 the sequence of creation was light, water, land, plants, stars and sun, birds and animals and fish, and, finally, humans. The key to this progression is that humans are created last, after animals. This sequence is reversed in Genesis 2. In this account, God creates the man *and then* creates animals *because* the man is lonely. Genesis 2:18–19 could not be more clear:

> [18] And the LORD God said, It is not good that the man should be alone; I will make him an help meet for him. [19] And out of the ground the LORD God formed every beast of the field, and every fowl of the air; and brought them unto Adam to see what he would call them. (KJV)

The reason for verse 19—God forming the animals—is because in verse 18 God said that the man should not be alone. According to the narrative of Genesis 2, God creates animals because the man is lonely. The man does not find a suitable companion among the animals, so God forms Eve out of the body of the man. This is the flow of the story. The story makes sense this way. This is not how many contemporary translations present it.

Notice how the NIV translates verse 19: "Now the LORD God had formed out of the ground all the wild animals and all the birds in the sky. He brought them to the man." Instead of translating the first verb as a simple perfect ("formed"), as in the KJV, the NIV renders it a pluperfect ("had formed"). Why? Grammatically, the verb is a narrative preterite. Narrative preterites indicate sequential actions that result from a previous situation.[16] They come after an initial verb in the perfect form (or less often nominal clauses, infinitives, etc.). The construction communicates a progression: this happened

---

in Fire' in 2 Chron. 35.13 and Related Passover Questions: Text, Exegetical Needs, Concerns, and General Implications," in *Biblical Interpretation in Judaism and Christianity*, ed. Isaac Kalimi and Peter J. Haas (Library of Hebrew Bible/Old Testament Studies 439; London and New York: T&T Clark, 2006), 238–50.

16. Bill T. Arnold and John H. Choi, *A Guide to Biblical Hebrew Syntax* (Cambridge: Cambridge University Press, 2003), 84–87.

(perfect) and then this happened (narrative preterite) and then this happened (narrative preterite). This is precisely what we have in Genesis 2—a whole string of events linked together with narrative preterites. So again, why did the translators of the NIV render the narrative preterite in verse 19 as a pluperfect?[17] Because they are the Chronicler's children. They couldn't stand contradiction. They felt the need to harmonize the orders of creation in Genesis 1 and 2. The pluperfect ("had formed") communicates the idea that God previously made the animals but held them in reserve and is only now bringing them out to Adam. It cuts against the grain of the story.[18] No one would propose this way of reading the passage if Genesis 1 were not before it. And yet this interpretation yields a consistent chronology in which animals are created before humans. Hence its appeal.

Consistency is crucially important in some areas and detrimental in others. A structural engineer would be negligent if she designed a building that both could and could not support the weight of the people inside it. A poet would be rather boring if he wrote pieces as logical as repair manuals. Most Bible readers understand this. They are not bothered by the fact that many proverbs speak in direct opposition to one another. For instance, Proverbs 26:4 and 5: "Do not answer fools according to their folly, or you will be a fool yourself. Answer fools according to their folly, or they will be wise in their own eyes." Which one of these is true? Should we summon the Chronicler to harmonize them? Of course not. Wisdom literature, by its very nature, trades on generalizations and must be applied to specific situations. Different situations call for different, even opposite, responses. More often than not, when ancient peoples discussed their thoughts about the creation of the world and imagined what God was like, they were not speaking the grammar of contemporary science but of the sages. Contradiction was not eschewed but embraced. The compilers of Genesis were far from the only editors in antiquity who were comfortable putting two contradictory accounts of creation side by side. The third-millennium priestess Enheduanna did the very same thing.[19]

---

17. The editors of another modern translation, the ESV, initially translated the first verb in Gen. 3:19 as a perfect ("formed") and then in later editions changed it to a pluperfect ("had formed") with a footnote that indicated the original translation as an option. The Chronicler sure had a lot of kids.

18. Interpreters who want to believe this often look to Umberto Cassuto's *A Commentary on the Book of Genesis* (Jerusalem: Magnes, 1961) for support, but his treatment is generally considered by scholars to be tendentious and highly idiosyncratic, and it is quite unconvincing to this reader.

19. This discussion is adapted from Charles Halton and Saana Svärd, *Women's Writing of Ancient Mesopotamia: An Anthology of the Earliest Female Authors* (Cambridge: Cambridge University Press, 2017), 54.

WHO'S AFRAID OF CONTRADICTION?

Enheduanna's father was the king of an empire in northern Mesopotamia around 2250 BCE. He installed his daughter as the priestess of one of the region's most important temples, the temple at Ur. Ur was located in an area that her father had recently conquered, and Enheduanna's mission, in part, was to help unify the country in religious observance. To this end she compiled a collection of forty-two hymns that celebrated the major temples across the new empire. Enheduanna tried to show that Mesopotamian people, north and south, were united in similar religious belief and practice.

The first hymn of this collection recounts the greatness of the Enlil temple in the northern city of Eridu. The temple is described as the foundation of heaven and earth—the geographic point at which the universe was created, the node that connects the divine and human realms. The second hymn celebrates Enlil's temple in the southern city of Nippur. This temple is also said to be the place that brings together heaven and earth. None of the other hymns make this claim, only these two that begin the composition.

Both of these assertions cannot be true. Only one temple can stand at the site where the earth came into being. If the Chronicler had been around in Enheduanna's day he would have chastised her careless logic and found a way to navigate the contradiction. As it stands, Enheduanna and her subsequent traditors felt just fine placing these hymns shoulder to shoulder and letting their competing claims remain unadjudicated and unharmonized. It reminds me of the way the biblical editors arranged Genesis 1 and 2.

When it came to religion, few in the ancient world were concerned about contradiction.[20] Harmonizers like the Chronicler were in the minority. Those of us who feel the need to maintain a consistent theology and bring the Bible's disparate parts into congruity might find in the Chronicler a justification, and even an imperative, to do so: "There's biblical warrant for this!" Indeed there is. But consider this: the presence of the conflicting accounts of creation in Genesis 1 and 2 begin the Bible. The Scriptures *start* with contradiction. The mere presence of these unharmonized texts shows that the Chronicler's approach did not win. It is even more profound than this. The editors of the

---

20. Mark Smith discusses the contradictory presentations of the divine pantheon within Ugaritic literature in "The Divine Family at Ugarit and Israelite Monotheism," in *The Whirlwind: Essays on Job, Hermeneutics and Theology in Memory of Jane Morse*, ed. Stephen L. Cook, Corrine L. Patton, and James W. Watts (Journal for the Study of the Old Testament Supplement Series 336; London: Sheffield, 2001), 40–68. And see Niek Veldhuis's discussion concerning the impossibility of forming a consistent abstract theology of Mesopotamian religion, in *Religion, Literature, and Scholarship: The Sumerian Composition* Nanše and the Birds (Cuneiform Monographs 22; Leiden: Brill, 2004), 15.

Old Testament were so open to including competing ideas within the writings they produced that they preserved the work of their ideological rival, the Chronicler, who tried to weed out contradiction! Ironically enough, the Chronicler's very presence in the pages of Scripture proves how tolerant of contradiction the editors of the Bible were.

Whenever we read a text—whether a blog post or the Bible—we bring our own situation, perspectives, questions, and expectations to the act of interpretation.[21] Accordingly, when we read the Old Testament we apply our previously assumed theological or philosophical musings of God onto the text. In extreme cases we pull a John Calvin and neuter passages that don't fit into our grid. Of course, we don't explain it this way—we create fancy terms to describe and legitimize this approach, but at the end of the day this is what happens. We all do this. We may differ on how thoroughly we do it and how much of this process is conscious, but there is no pristine interpretation that perfectly understands what is read. In my view, this is not the point of biblical interpretation in any case.

Old Testament scholar Brennan Breed says that instead of trying to understand what a biblical text originally meant, we should shift our focus to seeking to learn what a text can do. Instead of viewing a piece of literature as dead, as a housing that conveys an unchanged meaning to be received, we should regard texts as living things that take new shape as they encounter new audiences. Furthermore, texts have the potential to do things *to* us. They have energy that pulses. Here is how Breed puts it:

> Too often, biblical scholars ask, "What is the essential textual form of this biblical text? How should this text look? How should it be read? What does it mean?" Instead, we should think in terms of a text's potential. What can it look like? What can it do? The point of biblical scholarship is not containment. It is knowledge—to know what a biblical text is.[22]

When readers approach the Bible with the goal of achieving a consistent and uniform view of God that reflects the singular and original message of the author, it is almost inevitable that humanlike representations of God will be silenced or transmogrified. We should instead try to imagine how Scripture, and its underappreciated passages in particular, can shape our picture of God in new and surprising ways. Instead of trying to eliminate the Bible's contradictions and arrive at a single, harmonious theological understanding,

---

21. David H. Aaron, *Genesis Ideology: Essays on the Uses and Meanings of Stories* (Eugene, OR: Cascade, 2017), 9–10.
22. *Nomadic Text: A Theory of Biblical Reception History* (Bloomington: Indiana University Press, 2014), 117.

we should embrace contradiction as one of the fundamental ways in which the biblical authors teach us about God. The editors of Scripture knew what they were doing when they put together Genesis 1 and Genesis 2. They knew that these accounts, like the four New Testament Gospels, were different tellings. And like the two theories of light that Einstein pondered, if we downplay one of these accounts in favor of the other, our understanding of God will be diminished.

So how are we to think of the Bible, and how should we go about studying it? Biblical scholar David Aaron answered these questions regarding rabbinic literature, but his explanation applies just as well to the Old Testament:

> I mean that one should view rabbinic theology as a generative system that creates meaning through its own conceptual rules. Embedded within those rules will be the rubrics that allow seemingly contradictory statements of fact and fancy to stand side-by-side. By shifting the emphasis from theology as belief statements to theology as a hermeneutic activity, it should be possible to come closer to the intents of the rabbinic authors, and in the process, to abandon modern prejudices regarding theological discourse.[23]

I will explain this further in chapter 7. For now it is important that we view the contradictory presentations of God within the Bible not as problems to be solved but instead as catalysts that have the potential to draw us closer to God and lead us to a deeper understanding of the divine. If we apply Aaron's observations to Scripture, we learn to adjust our approach. Seeking to extract a harmonious and consistent belief system "actively works against the very conceptual structure" of biblical literature.[24] If the editors of the Bible purposely chose to retain contradiction within Scripture's pages, then we are actively resisting the understanding of the Bible's authors when we harmonize passages to create a singular picture of God.

Instead of seeing theology primarily as a belief-building act, we should approach it as a hermeneutic activity. Theology, in Aaron's conception, is not the task of forming a list of ideas we must get right. Rather, theology is a lifelong process of engaging with sacred texts, allowing them to draw us within their view of the world, wrestling with their difficulties, and persevering with them even when their ideas are off-putting to us.[25] I would also add, and I do not think Aaron would object to this, that we engage in this hermeneutic

---

23. David H. Aaron, "Shedding Light on God's Body in Rabbinic Midrashim: Reflections on the Theory of a Luminous Adam," *Harvard Theological Review* 90:3 (1997): 314.
24. Aaron, "Shedding Light on God's Body," 313.
25. This is similar to Walter Brueggemann's process of testimony, dispute, and advocacy described in his *Old Testament Theology: Testimony, Dispute, Advocacy* (Minneapolis: Fortress, 1997).

activity in community with other people. Theology is not merely an act of imaginative and speculative thought.[26] It does include that. Imagination is crucial to a deep, loving, and hopeful way of life.[27] As theologian Kwok Pui-lan writes, "Without the power of imagination we cannot envision a different past, present, and future."[28] But theology does not remain a topic for the mind. It is something we *do*.[29] It is an embodied practice that, we hope, will lead us closer to the people around us and to God.

Let me put this a different way. Knowing a person cannot be reduced to acquiring facts about them. We do not ask a friend to tell us the important data points of their lives and conclude from this information that we truly know them. Friendship requires living with someone, experiencing joys and disappointments together, getting frustrated at one another and forgiving each other. This process of friendship grows people together and causes them to know the other in far more significant ways than merely being able to recall the place in which someone was born. Facts are not unimportant. They *support* the relationship, but they do not constitute it. It is like this with God. The process of reading, interpreting, and then rereading Scripture, struggling through its challenges, and enjoying its beauty fosters a deeper appreciation for God than merely assenting to the idea of divine omniscience.[30]

To truly know God, then, we must continue the hermeneutic activity. We must imagine anew who God is, using the anthropomorphic passages in the Bible as the foundation of our thoughts—relying on Genesis 6:6 instead of Numbers 23:19. Once we have done this, we can bring these understandings of God into conversation with traditional ones. We can adopt two lines of discourse about the divine: the vocabularies of traditional theology and the humanlike presentations of God of the Old Testament. We could imagine these two ways of thinking about God as having different logics. They are internally consistent ways of imagining who God is but they conflict with one another when they are brought side by side. Instead of picking only one of these logics as the right one, we should "hold the two logics together without

---

26. Terry A. Veling, *Practical Theology: "On Earth as It Is in Heaven"* (Maryknoll, NY: Orbis Books, 2005), 4–5.

27. John O'Donohue, *Walking in Wonder: Eternal Wisdom for a Modern World*, ed. John Quinn (New York: Convergent, 2015), 122–24.

28. *Postcolonial Imagination & Feminist Theology* (Louisville: Westminster John Knox, 2005), 30.

29. Clemens Sedmak, *Doing Local Theology: A Guide for Artisans of a New Humanity* (Maryknoll, NY: Orbis Books, 2002), 6–20.

30. For further reflections on how repeated critical engagement with Scripture can deepen faith, see Ellen F. Davis and Richard B. Hays, eds., *The Art of Reading Scripture* (Grand Rapids: Eerdmans, 2003). The entire book is worthwhile, but for this topic see in particular two of the essays: Ellen F. Davis, "Critical Traditioning: Seeking an Inner-Biblical Hermeneutic," 163–80, and R. W. L. Moberly, "Living Dangerously: Genesis 22 and the Quest for Good Biblical Interpretation," 181–97.

jettisoning one, and without eliding the jagged edges that make the holding together difficult and imperfect."[31] For the remainder of the book I will focus on the biblical pictures of God as embodied. Before I begin, though, we should consider metaphor: what it is, how it works, and why biblical authors used it to communicate their ideas about God.

METAPHOR

It is common for scholars to assert that all language is metaphorical because it is nonliteral. That is, language points toward something else. It *represents* reality (or imagines an alternate one), but it is not reality itself. A chair is a thing. You can sit in one. You can't do this with language. The word "chair" isn't a thing. You can write it or speak it but it doesn't exist on its own as a physical chair does. The word "chair" points to something else—an object in the real world. Some also say that all language, since it is produced and interpreted by humans, is anthropomorphic. By this they mean that language is incapable of representing reality in an exact way. In every utterance there is a degree of imprecision and ambiguity. There is never complete and perfect overlap between what we say about something and that thing itself. This is because humans are limited and therefore unable to make comprehensive statements.[32]

I agree that language can never fully and finally mirror the world it describes. It is also true that language is a signifier, a series of signs that point to something, whether that be a concrete object or an abstract thought. Language is metaphorical in the sense that it is a vehicle which is used to transfer meaning from one person to another. I even agree that language is dependent upon humans. In this way, language is anthropological. Language conveys meaning within specific cultural, physical, and temporal environments.[33] Take a language out

---

31. Lauren F. Winner, *The Dangers of Christian Practice: On Wayward Gifts, Characteristic Damage, and Sin* (New Haven: Yale University Press, 2018), 114. This practice of holding together different logics can be helpfully applied to a variety of approaches. For instance, "The wisest course is neither to substitute a modern secular interpretation [of biblical passages] for the traditional religious one . . . nor to adhere to the traditional interpretation alone as if it were the plain sense of the book considered as a stand-alone composition." Jon D. Levenson, *The Love of God: Divine Gift, Human Gratitude, and Mutual Faithfulness in Judaism* (Princeton: Princeton University Press, 2016), 140.

32. For instance, Colin Turbayne, *Myth of Metaphor*, rev. ed. (Columbia: University of South Carolina Press, 1970); Terry Eagleton, *Literary Theory: An Introduction*, rev. ed. (Minneapolis: University of Minnesota Press, 1996), 126; George Lakoff and Mark Johnson, *Metaphors We Live By*, 2nd ed. (Chicago: University of Chicago Press, 2003); and Eberhard Jüngel, "Anthropomorphism," in *Theological Essays*, trans. John Webster (London: Bloomsbury T&T Clark, 2014), 91–92.

33. This is particularly true for metaphors. Renita J. Weems, *Battered Love: Marriage, Sex, and Violence in the Hebrew Bible* (Minneapolis: Fortress, 1995), 7.

of these contexts and very little of it is understandable.[34] All of these contexts—textual, cultural, and human—lend meaning to words. Even onomatopoeia—words that mimic sounds and that are presumably the words least dependent upon context—is conditioned on the way a certain group of people hears and interprets sound. For instance, the French say "cocorico" to imitate the noise a rooster makes while English speakers say "cock-a-doodle-doo."[35] No word or expression perfectly represents what comes out of a fowl's beak. In this sense, language is imprecise or, as some scholars are fond of saying, metaphorical.

But if we are talking about metaphor as a rhetorical phenomenon that is centered upon analogy, then it makes no sense to say that all language is metaphorical or anthropomorphic.[36] To do so would put analogy at the center of every utterance, yet most phrases make no use of analogy whatsoever. "That is an apple" is devoid of metaphor. So is "I am sad." These are simple indicative statements. Similarly, "Are you going to the theater?" is a straightforward question. A metaphor, properly speaking, is a figure of speech that uses one thing to represent another unrelated thing. The word itself comes from two Greek words that indicate a transference. The meaning of one word is given over, or transferred, to another. The seventh-century archbishop and scholar Isidore of Seville explained, "Metaphor is an adopted transference of some word, as when we say 'cornfields ripple' or 'the vines put forth gems.'"[37] In the two examples that Isidore provides, the last halves of the phrases use terms that are foreign to agricultural contexts to describe the nature of plants: stalks of corn sway in the breeze like the waves of the ocean and vines produce grapes that are as prized and beautiful as precious minerals. Bringing together these unrelated terms highlights the similarities between them and uses these similarities to help us more deeply understand the original referents, cornfields and vines. Metaphor in this instance is a specific rhetorical strategy.

We use metaphors for a variety of reasons. One of the most basic is that we suffer from deficiencies of language. We grope around trying to express our thoughts through the limited set of signs that exist within our vocabularies. It is impossible to have a word for every thing, phenomenon, experience, and emotion. So we make do by using the words we have and applying them to

---

34. A few studies have uncovered certain patterns within languages that make it possible for people with no knowledge of a language to discern some parts of it. Iain McGilchrist, *The Master and His Emissary: The Divided Brain and the Making of the Western World* (New Haven: Yale University Press, 2009), 119–20. Yet anyone who has tried to order off a menu written in a language one does not know understands how limited this ability is.

35. Thomas C. Daddesio, *On Minds and Symbols: The Relevance of Cognitive Science for Semiotics* (Berlin: de Gruyter, 1994), 240 n. 146.

36. Umberto Eco has a wonderful discussion on the sometimes absurd definitions people offer for metaphor in *Semiotics and the Philosophy of Language* (Bloomington: Indiana University Press, 1984), 87–129.

37. *Etymologiae* 1, 37.2.

different things and situations. Metaphor is particularly productive, and even necessary, for languages with small vocabularies.[38] This is particularly relevant when considering the Old Testament. Scholars estimate there are about 8,200 discrete words within the Hebrew Bible.[39] Compare this with the more than one million words in the English language and we can see how essential a tool metaphor was for the authors of the Bible.[40]

But metaphor does not merely help us overcome a limited vocabulary or discover similarities between two things. Metaphors reorganize our categories of thought and produce new knowledge.[41] They are generative, not merely associative. Reorganizing thoughts creates new webs of knowledge. Metaphors link together previously disparate things. Ideas acquire new relationships. Metaphors do not merely teach us what we already know; they also build out our comprehension of the world. They do this in an economy of space, using just a few words instead of a drawn-out explanation.

For instance, Aristotle examined the way in which pirates referred to themselves:

> Pirates now call themselves purveyors; and so it is allowable to say that the man who has committed a crime has "made a mistake," that the man who has "made a mistake" is "guilty of crime," and that one who has committed a theft has either "taken" or "ravaged."[42]

As Umberto Eco explains, before this metaphor was used no one associated pirates—who stole other people's property and transported it back to their home base or sold it abroad—with honest traders who made a living conveying goods from one location to another. The metaphor creates a hierarchy of organization that considers property along two planes: (1) property that is acquired through commercial versus violent means and (2) property that is transported over the sea. It disrupts previous assumptions by elevating the second plane above the first, and "in this way the metaphor unexpectedly suggests a socially useful role for the pirate, at the same time leading us to suspect that there may be something not altogether above board about the

---

38. Giacomo Leopardi, *Zibaldone*, ed. Michael Caesar and Franco D'Intino, trans. Kathleen Baldwin et al. (New York: Farrar, Straus & Giroux, 2013), §§1702–3.
39. Chaim Rabin and Ghil'ad Zuckermann, "Hebrew," in *Encyclopedia of Modern Jewish Culture*, vol. 1, ed. Glenda Abramson (New York: Routledge, 2004), 359. Certainly there were words in the Hebrew language that did not make it into the Bible, so the available vocabulary of Classical Hebrew was larger than 9,000 words but probably not more than twice that number.
40. Jean-Baptist Michel et al., "Quantitative Analysis of Culture Using Millions of Digitized Books," *Science* 331:6014 (January 14, 2011): 176–82.
41. Paul Ricoeur, *La métaphore vive* (Paris: Seuil, 1975), 246.
42. Aristotle, *Art of Rhetoric*, trans. J. H. Freese (Loeb Classical Library 193; Cambridge: Harvard University Press, 1926), §1405a.

transactions of the merchant."⁴³ Portraying pirates as purveyors blurs the moral and ethical boundaries between traders and bandits. It causes us to think about both of these groups in new and surprising ways. Saying that pirates are purveyors does not merely elucidate what pirates do and unpack what we already know; it creates a relationship between two groups of previously unrelated professions. This novel linkage reveals something new.

One of the most useful aspects of metaphors is that they are not strict referents. Metaphors are different from literal descriptions. Literal descriptions define things by talking about them concretely and delineating them with clear boundaries. Metaphors open the mind to imagination and freedom.⁴⁴ They break new paths and lead readers to new discoveries.⁴⁵ Metaphors are not suboptimal means of expression. Just because they lack the supposed precision of literal description does not mean they are second-tier levels of discourse that we occasionally, and regrettably, fall back on. The nineteenth-century Italian poet Giacamo Leopardi believed this very strongly:

> Strength and clarity consist in awakening an image of the object and not at all in defining it dialectically, as [literal uses of] words do when they are brought into the language. This is why metaphors of every kind are perfectly suited to the *natural* beauty and color of discourse.⁴⁶

Leopardi stressed that metaphors have value and accomplish specific things that only they can. They are not awkward add-ons to language; they are perfectly suited to the *natural* function of discourse. Metaphor is as important to communication as proposition.

In fact, metaphor is a very sophisticated and mature means of communication. Children younger than six do not employ it. They relay what they think directly. They speak propositions and indicative statements. They use literal expressions. When children are unable to say what they mean because of their limited vocabulary, there are several techniques they use to communicate, but they do not use metaphor. Metaphor comes later with more age and understanding.⁴⁷

Metaphor is an entirely appropriate, and in some circumstances a preferred, means of communication. This is true with metaphor in general. It is true

---

43. Umberto Eco, *From the Tree to the Labyrinth: Historical Studies on the Sign and Interpretation* (Cambridge: Harvard University Press, 2014), 65.
44. Denis Donoghue, *Metaphor* (Cambridge: Harvard University Press, 2014), 182–210.
45. The very fact that metaphors are surprising makes them more memorable. Teresa Delgado, *A Puerto Rican Decolonial Theology: Prophesy Freedom* (Cham, Switzerland: Palgrave Macmillan, 2017), 66.
46. Leopardi, *Zibaldone*, §111, emphasis in original.
47. Steven Pinker, *Language Learnability and Language Development* (Cambridge: Harvard University Press, 1984).

with metaphors about God. We should not regard propositional statements about God as more true or more accurate or a better foundation for thinking about God than metaphorical passages. Nor should we identify propositional statements about God as normative and metaphorical descriptions of God as aberrant or second-tier. This is the methodology, however, that interprets Genesis 6 as accommodation because of the so-called literal description of God in Numbers 23. It also underlies a hermeneutical approach that was outlined by leaders of the early church and is still an important method for many biblical interpreters today.

Early Christian interpreters developed a hermeneutical principle which states that the clear passages in Scripture should be used to make sense of unclear ones.[48] In principle, this is a sensible idea. Who would advocate that we begin our thinking with a muddled idea? Yet in practice what often happens is that so-called metaphorical passages are deemed unclear and then harmonized with propositional descriptions. Whole swaths of the Bible are ignored, interpreted to mean the opposite of what they say, or suppressed. The unique pictures of God they provide are set aside.

Before we move to another topic we should quickly correct another common trope. Like the linguists who say that all language is metaphorical, it is popular for theologians and biblical scholars to say that all language about God is metaphorical.[49] This is only true if we adopt a sloppy definition of metaphor. What theologians mean when they say that all language about God is metaphorical is that no language about God exactly mirrors what God is in reality.[50] To put it differently: all theological language is *approximate*. This is not the same as saying that all theological language is *metaphorical*. If we want to preserve a meaningful definition of metaphor as a particular rhetorical form, we cannot reduce its meaning to merely "nonliteral" or "approximate." Nor can we reduce metaphor to a second-tier method of communication. Metaphor and proposition are different ways of speaking. We should not privilege one over the other.[51]

---

48. Michael Graves, *The Inspiration and Interpretation of Scripture: What the Early Church Can Teach Us* (Grand Rapids: Eerdmans, 2014), 63–64.

49. For example, Sallie McFague, *Metaphorical Theology: Models of God in Religious Language* (Minneapolis: Fortress, 1982), 7; Marjo C. A. Korpel, *A Rift in the Clouds: Ugaritic and Hebrew Descriptions of the Divine* (Ugaritisch-biblische Literatur 8; Münster: Ugarit-Verlag, 1990), 35; Henry Jackson Flanders Jr., Robert Wilson Crapps, and David Anthony Smith, *People of the Covenant: An Introduction to the Hebrew Bible*, 4th ed. (New York: Oxford University Press, 1996), 103; and Herman Bavinck, *Reformed Dogmatics*, vol. 2, *God and Creation*, ed. John Bolt, trans. John Vriend (Grand Rapids: Baker Academic, 2004), 99.

50. McFague, *Metaphorical Theology*, 35.

51. Rowan Williams, *The Edge of Words: God and the Habits of Language* (London: Bloomsbury, 2014), 21.

GOD AS HYPEROBJECT

One of the difficulties in thinking about God—and one of the reasons why metaphor is so commonly employed to speak about the divine—is that most conceptions of God assume that God is far bigger than humans are capable of apprehending. In this, God is not unique. There are many things that are so "massively distributed in time and space relative to humans" that they are impossible to really *know*.[52]

There are objects, like an apple on a desk, that we can see in totality. We can hold the apple in our hand and look over its entire surface area. We could cut it open and examine its interior. A person can form a reasonably comprehensive knowledge of that apple. We can't do that with God.

Neither can we do that with concepts like the environment, the universe, or global warming. We can experience local manifestations of the environment—the wind running through our hair—but we cannot encounter *the environment* in toto. Similarly, scientists can detect discrete data points, such as a series of temperature readings in the Arctic, but they cannot see global warming. Localized manifestations of these concepts are parts that constitute the whole, but they are not the things themselves. Certainly, we can see the *effects* of global warming—flowers blooming earlier than before, receding glaciers, rising ocean temperatures—but global warming as an actual entity remains obscure.

Humans are parts of systems that are beyond our comprehension. We are bound up and living within the environment, the universe, and global warming.[53] The environment surrounds us and supports our life, much like God. We are very tiny members of the universe. The decisions we make contribute to or mitigate global warming. And yet, even though we cannot separate ourselves from these things (i.e., we cannot remove ourselves from the environment) our experiences of them remain partial and limited. In part, this is because of our position within these things. We can approach a comprehensive understanding of an apple because we exist outside of it. But we are inside the environment; examining it would be like trying to exhaustively study an apple while living in its core. We could make educated guesses as to how the exterior of its skin appeared but we could not see it for ourselves. Accordingly, our knowledge of things like the environment is necessarily restricted. If this is true for our relationship with the environment, it is all the more true for our experience of the God who—according to Paul's description that approvingly

---

52. Timothy Morton, *Hyperobjects: Philosophy and Ecology after the End of the World* (Minneapolis: University of Minnesota Press, 2013), 1.
53. Morton, *Hyperobjects*, 20.

quotes Epimenides—is the being in which we "live and move and have our being" (Acts 17:28). In Pauline conception we are inside God in a similar way as we are inside the universe.

Contemporary philosopher Timothy Morton created a term for things that are beyond human comprehension: hyperobjects.[54] Hyperobjects are objects that are so big relative to human beings that they defy our ability to encounter them as a whole. They are things that we can mentally define to an approximate degree but cannot know in a comprehensive sense. So far we have considered the physical size of hyperobjects. This size makes them elusive to human experience, but hyperobjects are also things that are larger than humans with respect to time.

What does it mean that the universe is almost fourteen billion years old? Mentally, we can accept this as a logical fact, but what does fourteen billion years *really mean*? Have we ever seen fourteen billion of anything, much less had direct experience with a span of time approaching anywhere near fourteen billion years? This is our difficulty in trying to comprehend hyperobjects. We cannot experience hyperobjects themselves, only small chunks of them. We can live for one hundred years, if we are lucky, in a tiny pocket of the universe, but we cannot reside in it for much longer than that. We can notice isolated effects that hyperobjects produce, but hyperobjects themselves remain hidden. Of course, we can come up with definitions for hyperobjects. The environment is, say, the ecosystem in which humans and animals live. We can understand various features of hyperobjects, such as the way that plants use light to create energy, but at the end of the day even if we know some things *about* the environment we still cannot say that we *know* the environment.

This is our predicament when it comes to God. We could say that God is the most hyper of objects. Even if we take at face value the reports of people who say that they have directly experienced God—whether in the form of the Holy Spirit or in encounters with the risen Jesus or in ecstatic states—these are still only partial and local manifestations of what Christians believe to be a universal and triune deity. Not only are our perceptions of God always and necessarily partial and local; even the descriptions of God that theologians use are hardly comprehensible. What does it mean for God to be infinite or unbound by time? Of course, we could posit mental schemes attempting to explain this. We could say that God exists outside of the fourth dimension. But how do we as creatures profoundly limited by space and time understand at all what this means, apart from a blind leap of the imagination? We can hardly wrap our minds around the fact that giant sequoias can live for three thousand years. How can we understand the idea of an infinite God in any meaningful sense?

54. *The Ecological Thought* (Cambridge: Harvard University Press, 2010), 130–35.

Viewing God as a hyperobject is a somewhat new way of thinking (or it applies a new word to an old way of thinking), but the challenge of coming to grips with the idea of God is not. Many thinkers have noted the difficulties of conceiving, much less explaining and defining, the divine. Plato thought it was really hard to form a mental concept of God and downright impossible to express God in words. One of the early church's greatest thinkers, Gregory of Nyssa (ca. 330–ca. 395), turned Plato's understanding on its head with the observation that it is "indeed impossible to express in words [what God is] but even more impossible to form a concept of him." The theologian who influenced Western Christian thinking more than perhaps any other, Augustine of Hippo (354–430), said, "If you comprehend, it is not God; if you were able to comprehend, you comprehended something in place of God; if you were able as if to understand, your thought has deceived you."[55] Yet theologians, including Gregory and Augustine, had much to say about the character and nature of the God they believed to be beyond their comprehension. Just as we must hold certain contradictions between biblical passages in tension, we must also hold in tension the contradictory notions that God is at once knowable and mysterious. Metaphors are useful in making it easier to contemplate this confoundingly elusive God.

ANTHROPOMORPHISMS

Metaphors come in many different varieties. Relationships can, in theory, be created between almost any things. For instance, we commonly employ metaphors that use agricultural images, sports terminology, and nautical features. For the purposes of this book I will focus on the metaphors scholars refer to as anthropomorphisms. There are many definitions of anthropomorphism, but what is common to them all is the act of attributing human characteristics to a nonhuman entity. Human characteristics can be applied to almost anything from (the feminine shape of) a car to the stars (blinking) in the sky. Since we are discussing theology I am particularly interested in studying the instances in which biblical authors attribute human characteristics to God.

Many prominent thinkers looked down on metaphor and warned their readers not to use it.[56] About two and a half millennia ago the Greek philoso-

---

55. All of these quotes are from Hans Urs von Balthasar, *Theo-Logic*, vol. 2, *Truth of God*, trans. Adrian J. Valker (San Francisco: Ignatius, 2004), 100.

56. I've adapted the following discussion from Stewart Elliot Guthrie, "Anthropomorphism: A Definition and a Theory," in *Anthropomorphism, Anecdotes, and Animals*, ed. Robert W. Mitchell, Nicholas S. Thompson, and H. Lyn Miles (Albany: State University of New York Press, 1997), 51–52.

pher Xenophanes said that people fashion their gods by looking at the mirror. In his mind, this was not a good thing. The many gods in the Greek pantheon were organized into a hierarchical royal court. Xenophanes observed that the divine court of the Greek pantheon was identical in structure to the organization of Greek political life. He concluded that religious thoughts are merely human ideas projected into heaven. They say much about human culture but do not reveal anything about the divine. Baruch Spinoza (born 1632) and David Hume (born 1711) argued in a similar vein, cautioning against anthropomorphic thought since, in their views, it is inherently self-referential. That is, attributing human characteristics to nonhuman entities does not tell us anything about these entities. It only reveals what we already know about ourselves.

These critics believed that a worldview based upon anthropomorphism is little more than an echo chamber of what a person already believes. As such, metaphor does not qualify as genuine knowledge. Behind these criticisms is the belief that applying human traits, shapes, or patterns of thinking onto nonhuman things is improper. It is a category error that mistakenly ascribes an aspect of one thing to something entirely unrelated to it. But the meaning of anthropomorphic metaphors, as is the case with every metaphor, arises out of this very tension. In fact, contemporary philosopher Charles Taylor argues that inappropriateness of comparison is necessary for metaphors to be powerful and vivid.[57] A comparison between two roughly synonymous things would reveal very little. Equating pirates with purveyors reorganizes our conception of both occupations because of their superficial incongruity. This incongruity also makes the metaphor memorable. There are instances in which anthropomorphisms are unhelpful, but on the whole they are valid and powerful ways of exploring and remembering the nature of God.

The writers of the Old Testament embraced stories which taught that humans are made in the image of God. The reason humans are able to speak, these stories imply, is because God speaks.[58] If there are kings in this world, it is because God was a king first.[59] The human experience reflects God not because humans project their thoughts into heaven but because God imprinted the divine form onto humanity. If we take this as true, we could

---

57. Charles Taylor, *The Language Animal: The Full Shape of the Human Linguistic Capacity* (Cambridge: Harvard University Press, 2016), 139–40.

58. Javier A. Alanís, "God," in *Handbook of Latina/o Theologies*, ed. Edwin David Aponte and Miguel A. De La Torre (St. Louis: Chalice, 2006), 12–13.

59. Gerhard von Rad, *Old Testament Theology*, vol. 1, trans. D. M. G. Stalker (New York: Harper & Row, 1963), 145. Marc Brettler has a profoundly different approach. He assumes ancient Israelites employed these metaphors to bridge the gap between humanity and an incomparable deity. *God Is King: Understanding Israelite Metaphor* (Journal for the Study of the Old Testament Supplement Series 76; Sheffield: Sheffield Academic, 1989), 162.

reverse engineer our humanity to better understand the nature of God. If God stamped the divine image onto humans, one way we can better understand who God is is to understand God *in light of ourselves*. This may explain what the writers of the Old Testament were doing when they pictured God in humanlike ways.[60]

BUT ARE THEY METAPHORS?

Most people assume the anthropomorphic passages in the Bible are metaphors. They take for granted that the authors of the Bible thought their humanlike representations of God were nonliteral. For instance, Janet Soskice:

> It is difficult to believe that the prophets, although perhaps lacking a developed set of grammatical distinctions which enabled them to designate metaphors as metaphors, were unaware that in speaking of God as a herdsman or planter they were using language not strictly appropriate to him.[61]

Soskice says that even though the biblical passages which she believes are metaphors are never flagged as such within the text itself (she hypothesizes without evidence that the Israelites lacked markers for this) they are nonetheless nonliteral because she has a hard time believing otherwise. One of the problems with this line of thinking is that Soskice equates her assumptions with those of ancient Israelites. If it is hard for her to believe that God is a herdsman, it must have been hard for the authors of the Bible to believe this too. Soskice universalizes her individual experience.

Another flaw in her assertion, and this is common in discussions of biblical metaphor, is her assumption that unless God fully represents the terms applied to God, these terms must be metaphors. It is as if there is a checklist of characteristics that make a herdsman a herdsman. Unless there is absolute correspondence between objects—unless someone is able to tick off every last characteristic on the list—scholars assume that an ancient author used a metaphor. But there are very few concepts that function this way. As David Aaron points out, the overwhelming majority of expressions within any language

---

60. James Barr rejects this approach because he does not see a connection between the older literary sources that contain anthropomorphism and the later passages that speak of the image of God. "Theophany and Anthropomorphism in the Old Testament," in *Congress Volume: Oxford 1959* (Supplements to Vetus Testamentum 7; Leiden: Brill, 1960), 38. Even though different sources contain different perceptions of God, they were combined into an anthology of sacred literature. This analogy, then, became a new entity that invites readers to interpret the various sources together. Privileging one stratum over another is, in most cases, quite arbitrary.

61. *Metaphor and Religious Language* (Oxford: Oxford University Press, 1985), 77.

employ "a matrix of general principles that one might describe as floating or graded."[62] There is hardly ever complete correspondence between a term and the thing it indicates.

If we stay with the example of a herdsman, we discover that it can mean different things in different geographic places. A herdsman in the Levant may stay with his sheep as they move between grazing grounds. He sleeps with the animals, constantly protects them, and makes sure individual sheep do not wander off. A herdsman in the Lake District of England, on the other hand, releases his flock into the mountains in December and does not return for them until April. The sheep are hefted; they have an instinctual tie to the mountains and they do not stray from them.[63] The sheep wander around unsupervised for months at a time while the herdsman stays nice and warm in his living room. We do not say that the overseer of sheep in the Lake District is not a real herdsman because he does not remain with his sheep year-round. The checklists that define what a herdsman is in these two places do not match. But there is enough overlap between them for the same word to describe them both. We do not coin a new term for every unique occurrence of the tending of sheep. We extend existing terms to new situations.[64] This may expand a definition as we apply it to different things or revise it in some way, but what we do not do is assume that the Lake District herdsman is a metaphorical herdsman while the Levantine herdsman is a literal one.

This example illustrates the difficulty in determining when a statement is a metaphor and when it is not. In order to make a correct assessment, the reader and author must share an understanding of what the text conveys.[65] This involves collaboration. An author encodes meaning into a string of symbols and the reader unlocks the symbols' code and tries to make sense of what the words say. To be successful, the reader must have a sense of the statement's content and what the author was trying to accomplish with it. There are situations in which readers can understand a literary work with little knowledge of its context, but this is only possible for highly stereotypical language such as codified legal terminology.[66] Even in this case there is still context. The reader brings to the act of reading their knowledge of the history

---

62. *Biblical Ambiguities: Metaphor, Semantics and Divine Imagery* (Brill Reference Library of Ancient Judaism 4; Leiden: Brill, 2001), 40.

63. James Rebanks, *The Shepherd's Life: Modern Dispatches from an Ancient Landscape* (New York: Flatiron Books, 2015).

64. Umberto Eco, *The Search for the Perfect Language*, trans. James Fentress (Oxford: Blackwell, 1995), 57–58.

65. Jonathan D. Culler, *Structuralist Poetics: Structuralism, Linguistics and the Study of Literature* (Ithaca, NY: Cornell University Press, 1975), 3–36.

66. Lawrence M. Solen, "Learning Our Limits: The Decline of Textualism in Statutory Cases," *Wisconsin Law Review* 2 (1997): 235–81.

of how the term has been used and accepted in the history of legal discourse. There may not be much immediate grammatical context surrounding the use of the term but there are loads of historical and situational context a trained professional brings to her engagement with it.[67]

This collaborative effort between author and reader is more difficult the further apart the participants are in time, culture, language, and space. We should proceed with a healthy sense of caution when reading the Bible since there are thousands of years, entirely different cultures, completely different languages, and a lot of physical distance between us and its authors. It does not mean that we can understand nothing of what they wrote, but it does mean that it is unwise for us to make the assumption that our intuitions and levels of credulity are the same as those of the people who wrote and compiled the Hebrew Bible.

In almost every case, when a scholar labels an Old Testament statement as anthropomorphic the only reasoning behind this decision is their intuition regarding the literalness of the passage. If we take our assumptions out of the equation, there is very little to make us think the Israelites understood these statements as metaphors. The passages that depict God in human ways do not include disclaimers denying their literal reality. They scan just like the statements we regard as propositions. Soskice hypothesized that Israelites lacked markers to indicate metaphors. But what kind of markers does she think they need? An author can always say: *God isn't like this in reality but I picture him as a bearded old man.* There are plenty of similes in the Old Testament that are clearly marked as nonliteral descriptions—Psalm 78:65, for instance, "Then the LORD awoke as from sleep, like a warrior [*kəgibbôr*] shouting because of wine." In this psalm God shouts *like* a drunken warrior. The nonliteral nature of the expression is marked with a preposition (*k*). The authors of the Bible had ample ability to signal figurative statements when they wanted to.

It seems to me that in very many cases the people who wrote the Old Testament understood their so-called anthropomorphic statements as literal expressions of fact. God is a king. God has a body. That is just how God is. We might be tempted to regard these passages as metaphors because *we* doubt their reality, but the writers of the Bible almost never indicate that *they* did. David Aaron insists that when biblical scholars label these passages as metaphors they "project post-biblical conceptualizations of language and transcendence upon the Bible, all while assuming that the ancients recognized

---

67. John Berger's observation about translation also applies to reading: "True translation is not a binary affair between two languages [or writer and reader] but a triangular affair. The third point of the triangle being what lay behind the words of the original text before it was written." *Confabulations* (London: Penguin, 2016), 4.

the same philosophical problems that occupy us."[68] In other words, when we label passages as anthropomorphic metaphors we are interpreting the Old Testament as if we were the ones writing it. This is not a sound assumption.

To more fully understand the ways in which Old Testament authors understood God, we need to analyze their depictions of God as if they are literal descriptions. Unless, that is, they contain disclaimers or markers that clearly delineate them as metaphor. This methodology is not perfect. Inevitably, there will be passages that were intended as metaphors and are not marked as such. There may be many of them. Nonetheless, I think this is a better approach than the typical practice of regarding all humanlike depictions of God as metaphorical. Perhaps I've swung too far in the opposite direction, but if so I will at least provide a counterpoint to a long-standing imbalance. In any case, it is not my intention that we view the Old Testament God from only this angle. After we have understood God anthropomorphically we can then bring this picture of God into conversation with more transcendent views of the divine.

The Old Testament pictures God in at least two distinct and parallel forms: (1) a deity who takes concrete form and local manifestation and (2) a god who is spirit and whose presence is everywhere at the same time, unrestricted in time, space, and location. This is totally contradictory. So is saying that light is a wave and a particle. If we want to more fully understand the God of Scripture, we need to embrace these two, very different representations of God as equally valid instead of regarding one as superior to the other.[69]

---

68. Aaron, *Biblical Ambiguities*, 35.

69. The latter approach is incredibly common even within scholarly circles. One of the most influential Old Testament theologians of the twentieth century had precisely this opinion: "Among the great mass of the people, and especially in the earlier period, the deity was frequently conceived as restricted to physical modes of living and self-manifestation. They understood the anthropomorphic expressions in a quite literal and concrete way, and so managed to acquire a most inadequate conception of the divine supremacy." Walther Eichrodt, *Theology of the Old Testament*, vol. 1, trans. J. A. Baker (Philadelphia: Westminster, 1961), 104–6.

3

God's Body

If someone asked an ancient Israelite where God was, he could stick out his finger and point. God might be above the sky or dwelling in the temple or within the fire of a burning bush, but one thing God was not was the omnipresent spirit that many today imagine God to be.[1] Instead of God being fully present everywhere at all times, the writers of the Old Testament stress that God has the ability *to go* anywhere God chooses, but the divine person is not everywhere simultaneously.[2] Ancient Israelites believed that God has similar physical limitations as humans. God is present in one place and not in another. And yet, they believed that God has the ability to travel across boundaries that restrict human movement. God is, to them, a being who has a localized presence but who can travel to any point God chooses. God lives in heaven, visits earth, and has very little to do with the realm of the dead. God has superhuman abilities that allow God to move between these spaces with ease, but God's presence is nonetheless restricted to particular locales. This is because many of the writers of the Bible assumed God has a body.

---

1. For instance, Karl Barth: "There is no place where He is less present than in all others. On the contrary, He is everywhere completely and undividedly the One He always is, even if in virtue of the freedom of His love He is this in continually differing and special ways." *Church Dogmatics*, II/1, *The Doctrine of God*, ed. Geoffrey W. Bromiley and Thomas F. Torrance, trans. T. H. L. Parker et al. (London: T&T Clark, 1957), 470. See also Mark Smith, *How Human Is God?* (Collegeville, MN: Liturgical Press, 2014), 3–4.
2. John Goldingay, *Old Testament Theology*, vol. 2, *Israel's Faith* (Downers Grove, IL: IVP Academic, 2006), 102.

WHAT IS A BODY?

Before we go further I should define what I mean by the term "body." We might think of a body as a collection of bones, muscles, tendons, and organs sealed inside a sack of skin. It may be that some Israelites thought of God's body in this way. If they did, they adopted a common belief of the people of their time. Creation accounts from neighboring cultures depict gods of flesh and blood. These stories are quite earthy.

For instance, the Babylonian creation epic Enuma Elish describes heaven and earth as the products of two halves of the goddess Tiamat.[3] Marduk, the chief deity in the Babylonian pantheon, fought Tiamat when she rebelled against him. He split her body down the middle—head to toe—and formed heaven and earth with the two halves. Marduk also killed the god who incited Tiamat to riot and formed humans from his spilled blood. In another story, this one from Egypt, the creator god Atum generated a pair of lower-ranking gods by masturbating into his own mouth. As Atum's seed mingled with his saliva, the plebeian gods somehow came into being and Atum spat them out.[4] These stories, bizarre as they seem to us, reveal that it was common for ancient people to imagine divine beings as having humanlike bodies. It doesn't get more corporeal than blood and semen.

There are passages in the Old Testament that seem to indicate ancient Israelites thought of God's body in similar ways. In Genesis 2:7 God breathes life into the nostrils of the first human. Unless we regard this passage as completely allegorical, God would need a mouth or something like it (not to mention lungs and a throat) to impart breath to creation. Jump-cutting to the prophet Amos, we read these words that preface an oracle: "I saw the Lord standing beside the altar" (9:1). Children immediately understand the implication of this verse: in order to stand, one needs legs. If we interpret the Genesis and Amos verses straightforwardly, we would conclude that God has a body like ours. God has two legs, a head, and a torso, at the least. Not to mention internal organs like lungs.

Once we grow up we often lose the sensitive reading strategies of our youth. Our minds are blunted by the assumption that passages like these cannot, under any circumstances, relay accurate facts about the physical structure of God because, we assuredly know, God has no physical structure.[5] We

---

3. A translation of Enuma Elish can be found in William Hallo and K. Lawson Younger, eds., *The Context of Scripture*, vol. 1 (Leiden: Brill, 2003), 390–402.

4. Erin E. Fleming, "Creation," in *The Oxford Encyclopedia of the Bible and Gender Studies*, vol. 1, ed. Julia M. O'Brien (Oxford: Oxford University Press, 2014), 62.

5. This assumption is so widespread that even in a monograph that discusses the meanings of Hebrew terms relating to humanity the author does not even entertain the possibility that the

dismiss the questions that came naturally to us as children. They seem silly and unbelievable. But, for the sake of argument, let's say that our adult readings are true. Let's say that these passages are metaphors and do not mean to convey the idea that God actually has a body. It is still important to note that God *is described* as embodied even if the person who wrote or said these statements did not literally believe this. By describing God in these ways, these authors wanted their readers to imagine God as having lips and lungs even if, at the end of the day, these pictures were merely imaginary. God's corporeality must teach us something about the divine or else Scripture's authors were very poor communicators. The reason these pictures teach us something is because there is at least some continuity between the metaphors used and the being of God (if they are, in fact, metaphors and not literal depictions!).[6] If there is no continuity between the two, then we could learn nothing from these identifications and we are back to thinking that Scripture's authors were inept at describing God.[7]

To appreciate the Old Testament portrayals of God more fully, we must redefine our understanding of the word "god." The Old Testament writers use this word differently than we do. For them, "god" encompassed more types of being than the supreme being in the universe. One passage that reveals this, and also implies something profound about God's body, is 1 Samuel 28. In this passage Saul asks a diviner to conjure a dead man. The diviner succeeds. The narrator reports the diviner's description of what happened: "The woman said to Saul, 'I see a divine being [ʾĕlōhîm] coming up out of the ground'" (v. 13). This divine being was the prophet Samuel, long dead at this point. The diviner used the same term (ʾĕlōhîm) to describe Samuel—a dead human coming back to earth—that the writers of Scripture commonly used to designate God.

Genesis passages that say God created humanity in the divine image could mean that humans look like God. John W. Rogerson, *Anthropology and the Old Testament* (Atlanta: John Knox, 1979), 159–61. Instead, this scholar assumes that the idea of humans created in the divine image means God created humans as relational beings. This interpretation is nowhere in the Genesis texts themselves nor does it have anything to do with the etymology or ancient contexts of the Hebrew words this scholar explains. Our assumptions about God are strong indeed.

6. As Terence E. Fretheim observes about the nature metaphors that biblical authors used to describe God: "If God is a rock or a mother eagle, for example, rocks and mother eagles are reflective in some sense of the identity of God. That is to say, there are continuities between rocks and eagles and the reality of God." *God and World in the Old Testament: A Relational Theology of Creation* (Nashville: Abingdon, 2005), 256.

7. "To diminish the thrust of the metaphors as though they were a merely figurative device with no precise theological significance is to stop one's ears to what the writers were saying. The point of the Old Testament analogies, especially the metaphors drawn from human experience, is that they are the most appropriate form of speech for talking of a God who, as they fundamentally believed, is committed to a reciprocal relatedness with the world and has an affinity with it." John V. Taylor, *The Christlike God* (London: SCM, 1992), 149.

For ancient Israelites, any being that does not primarily reside on earth is a "divine being"—whether that being lives in the underworld, as Samuel would have, or in heaven where God and the divine attendants dwell. Perhaps it is more accurate to translate ʾĕlōhîm as "otherworldly being." Gods are beings who do not reside on earth's crust. Yet they resemble humans to a striking degree. Saul asks the diviner to tell him what she sees. She says, "An old man is coming up; he is wrapped in a robe" (v. 14). The deceased prophet, the person whom the woman calls an "otherworldly being," was shaped like a man and even wore clothes. The dead do not become amorphous spirits once they die—they retain the forms they took when they were alive. They have arms and legs and even wear robes.

When Samuel was conjured from the dead he had a different material composition than he did when he was alive. He retained the form of a human body, but he rose up out of the ground. This is obviously something a corporeal body cannot do. Nonetheless, this otherworldly version of Samuel occupied a particular space and had a recognizable shape. Samuel's body was different from ours—it could pass through dirt—but it retained aspects of its previous version, such as a localized presence and a unique anthropoid appearance.

Biblical passages like Amos 9:1a ("I saw the Lord standing beside the altar") seem to indicate God's body was similar to the shape of the conjured Samuel's. In Amos's vision God had legs that enabled God to stand. There are other accounts that make God's body seem very different and imply that we need to expand our understanding of what it means for God to have a body. For instance, the account of God's appearance at Mount Sinai. Exodus 24 recounts the story of Moses spending forty days atop a mountain in order to meet with God. Moses goes up and waits for the divine presence to arrive. The fact that Moses waits is important. Moses does not think God is already there. That is, Moses does not assume that God is omnipresent, or everywhere at the same time. Moses waits. He waits because God needs to travel from heaven, or wherever else God was at the moment, to Mount Sinai. This story assumes that God has a localized presence.

When God arrives, thunder shakes the earth and lightning flashes across the sky. Exodus 24:15–18 says there was also a cloud of smoke. The reason for the smoke? "Now Mount Sinai was wrapped in smoke, because the Lord had descended upon it in fire" (Exod. 19:18). Like God's appearance to Moses in the burning bush (Exod. 3), God's presence on Mount Sinai takes the form of fire. This is a far cry from the arms, legs, torso, and head that make up the human frame. It is also very different from Amos's image of God standing in the temple. And yet, there is a common theme running through all of these presentations. There is a particular place where God is. In Exodus 19, God's fiery presence is atop a mountain. The Israelites could point to Mount Sinai's summit and say, "There's our God."

Throughout this book I assume Benjamin Sommer's definition of a body: *something located in a particular place at a particular time, whatever its shape or substance*.[8] This definition is broad enough to account for the variety of forms that God takes within the Old Testament yet specific enough to reflect fundamental ideas that the authors of Scripture had about God—that God was located in a particular place, at a particular time, and that God took particular shapes. We will first look at what it means for God to be located in a particular place.

LOCALIZED PRESENCE

Ancient Israelites, along with most other contemporaneous Near Eastern peoples, thought of the universe as a three-tiered expanse.[9] The three spaces were inhabited by different types of beings. God and the heavenly court occupied the heavens above, humans populated the earth in the middle, and the dead collected dust in the netherworld below. Psalm 115:16–17 reflects this scheme:

> The heavens are the LORD's heavens,
>   but the earth he has given to human beings.
> The dead do not praise the LORD,
>   nor do any that go down into silence.

In Psalm 115 the dead descend beneath the ground into a quiet existence. They are cut off from God and do not even bother to give the Lord praise.[10] The polar opposite of this space, the place farthest from this depressing holding tank of the noiseless deceased, is God's residence. It is a place we call heaven but is termed the "skies" in the Hebrew Bible. Let's consider a bit more deeply the geography of the divine realm because, like God's body, the Israelites believed that the place where God lives has a defined location and takes a particular form and shape.

---

8. *The Bodies of God and the World of Ancient Israel* (Cambridge: Cambridge University Press, 2009), 2.

9. Kyle Greenwood provides a good summary of this idea in *Scripture and Cosmology: Reading the Bible between the Ancient World and Modern Science* (Downers Grove, IL: IVP Academic, 2015), 71–102.

10. Gregorio del Olmo Lette, "La religion cananéenne des anciens Hébreux," in *Mythologie et Religion des Sémites Occidentaux*, ed. Gregorio del Olmo Lette (Orientalia Lovaniensia Analecta 162; Leuven: Peeters, 2008), 2:246.

In Genesis 1:6–7 we read of God creating a "firmament," or dome, that forms a ceiling over the earth. This firmament "separated the waters that were under the dome from the waters that were above the dome." This thin dome supports an ocean in the sky and keeps the waters from flooding the earth. They thought of the sky as a holding tank of water. This makes a lot of sense given that rain falls down from above. In fact, they believed there are windows in the dome that God opens to shower the ground with rain.[11] Above this supposed ocean in the sky is the place where divine beings, including God, live.

The firmament is a physical barrier between two worlds. Below it is the space where humans and animals live. Everything above the firmament belongs to the divine realm. Deuteronomy 10:14 calls the divine residence "the heaven of the heavens" (or sky of the skies). Pillars with bases on the firmament's dome supported a palace complex above the heavenly ocean (Job 26:11). God's heavenly palace is a lot like the city of Venice, where merchants created homes for themselves in the middle of a lagoon by sinking tree trunks into the water and pounding them deep into the mud. They built elaborate palaces and grand homes atop the pylons. If only these supports rested on a solid firmament, Venice wouldn't be sinking. In any case, Yahweh's residence was built upon pylons, too. And like earthly palaces, God's residence has space for attendants. God, like us humans, needs a house to live in.[12] After all, it would be unseemly, not to mention tiring, for divine beings to tread water for eternity.

It is from this palace, far above the earth, that God watches over the world:

> The LORD looks down from heaven;
>   he sees all humankind.
> From where he sits enthroned he watches
>   all the inhabitants of the earth—
> he who fashions the hearts of them all,
>   and observes all their deeds.
>   Ps. 33:13–15

This description of Israel's god is similar to the way Mesopotamians conceived of the sun god, Shamash. Each day Shamash would make a journey

---

11. For instance, Gen. 7:11; 8:2; 2 Kgs. 7:2; Isa. 24:18.
12. Divine attendants include the members of the heavenly royal court that make up the "host of heaven" (1 Kgs. 22:19) and "sons of God" (Job 1:6; 2:1); the seraphs, or assistants that apparently were on fire (Isa. 6:2); divine messenger-warriors that ferried dispatches from heaven to earth (2 Sam. 24:10–17 and 2 Kgs. 19:35); named angels such as Gabriel (Dan. 8:16; 9:21) and Michael (Dan. 12:1); cherubim that guard the sanctuary and carry God's throne (Exod. 25 and Ezek. 10); and the Accuser (Job 1:6–12). See Samuel A. Meier, *Themes and Transformations in Old Testament Prophecy* (Downers Grove, IL: IVP Academic, 2009), 19–27, and Greenwood, *Scripture and Cosmology*, 92–93.

through the sky, rising in the east and setting in the west. He looked down from his perch and observed everything that happened on the ground below. He was thought of as "the great judge of heaven and earth."[13] He could act as a judge because he saw everything that took place and therefore could correctly arbitrate disputes. While a global vision like this has its advantages, it also comes with a weakness. One is able to comprehensively survey the activity of humanity but it is hard to get beyond a general impression.

The details of a particular happening in Babylon are hard for God to chart out when the divine throne room is in the upper heavens. It's like watching people ice skate in Central Park from the hundredth floor of a skyscraper. The writers of the Old Testament understood this. They represented the god of Israel as sometimes leaving the heavenly palace and going down to visit the earth. The reason for this? God wanted to spy out the details of what was taking place. For example, Genesis 11:5: "The LORD came down to see the city and the tower, which mortals had built." In this story humans had banded together and were building a tower they thought would enable them to reach heaven. God leaves the palace above the firmament and comes down to earth to investigate. This act—God's presence moving locations so that God could better observe human actions—implies "that Yhwh does not know everything by inherent omniscience but is capable of discovering everything when desiring to do so."[14] God's localized yet potentially boundless knowledge coincides with God's localized yet potentially boundless presence. God's body puts a limitation on the knowledge God possesses at any given time. God has the ability to learn something when God wants, but the divine mind does not automatically know everything. I will discuss this further in chapter 4. What is important for our discussion here is to underscore that underlying all of the passages I have mentioned is the idea that God's presence is local. God must journey to a different space to more fully comprehend the details of what is taking place. God is not everywhere at the same time. God is limited to certain locations.

Before we examine some of the locations God inhabits, we should briefly pause to remember that if God inhabits certain locations, God is necessarily absent from other places. As Abraham Joshua Heschel put it, "There is an alternative to God's presence, namely His absence. God may withdraw and

---

13. This epithet is from the epilogue of Hammurabi's Laws, xlvii 79–xlviii 2, in Martha T. Roth, *Law Collections from Mesopotamia and Asia Minor* (Writings from the Ancient World 6; Atlanta: Scholars Press, 1995), 134. For a short description of Shamash, see the entry "Shamash" in *The Dictionary of the Ancient Near East*, ed. Piotr Bienkowski and Alan Millard (Philadelphia: University of Pennsylvania Press, 2000), 263–64.

14. John Goldingay, *Psalms*, vol. 1, *Psalms 1–14* (Baker Commentary on the Old Testament Wisdom and Psalms; Grand Rapids: Baker Academic, 2006), 470.

detach Himself from history."[15] According to the biblical prophets, God is not always immediately present with us. There are times when God is in the vicinity, but for humans to feel a connection to God they have to search. For instance, Isaiah 55:6 warns people to act on the opportunities to look for God when they arise because there could come a time when they will not be able to find God at all. "Seek the LORD while he may be found, call upon him while he is near."

GOD IN A LAND

Almost every culture in the ancient world believed that divine beings live in the heavens and that earth is the dwelling place of humanity. These gods make occasional forays to earth or they send messengers in their place. Gods were not thought to be omnipresent. Nor did ancient peoples imagine gods as enjoying universal authority on earth. Each locality—a nation or city—had its own protective deity. Protective deities were tied to particular patches of ground, and their jurisdiction stopped once a person crossed over into a new territory.[16] Second Kings 5 presents a fascinating example of this.

Naaman, the commander of the Aramean army, asks Elisha, an Israelite prophet, to heal his skin disease. Elisha tells Naaman to wash himself seven times in the Jordan River. The commander obeys and is healed. He returns to Elisha's house to ask for permission to take some of Elisha's dirt. What an odd request. Why would an Aramean want to take home Israelite dirt? Naaman reveals his reason: "Please let two mule-loads of earth be given to your servant; for your servant will no longer offer burnt offering or sacrifice to any god except the LORD" (2 Kgs. 5:17). After Naaman is healed he pledges to worship only Israel's god. Naaman is leaving Israel and going back home, and he does not believe it would be possible to worship Yahweh from there without Israelite dirt. Naaman operates with an idea common to ancient Near Easterners: deities are constrained to certain lands. If Naaman wants to sacrifice to Yahweh after returning to Aram, he would need Israelite dirt to do it. By schlepping a couple loads of Israelite soil to Aram, Naaman is taking Yahweh with him.

Commentators point out that Elisha doesn't correct Naaman. The prophet merely responds with a blessing: "Go in peace" (5:19). Commentators also point out that Elisha does not affirm Naaman's view that Yahweh is bound

---

15. *The Prophets*, vol. 2 (New York: Harper & Row, 1962), 211–12.
16. Daniel I. Block, *The Gods of the Nations: Studies in Ancient Near Eastern National Theology*, 2nd ed. (Grand Rapids: Baker, 2000).

to the confines of Israel's land. That is, commentators take pains to say that the Israelite prophet does not explicitly endorse the Aramean's understanding that to worship Yahweh in Aram, Namaan would need to take Israel's dirt. These commentators posit that Elisha was being charitable and ignored Naaman's theological blunder. Naaman was new to faith in Yahweh, after all. His heart was in the right place even though his head was not in the game. They opine that Elisha understood that Naaman was sincere in his commitment to worship Yahweh even while he was profoundly mistaken in thinking that God was limited geographically.[17] Elisha was not so foolish as to think that hauling dirt was a precondition to pray to Yahweh beyond the boundary of Israelite territory. Elisha was kind and nonjudgmental. He accepted this Gentile's statement of faith, warts and all. While this interpretation is popular, I do not think this is a good reading of the text. There are indicators within the passage which show that Elisha shares Naaman's perception that Yahweh is geographically limited.

When Naaman approaches Elisha for healing, Elisha specifies that he must wash in the Jordan River. Apparently, no other stream will do. Naaman becomes angry and says, "Are not Abana and Pharpar, the rivers of Damascus, better than all the waters of Israel? Could I not wash in them, and be clean?" (5:12). This is a fair question, particularly if one assumes that God is omnipresent. If God is everywhere at the same time, then it shouldn't matter which river one bathes in.[18]

The Abana (modern-day Barada River) and the Pharpar (el Awaj River) supply Damascus and its environs, while the Jordan River gives life to the land of Israel. Naaman argues that the rivers of Damascus should be just as effective for his healing as Israel's source of water. Naaman's servants point out that for the healing to work he must follow the prophet's instructions exactly.[19] But why the Jordan in particular? Why couldn't Naaman wash seven times in any watercourse? Because the Jordan is under Yahweh's control and the waters of Damascus are outside his jurisdiction. By restricting Naaman's washing to the Jordan, Elisha is saying that only the god of Israel can heal him. And Elisha assumes that if Yahweh is to cleanse a person, it has to happen within the confines of Israel. This matches exactly Naaman's assumption

---

17. For instance, Richard D. Nelson, *First and Second Kings* (Interpretation; Louisville: John Knox, 1987), 182–83. To be charitable to Nelson and the many other commentators who follow his line of thought, at least they understand the real significance of Naaman's request for dirt.

18. As I have discussed before, Naaman did not believe in the omnipresence of God. His question challenges the idea that only Israel's God can heal him. In essence, Naaman asks: Why can't my Aramean god help me?

19. Marvin A. Sweeney, *I & II Kings* (Old Testament Library; Louisville: Westminster John Knox, 2007), 300.

that if he is to pray to Yahweh he must do it on Israelite dirt. Both Naaman and Elisha believe the same thing: Yahweh's presence on earth is confined to a particular plot of dirt.

GOD AND THE TEMPLE

Many writers of Scripture assumed that, like an earthly king, God's power extends only to the boundaries of the land of Israel. They also assumed that, like an earthly king, God had a residence where God's actual presence could be found.[20] Early in the Pentateuch Yahweh resided in a movable tent, and later God moved to the Jerusalem temple. Not only did God live in one particular house but God's presence filled only one particular room within the temple: the Holy of Holies. The Holy of Holies was God's earthly bedroom, living room, and throne room combined. There was furniture in this room for Yahweh to use—a lamp, a table, and a backless chair called the ark.[21] In some inexplicable way, God lived in heaven and on earth at the same time within a temple in each of these realms. This is how casual Bible readers understand God's presence in Old Testament times. It is not, however, the way that some Old Testament writers imagined it. There is disagreement among biblical authors regarding the precise way in which God's presence appeared on the earth. I'll mention four of these views.

God outside the Camp

The pentateuchal author contemporary scholars term "E" because he often refers to Yahweh with the generic title for God, Elohim, understood that God was present at the tabernacle/temple only on special occasions.[22] For instance, Numbers 12 recounts a disagreement between Moses and his sister Miriam. This occurs during the time the people of God are dragging their camp and a portable shrine around the Sinai Peninsula. God summons Moses, Aaron, and Miriam to *come out* (*wayyēṣ'û*) to the tent of meeting, the structure that other writers refer to as the tabernacle. The verb that God uses here is important. It indicates that the tent of meeting—the place where

---

20. The idea that a deity's presence dwelled in a temple was common throughout the ancient Near East. Michael B. Hundley, *Gods in Dwellings: Temples and Divine Presence in the Ancient Near East* (Atlanta: SBL Press, 2013).

21. Menahem Haran, *Temple and Temple Service in Ancient Israel* (Oxford: Clarendon, 1978), 236–53.

22. Alexander Rofé, *Introduction to the Literature of the Hebrew Bible* (Jerusalem: SIMOR, 2009), 206–13.

Moses, Aaron, and Miriam will find the presence of God—is outside the camp.[23] They have to *go out* from the camp to reach it. Once Moses, Aaron, and Miriam reach the tent of meeting, God *comes down* (*wayyēred*) in a cloud and hovers over the entrance to the tent (12:5). God speaks to Moses and Miram, and then the cloud *leaves* (*sār*) from above the tent (12:10). The presence of God returns to heaven.

The verbs of movement in this passage depict God's presence as ethereal, peripheral, and temporary. From the people's perspective, God is "out there." One must leave the congregation of Israel and *go out* to meet with Israel's God. What's more, God does not actually reside in the tent of meeting. This structure is not the tabernacle of popular imagination. It is not a place where God lives but a space that God visits. The divine presence comes down from heaven and then returns once the special mission is complete. What's more, while the divine presence is on earth, it does not actually enter the tent of meeting but remains above it. God is not easy to pin down in these accounts. If someone asked the author of Numbers 12 where God was, he would point outside the camp and say, "Sometimes God appears way over there."

God in the Middle of the Camp

Other pentateuchal writers imagine God's presence very differently. In the so-called Priestly tradition, God is a constant presence in the middle of the community of Israel. This author describes, in elaborate detail, the camp as a concentric ring of circles that radiate out from the tabernacle like a target. God is in the center of the bull's-eye, the priests form the first ring, then the Levites. The tribes of Israel are at the edges organized in clusters that flank each of the tabernacle's sides. The tents of each family face inward toward God's presence at the center of the camp (Num. 2).[24] The tribes are positioned around the tabernacle to reflect their prominence within the community. Their locations are fixed and organized hierarchically. Surprisingly, in the Priestly tradition Judah usurps Reuben's position as the preeminent tribe (according to Genesis, Reuben was the first of Jacob and Leah's sons). Judah is given the most coveted spot at the tabernacle's entrance.[25] The rest of the tribes encircle the tent. According to this arrangement, if you asked an Israelite where their God was, they would point to the very heart of the camp and say, "God lives right here."

---

23. E's conception of the tent outside the camp is made even more clear in Exod. 33.
24. Samuel E. Balentine, *The Torah's Vision of Worship* (Overtures to Biblical Theology; Minneapolis: Fortress, 1999), 177–78.
25. Dennis T. Olson, *Numbers* (Interpretation; Louisville: John Knox, 1996), 19–24.

God's Presence Is Close and Constant

There is yet another depiction of God's presence. Numbers 9:15–23, a passage contemporary scholars assign to the Priestly tradition, says that a cloud shielded the presence of God. So far, this is similar to Numbers 12 of the Elohim tradition. Also similar to the Elohim tradition, in Numbers 9 this cloud does not enter the tabernacle but hovers above it. A key difference with Numbers 9 is that God's presence is constant, not temporary as in Numbers 12. In Numbers 9 the cloud hovers above the tabernacle as a simple cloud by day and a glowing one at night. When God wants the people to break camp and move to another location the cloud rises (*wanaʿălâ*) and when God wants them to stop the cloud settles back down (*yiškōn*; 9:17, 21). The cloud acts as a signal when it rises and falls but it never returns (*sār*) to heaven as it does in Numbers 12. God's presence stays with the people, floating above the tabernacle, never quite touching the earth, as a constant presence close enough for everyone to see.[26]

God in a Box

The location of God's presence gets even more complicated than this. The tabernacle / tent of meeting was not the only portable structure in which God's presence was located. Some passages speak of God using the ark not merely as a seat to rest on but as a house in which God lived. According to Exodus 25:10–22, as well as the book of Deuteronomy, the two tablets containing the instructions that God gave to Moses at Mount Sinai were placed within the ark. This was the function of the ark for the authors of these accounts. The ark was a portable safety deposit box. It kept God's revelation safe and, as a secondary function, it was a seat on which God sat or an ottoman on which God propped God's legs as God lounged in the Holy of Holies. These purposes are not mentioned in the battle song of Numbers 10, which provides a very different account of the ark's function.

After Moses comes down from meeting with God on Mount Sinai and the cloud of God's presence lifts from the mountain, the Israelites break camp and continue their journey through the wilderness. They send the ark of the covenant ahead as a vanguard. It is worth quoting the entire description of this event because it reveals a very different perspective regarding God's presence from what we have encountered so far:

---

26. For a more detailed comparison of the differences between E's tent of meeting and P's tabernacle, see Israel Knohl, "Two Aspects of the 'Tent of Meeting,'" in *Tehillah le-Moshe: Biblical and Judaic Studies in Honor of Moshe Greenberg*, ed. Mordechai Cogan, Barry Eichler, and Jeffrey Tigay (Winona Lake, IN: Eisenbrauns, 1997), 73–79.

> So they set out from the mount of the LORD three days' journey with the ark of the covenant of the LORD going before them three days' journey, to seek out a resting place for them, the cloud of the LORD being over them by day when they set out from the camp.
> Whenever the ark set out, Moses would say,
>
> "Arise [qûmâ], O Lord, let your enemies be scattered,
>   and those hating you flee before you."
>
> And whenever it came to rest, he would say,
>
> "Return [šûbâ], O Lord of the ten thousand thousands of Israel."
>   Num. 10:33–36[27]

When the camp broke and the people set out for a journey, Moses was to preside over a ritual that summoned God out of the ark. Yahweh would emerge from the box and scatter the enemies who stood in their way. When the people came to a resting place, Moses would invite God to return into the box. In this passage the ark functions as a storage container not for the Decalogue tablets but for the martial presence of the Israelite god.[28] There is no cloud shielding God's appearance, God's presence is not hovering over the tabernacle, the ark is not a footstool or a throne. In this passage the ark is imagined as a bottle and God is the genie. Moses says a few words and Yahweh hops out. If we were to ask Moses where God was, he would point at the ark and say, "He lives in there. Would you like me to summon him?"

Numbers 10 is not the only biblical passage that views the ark in this way. Psalm 68 looks back on the nomadic presence of God and uses the same trope that is contained in Numbers 10 to explain God's *stationary* presence on the holy mountain in Zion.[29] The first verse of Psalm 68 uses the exact wording of Moses's incantation: "Let God rise up, let his enemies be scattered; let those who hate him flee before him."[30] Verse 7 also refers to the wilderness sojourn: "O God, when you went out before your people, when you marched through the wilderness." The psalmist used the first line of the wilderness incantation as the inspiration of a song intended for worship at the Jerusalem temple. But instead of merely pasting the ideology of Numbers into his song, the author

---

27. I have slightly altered the NRSV in verse 35 so that the parallels with Ps. 68 will be more clear.

28. Samuel Terrien notes that this passage appears within the same chapter in which a narrator says that "the cloud of Yahweh was over them by day" (Num. 10:33–34). Terrien underlines the tension between these two perspectives—God in the cloud versus God in the box—since the source material for this chapter comes from at least two different traditions. *The Elusive Presence: The Heart of Biblical Theology* (Religious Perspectives 26; New York: Harper & Row, 1978), 165.

29. Or was this idea inserted into the book of Numbers . . . ?

30. A couple of the verbs are in different forms and "God" is used in place of "Yahweh," but other than that Ps. 68:1 is identical to Num. 10:35.

of Psalm 68 refashioned the wilderness narrative to fit a new understanding of God's presence. Instead of God emerging from the portable ark, in this psalm God comes out of the stationary palace that sits atop Jerusalem (*mēhêkālekā ʿal yərûšālāim*; 68:29 [30 Heb.]).[31] God is no longer nomadic but stationary. Israel no longer carries their god around in a box but has built a divine palace comparable to a king's.

The passages we have considered display strikingly different perspectives regarding the nature of God's presence on earth. God's presence either remains over the tabernacle at all times or it descends from heaven only on special occasions. Yahweh lives in a permanent temple above Jerusalem or within a movable box. In spite of their differences, these passages share a fundamental idea—God's presence with humanity is linked to a particular structure. This structure may be portable like the ark or stationary like the temple. It may be associated with the abiding presence of God like the tabernacle or with temporary appearances like the tent of meeting. Nonetheless, the writers of the Old Testament believed God needed a house. Some of them conceived it as a billionaire's mansion while others thought it a hipster's tiny house on a trailer. But all of them thought that, like a human, God needs four walls and a roof (or four sides and a canopy) to call home.

GOD IN WOOD AND STONE

Throughout the ancient Mediterranean world it was common for people to believe that gods inhabited the natural world. To borrow Charles Taylor's term, their world was enchanted—alive with deified rivers, sacred stone outcroppings, and divine arboretums.[32] The objects that fill the world and the geographic features that mark its surface are not inert matter but vessels capable of hosting divine forces. Trees often marked sacred spaces—places where deities could be worshiped, where gods were more present than at other spots. The Greeks, for example, went to a sanctuary in Epirus and asked questions of Zeus, the king of their gods, at a sacred oak. Zeus was thought to respond to the queries by rustling the oak's leaves or speaking through the

---

31. David H. Aaron, *Etched in Stone: The Emergence of the Decalogue* (New York: T&T Clark, 2006), 111–13.

32. Charles Taylor, *A Secular Age* (Cambridge: Belknap Press of Harvard University Press, 2007), 33–34. Contrary to Taylor, I do not believe that the contemporary world is "disenchanted." Rather, Eugene McCarraher demonstrates that contemporary and industrialized societies have merely shifted their enchantment to money and the capitalist economy. *The Enchantments of Mammon: How Capitalism Became the Religion of Modernity* (Cambridge: Belknap Press of Harvard University Press, 2019).

birds sitting in its branches.[33] The oak tree was not merely a plant that provided shade. It was a portal that connected heaven to earth, the divine world with the human one. We see echoes of this kind of thinking within the Old Testament.

Genesis 35 hints that trees marked spaces where God was present in ways that God wasn't in other spots.[34] Genesis 35 is a narrative with several scenes that occur in different locations. It starts with God telling Jacob to rid his family of figurines that depict other deities. Jacob rounds them up along with all the family's taboo religious jewelry and buries them underneath an oak tree near Shechem. We could suppose that Jacob buried the objects under the oak tree in case he had second thoughts about his allegiance to Yahweh; if so, he could come back and dig them up. The oak tree served as an X on a pirate's treasure map. This might be a possible reading of the passage, but it is not a strong one.

After Jacob buries his family's forbidden cultic objects he moves on to another city, Luz, in the land of Canaan. He builds an altar there because "it was there that God had revealed himself to him when he fled from his brother" (Gen. 35:7). In other words, it was a particular spot in the city where God appeared to him. The next verse states that Rebecca's nurse, Deborah, died and was buried under an oak near the city. At first blush the story may seem disconnected, but here is the flow: Jacob hears God speaking to him and buries objects under an oak tree, then Jacob goes to another town and sees God and afterward buries a beloved person under an oak. Both of these situations fuse God's special manifestation with a particular kind of tree. Like the Greeks, ancient Israelites thought of trees as portals between earth and the realms of the divine and dead. Trees were nodes that connect these spaces. Possibly this thought was derived from the fact that tree roots extend down into the ground while their branches reach up into the sky?

Perhaps this is just coincidence, though. Correlation does not imply causation. Just because we read that Jacob buried Deborah underneath a tree, it does not mean he did that because that place was a special node that connected metaphysical places. He might have buried her there because, like the jewelry he hid, he wanted to be able to locate the grave so that he could return to that spot later on. Yet these are not the only times in the Bible where

---

33. "Dodona," in *The Oxford Classical Dictionary*, 4th ed., ed. Simon Hornblower, Anthony Spawforth, and Esther Eidinow (Oxford: Oxford University Press, 2012), 471.

34. This understanding behind the Gen. 35 narrative is clearly at odds with that behind Deut. 16:21–22. R. W. L. Moberley, *The Old Testament of the Old Testament: Patriarchal Narratives and Mosaic Yahwism* (Overtures to Biblical Theology; Minneapolis: Fortress, 1992), 92–93. As I noted in chap. 2, theological consistency is not something the editors of the Bible were ultimately concerned about.

trees are connected to the presence of a deity. For instance, Joshua 24:26–27 describes the placement of an altar near a tree in Yahweh's sacred area in Shechem, an angel appears to Gideon near a tree in Judges 6:11, Isaiah condemns sacred oak trees in 1:29–30, and Hosea 4:13 condemns pagan sacrifices done underneath a variety of trees.[35] Also, if we keep reading in Genesis 35 we find something else.

After burying Deborah, Jacob eventually returns to Luz and God appears to him. In the spot where Jacob has this encounter with God, Jacob erects a pillar of stone, pours out a drink offering, and anoints the standing stone with oil (Gen. 35:14). The description of the stone's installation is brief—just a single sentence—but Jacob's actions resemble Mesopotamian rituals that prepared statues of deities to be filled with the presence of the gods they represented. If a temple contained a statue of Marduk, for instance, people believed that Marduk's presence would enter it. Just like cleaning your house when you expect guests, priests would ready the idols for gods to enter. The statues were washed with water and their mouths were rubbed with honey, ghee, cedar, and cypress.[36] After this it was thought that the deity would take up residence there. The god or goddess would use the statue as a body.

In Genesis 35 Jacob pours a drink offering on top of his pillar (parallel to washing the Mesopotamian statue?) and then smears it with (scented?) oil (parallel to rubbing the idol with cedar and cypress?). Jacob does not merely erect a historical marker that documents his experience. He officiates a sacred ritual. Likely, he prepared this pillar, and concomitantly this particular place, for the continued presence of Yahweh.[37] Even if he wasn't doing this, by erecting the pillar Jacob marks the spot as special, as the place where God made an appearance. He sets apart that space as sacred ground. In the previous two scenes in Genesis 35 Jacob performs a religious observance at a place that was already considered sacred. These sacred places were marked with trees. Now, Jacob recognizes a spot as sacred by erecting a stone. The spot was special because God had visited it. Jacob marks this new holy site and officiates a ceremony that may have invited Yahweh to inhabit it more permanently. Genesis 35 operates with the understanding that God inhabits objects—trees and stones—and infuses places with his special presence. Before moving on we should consider one other passage that further

---

35. This list is from Mark S. Smith, *The Early History of God: Yahweh and the Other Deities in Ancient Israel*, 2nd ed. (Grand Rapids: Eerdmans, 2002), 114–15.
36. Christopher Walker and Michael B. Dick, "The Mesopotamian mîs pî Ritual," in *Born in Heaven, Made on Earth: The Making of the Cultic Image in the Ancient Near East*, ed. Michael B. Dick (Winona Lake, IN: Eisenbrauns, 1999), 70.
37. Thomas Römer, *The Invention of God*, trans. Raymond Geuss (Cambridge: Harvard University Press, 2015), 142–44.

illustrates how widespread the assumption was in ancient Israel that God inhabited objects of wood and stone.

Second Kings 13 describes the reign of Jehoahaz, king of Israel. It includes a line that we might be inclined to regard as typical and inconsequential, but the last phrase reveals something profound about ancient Israelite perceptions of God: "Nevertheless they did not depart from the sins of the house of Jeroboam, which he caused Israel to sin, but walked in them; the sacred pole also remained in Samaria" (13:6). In this line the author of Kings castigates many Israelite leaders for guiding the people into sin. That part is not unusual. The situation surrounding Jehoahaz's reign, however, was very odd, and the last phrase of this verse is odder still.

Jehoahaz was the son of Jehu. We read in 2 Kings 10 that Jehu led a rebellion against Ahab, king of Israel, and his Phoenician consort, Jezebel. The author of Kings tells us that Ahab and Jezebel underwrote the worship of the Phoenician storm god Baal. The author of Kings regarded this as abominable. There you had the Israelite royal family fostering the worship of a pagan deity. Anathema! But then, the author of Kings tells us, along comes Jehu, who toppled Ahab's regime. Jehu didn't merely push Ahab to the side; he slaughtered him, his sons, Ahab's advisers, his priests, and his friends. Jehu purged the nation of pretty much anyone connected to Ahab and his worship practices. Jehu was on a mission to destroy any hint of pagan worship. The only god that was to be worshiped within the land of Israel was Yahweh. Jehu killed everyone who violated this.

To accomplish this Jehu concocted a trap. He announced a religious festival devoted to Baal. He boasted that his patronage of Baal would make Ahab's look paltry in comparison. People from all over the country came to participate. The temple of Baal was filled wall to wall. Jehu looked at the congregation and ordered all those who did not worship Baal to leave. Then, acting on previous instructions, Jehu's men burst in and hacked the congregation to death. Not a Baal worshiper remained alive. Jehu and his men dragged the corpses from the shrine and ripped out every object devoted to Baal. They turned the temple into a latrine. All this seems a bit extreme to my sensibilities, but Yahweh affirmed Jehu's actions (10:30). The narrator of Kings goes even further. He tells us that Jehu did not go far enough.

Jehu left in place statues of calves in Bethel and Dan that Jeroboam, the first king of Israel, had made.[38] First Kings 12:28 says that these calves represented Yahweh—they were depictions of Israel's own God. Jeroboam made

---

38. These were not the only golden calves used in cultic service within Israel, but perhaps they were the most prominent ones. For instance, there was also a calf at Gilgal (Hos. 12:11 [12 Heb.]; see Gösta W. Ahlström, *The History of Ancient Palestine* [Minneapolis: Fortress, 1993], 622–23).

them because he was worried that after David's united kingdom was split in two, residents of the northern country—the part Jeroboam controlled—would cross the border into the southern state of Judah to worship at the temple in Jerusalem. Jeroboam ruled the northern kingdom that did not include Jerusalem. Jeroboam had a suspicion, likely a well-founded one, that his citizens would journey south and out of his jurisdiction to worship Yahweh in Jerusalem because there was a big, fancy temple there that housed the divine presence. If you want God to hear your prayer, you better be in shouting distance. Naturally, pilgrims would bring their offerings and donations with them and deposit them at the temple. Again, these riches would be deposited at a temple that was under the control of Jeroboam's rival. Jeroboam needed something to keep his people—and their tithes—within his kingdom. So he built two statues that represented their god and placed them in the prominent cities at the northern and southern boundaries of the land. The people probably assumed that, similar to the statues of deities in temples throughout the ancient Near East, the idol was filled by the deity the statue represented. Jeroboam was telling his people that while Yahweh's house might sit in Judah, Yahweh's presence was there at Bethel and Dan. The people no longer had to go to Jerusalem to meet with God. They could meet Yahweh right there in the northern kingdom. God resided within those two calf statues. All of this is completely standard for the ancient world. What's interesting about 2 Kings 13:6 is that it reveals that Jehu did not destroy the golden calves when he purged the nation of idolatrous worship. Not only did Jehu leave these calves in place even after he completely obliterated the worship of Baal from Israel, but 2 Kings 13:6 reveals that he also kept the sacred pole within the Israelite temple in Samaria.

At first glance, this is shocking because sacred poles were used in pagan worship and often condemned by Israelite prophets. Yet, as Benjamin Sommer explains, the most logical thing to conclude from this is that Jehu did not find the sacred pole, specifically an asherah pole, objectionable because it functioned as a representation of Yahweh, much like the golden calves.[39] Since Jehu was quite literally dead set on destroying every hint of non-Yahwistic worship, the only way he would conceivably leave the calves and pole in place was if he thought they were used to venerate Israel's god. Jehu did not mind if people used material objects as vehicles to worship God. Nor did Jehu blink an eye when people believed that Yahweh inhabited golden statues or upright

---

39. Sommer, *Bodies of God*, 46. Many other scholars, including William G. Dever (*Did God Have a Wife? Archaeology and Folk Religion in Ancient Israel* [Grand Rapids: Eerdmans, 2005], 211–13), believe that Jehu did not destroy the asherah poles because the worship of the goddess Asherah, Baal's consort, was so popularly ingrained that the people wouldn't have stood for it. I think Sommer's treatment is more convincing.

poles. To him, all of this was perfectly appropriate as long as worship was fixed upon Yahweh. But asherah poles did not always represent Yahweh. This was a fairly new development in Israelite religion.

The asherah pole spoken of in 2 Kings was likely a manufactured cultic object—a tree chopped and limbed and then placed upright in the temple. In earlier times, and in other places, an asherah could be a living tree or a sacred grove.[40] The verdant tree was a symbol of fertility and, as such, originally represented a female deity.[41] Within monarchic Israel, however, Yahweh assumed within himself the functions and symbols that surrounding nations divided into separate gods. For instance, within Ugaritic literature Baal was said to "ride on the clouds," but to the biblical writers it was Yahweh who was the "rider in the heavens" (Deut. 33:26; see also Isa. 19:1; 2 Sam. 22:11; and Ps. 18:11).[42] I mentioned earlier that the sun god, Shamash, was for Mesopotamians the judge of earth. In the pages of Scripture, Yahweh assumes the role of the judge of heaven and earth (e.g., Ps. 50). In addition, an inscription from the Judean lowlands dating to around 700 BCE equates Yahweh with the Canaanite god El.[43] Yahweh takes into himself the descriptions and roles of neighboring gods.[44] He is like a giant vacuum that sucks up the features of every deity around him. This isn't an uncommon development within Mediterranean religions. A similar thing happened in Babylonia.

Enuma Elish is often referred to as the Babylonian creation epic, yet, as many scholars note, this description does not represent the true purpose of the story.[45] Its primary goal is not to explain the way the earth was created but to recount how Marduk, a middling deity, subsumed fifty other gods into himself and became the head of the Mesopotamian pantheon. This is perhaps what happened in the case of Asherah within ancient Israel. Over time the poles that had represented the goddess Asherah became seen as stylized representations of the abundance and fecundity that Yahweh brought to his people and their land.[46] Asherah was no longer the wife of Baal, as she was in Canaanite religion, but a divine attendant who brings God's provision to

---

40. Ziony Zevit, *The Religions of Ancient Israel: A Synthesis of Parallactic Approaches* (London: Continuum, 2001), 263–65.

41. Smith, *Early History of God*, 108–47.

42. W. Herrmann, "Rider upon the Clouds," in *The Dictionary of Deities and Demons in the Bible*, ed. Karel van der Toorn, Bob Becking, and Pieter W. van der Horst (Leiden: Brill, 1999), 703–5.

43. Othmar Keel and Christoph Uehlinger, *Gods, Goddesses, and Images of God in Ancient Israel*, trans. Thomas H. Trapp (Minneapolis: Fortress, 1998), 311–12.

44. For a detailed discussion of the transition from polytheism to monotheism, see Römer, *Invention of God*.

45. For instance, William W. Hallo, *The World's Oldest Literature: Studies in Sumerian Belles-Lettres* (Leiden: Brill, 2010), 559.

46. Keel and Uehlinger, *Gods, Goddesses, and Images of God*, 237.

his people or, perhaps, an abstracted symbol for Yahweh himself. This is why Jehu did not hew the asherah pole that stood in Samaria. It represented, like the calves in Bethel and Dan and even the temple in Jerusalem itself, the abiding presence of God in a particular place.

It is certainly true that regardless of what Jehu or any other Israelite monarch believed, the narrator of the books of Kings regards the golden calves and asherah pole as sacrilegious. They are evidences of Israel's continued sin and stubborn insistence on embracing heretical ideas. In spite of this, the author of Kings, and the authors of other portions of Scripture, still share a basic understanding with the folks they brand as heretics. All of them believe that God's presence could be found in particular localities. Some thought that God lived in the trunk of a tree or a stylized version of one. Some thought Yahweh's presence infused golden calves. The author of Kings believed God resided in the Jerusalem temple. Jehu's idea that Yahweh inhabits trees (or, again, stylized versions of trees) is not so far-fetched. The author of Deuteronomy, who most scholars believe had a large influence on the books of Kings,[47] referred to Yahweh as "him who dwells in the bush" (Deut. 33:16 ESV). The idea that God inhabited wood was very old. We should take a closer look at this thought and what it represents.

TEMPORARY THEOPHANIES

The description of God as someone "who dwells in the bush" in Deuteronomy 33 likely recalls Moses's first encounter with Yahweh, in which God appeared as a burning bush (Exod. 3).[48] This story again shows that God's presence appeared in specific locations, even a location as humble as desert scrub. We saw a similar understanding in the cloud and fire theophanies of the wilderness sojourn. These temporary divine manifestations guided the people through the Sinai wilderness. Once they reached the land of Canaan, the need for Yahweh's visible presence was no longer essential, so the cloud and fire disappeared. Yet God's localized nature did not.

Of course, there is the Jerusalem temple—the most prominent sign in the Old Testament of God's localized presence. But Yahweh had other presences throughout Canaan in addition to the temple. For instance, the book of Samuel opens with a story of a man with two wives. This man, along with his

---

47. Mordechai Cogan, "1 and 2 Kings," in *The Oxford Encyclopedia of the Books of the Bible*, vol. 1, ed. Michael Coogan (Oxford: Oxford University Press, 2011), 537–40.

48. That is, if we should understand the last word in that phrase as "bush" (*hns*), as it is written in the Masoretic Text. The translators of the NRSV thought this reading was an ancient corruption of "Sinai" (*yns*).

family, "used to go up year by year from his town to worship and to sacrifice to the Lord of hosts at Shiloh" (1 Sam. 1:3). We could read over this verse and think it is nothing special, merely recounting that a person traveled to Shiloh to the temple of Yahweh that happened to be there.[49] But this misses what is really going on. Instead of reading the last phrase as the name of god paired with a title ("Lord of hosts") and a location of this god's temple ("at Shiloh"), it is more likely that this phrase should be read as one long name: The-Martial-Yahweh-of-Shiloh. In Hebrew "host" means army, and grammatically it makes more sense to connect the words than to separate them. In like manner, when Absalom says, "I will worship the Lord in Hebron" (2 Sam. 15:8), we should read this as "I will worship Yahweh-of-Hebron." The towns mentioned in conjunction with God's name indicate a unique local presence of Yahweh that was not experienced elsewhere.[50]

It was common in ancient Israel for residents of towns to venerate a particular presence of Yahweh. These towns would erect their own shrines that commemorated the theophanies they witnessed. Towns would also create their own set of cultic traditions that they incorporated into common liturgies. An inscription found in an outpost of the northern kingdom of Israel mentions a blessing from "Yahweh of Samaria." Scholars debate whether the term "Samaria" in this inscription refers to the town of Samaria or the entire nation (i.e., the part representing the whole, as "Washington" could be used in the place of "United States of America").[51] That is a fairly peripheral discussion. What most scholars agree on is that the person who wrote this blessing differentiated between the Yahweh who appeared to the residents of the city (or nation) of Samaria and the Yahweh of the southern kingdom of Judah. The northern Yahweh was somehow different from the southern one in the mind of the person who wrote this inscription.

None of this should surprise us. It is not so strange that the residents of Israel would differentiate the Yahweh they worshiped from the Yahweh of their Judean neighbors. It is also not odd that the residents of Hebron petitioned a version of Yahweh that was distinct from the Yahweh the citizens of Shiloh venerated. Let me give you a modern analogy. When I drive to my neighborhood hardware store I pass a church named Our Lady of Lourdes.

---

49. This temple in Shiloh is designated with the same term as the temple in Jerusalem. There was also a cherub throne in Shiloh just as in Jerusalem. These temples seem to be of a similar kind. Tryggve N. D. Mettinger, *In Search of God: The Meaning and Message of the Everlasting Names*, trans. Frederick H. Cryer (Philadelphia: Fortress, 1988), 148.

50. Rainer Albertz, *A History of Israelite Religion in the Old Testament Period*, vol. 1, *From the Beginnings to the End of the Monarchy*, trans. John Bowden (Louisville: Westminster/John Knox, 1994), 83.

51. Karel van der Toorn, *Family Religion in Babylonia, Syria and Israel: Continuity and Change in the Forms of Religious Life* (Leiden: Brill, 1996), 278.

This church in Louisville, Kentucky, is devoted to the apparition of Mary, the mother of Jesus, which is thought to have appeared near Lourdes, France. In 1858 a fourteen-year-old girl told her mother that a lady spoke to her in a cave as she gathered firewood. Her sisters accompanied her on a return visit some days later. The girl went into an ecstatic trance and she again heard the voice of Mary. A variety of miracles were experienced and witnessed. The people of Lourdes believed that Mary herself had made an appearance, and a church was built to commemorate it. Millions of pilgrims visit Lourdes each year—so many people that Lourdes has become, after Paris, the city with the most hotel rooms in France. Maybe it's not so weird that the writers of Scripture distinguish between Yahweh of Shiloh and Yahweh of Hebron. If the Mary who appeared in France (remember, this is not generic Mary, since the church is named Our Lady *of Lourdes*) can be venerated in Kentucky, then it shouldn't surprise us that ancient peoples honored distinct theophanies of Yahweh which occurred a few hillocks apart.

EMBODIMENT

For the writers of the Old Testament, not only was God's presence localized to a particular place, it occasionally resembled the human form. I mentioned this in passing above, but it deserves fuller treatment. God appeared as a human in the visions of three Hebrew prophets—Isaiah, Ezekiel, and Daniel.[52] These prophets did not see Yahweh as a fluffy cloud or an angular disk or a pulsing splotch. Nor was God an abstract spirit or a gentle wind. What they saw was a god who looked human. Some scholars counter that in all three cases the prophets' descriptions are shadowy—the form of God is visible but God's actual appearance is hidden.[53] The prophets focus on God's clothing (Isa. 6:1) or the color of the divine throne (Ezek. 1:26). They never say whether the shape of God's nose is round or Roman. Of the three, some say, Daniel gives us the most intimate picture. But even that is sketchy. Daniel says that Yahweh's clothing was "white as snow" and that God's hair was a similar hue, "like pure wool" (Dan. 7:9). This leaves much to the imagination. Since God is so shadowy, these scholars argue, we shouldn't push the imagery in these passages too far. I disagree.

---

52. While there are many anthropomorphic representations of God in the Old Testament, James Barr identified only three full-fledged anthropomorphic theophanies—Isa. 6:1–5; Ezek. 1:26–28; and Dan. 7. "Theophany and Anthropomorphism in the Old Testament," in *Congress Volume: Oxford 1959* (Supplements to Vetus Testamentum 7; Leiden: Brill, 1960), 31–38.

53. Rolf Rendtorff, *The Canonical Hebrew Bible: A Theology of the Old Testament*, trans. David E. Orton (Leiden: Deo, 2005), 58.

It may be, for instance, that Isaiah's picture of God is far more human than we typically realize. Translations of Isaiah 6:1—from the 1611 King James Version to the 2011 Common English Bible—say that the "train" (KJV) of God's robe or the "edges of his robe" (CEB) spilled out from the throne and extended to the walls of the temple. God's attire reflects the extent of divine majesty. Yahweh's robe fills the temple in the same way that God's glory occupies the entire universe. The size of God's robe is a metaphor pointing to an abstract feature of God's character. At least that is how this passage is commonly understood.[54] Yet every lexical study I am aware of concludes that the meaning of the Hebrew word (*šûl*) that is behind this translation means "things that hang down," "lower limbs," "physical extremities," even, in some situations, "pudenda." It's rather shocking to think of the prophet using such a word, particularly the latter definition, to describe his vision of the creator of the universe. But as I already mentioned, it is not legitimate to disbelieve that an ancient author would say something merely because modern folks are disinclined to believe it.

After an exhaustive study of *šûl*, Lyle Eslinger concluded that personal bias is why translators render this term as an article of clothing—"train" or "edges of his robe"—in Isaiah 6 instead of as an anatomical feature. Eslinger showed that translators use the other reflexes—lower limbs, physical extremities, etc.—in biblical passages that do not involve God.[55] It is not etymology or context or any other scientific or scholarly reason that determines how contemporary Bible editors translate this word in Isaiah 6; rather, it is their expectations regarding what God is like. Their aversion, perhaps subconscious, to anthropomorphic representations of God leads them to conclude that Isaiah was describing God's clothing but not the actual divine person. Lexically, the case for this opinion is very thin.

This is not to say that Isaiah saw Yahweh's genitals. There is a theme of modesty that runs through Isaiah 6 which makes this interpretation unlikely. The winged creatures that attend to God have three sets of wings. They use one to fly around, one to cover their faces (so as not to see God's glory), and another to cover their feet (a common euphemism for genitalia). Isaiah informs us that God employs decorous servants. These creatures are animal-like (they have wings) and are apparently unclothed. But they are polite. They use one set of wings as fig leaves.

---

54. For instance, Izaak J. de Hulster, "Of Angels and Iconography: Isaiah 6 and the Biblical Concept of Seraphs and Cherubs," in *Iconographic Exegesis of the Hebrew Bible/Old Testament: An Introduction to Its Method and Practice*, ed. Izaak J. de Hulster, Brent A. Strawn, and Ryan P. Bonfiglio (Göttingen: Vandenhoeck & Ruprecht, 2015), 154.

55. "The Infinite in a Finite Organical Perception (Isaiah VI 1–5)," *Vetus Testamentum* 45:2 (1995): 145–73.

So, God seems to be modest. We still have not figured out what the description of God in Isaiah 6:1 actually means. I think we are to understand that Yahweh is gigantic and can barely cram his frame into the heavenly throne. He must fold his legs up tight to make them even fit into the room. Yahweh is huge. Not only metaphorically but in fact. This is not as far-fetched as it may seem. We know from other verses that Yahweh has very long legs. Later on in the book of Isaiah, Yahweh says, "Heaven is my throne, and the earth is my footstool" (66:1). In Isaiah 66 Yahweh's legs are even longer than they are in Isaiah 6. They stretch all the way from heaven to earth!

It is not only the prophets who saw God in human form. Genesis 32 recounts the story behind Israel's name. Long, long ago there was a guy named Jacob. Jacob ran away from his family because he was afraid that his brother would seek revenge against him after Jacob swindled his brother out of his inheritance. Jacob returns home a number of years later with the hope of reconciling with his brother. Before entering his homeland Jacob separates himself from the rest of his camp and spends the night by himself alongside the Jabbok River. Genesis 32:24 (25 Heb.) reads quite sparingly and not a little mysteriously: "Jacob was left alone; and a man wrestled with him until daybreak." At first, it is unclear who wrestled with Jacob.[56] Was it a bandit or even his brother, who found the little trickster alone and decided it was time to exact his long-awaited vengeance? At the beginning of the story we are not sure. All we know is that this assailant is a man.

The narrator makes it clear that Jacob wrestles with a person. Throughout the story Jacob's opponent is said to be a "man" (אִישׁ). Not a god; not a spirit.[57] There are two tantalizing hints, however, that this man is no ordinary person. They come at the end of the story in the form of (1) an enigmatic statement the man makes at the conclusion of the encounter and (2) the name Jacob gives to the spot where the altercation took place. The two men grapple until daybreak, at which time the assailant realizes that he will not be able to subdue Jacob by fighting clean. He inflicts a cheap shot: "When the man saw that he did not prevail against Jacob, he struck him on the hip socket; and Jacob's hip was put out of joint as he wrestled with him" (Gen. 32:25 [26 Heb.]). But even with his hip out of joint, Jacob would not relent. Jacob makes the man beg to let him go. And beg the man does. Apparently, the man is afraid to be seen, because he pleads with Jacob, "Let me go, for the day is breaking."

---

56. Oswald Bayer, *Martin Luther's Theology: A Contemporary Interpretation*, trans. Thomas H. Trapp (Grand Rapids: Eerdmans, 2008), 40.

57. Many interpreters have understood this figure as a river demon or other being that modern people would, rightly or wrongly, categorize as a spirit. See Esther J. Hamori's excellent discussion on the history of interpretation of אִישׁ in *"When Gods Were Men": The Embodied God in Biblical and Near Eastern Literature* (Berlin: de Gruyter, 2008), 1–27.

Jacob doesn't bend. He tells this individual that he will not let him go until he gives him a blessing. The man asks his name, and Jacob tells him. The person responds, "You shall no longer be called Jacob, but Israel, for you have striven with God [*ĕlōhîm*] and with humans, and have prevailed."

There is much in this response that is worthy of comment, but the most striking thing to me is that it reveals that the man (*'îš*) with whom Jacob has wrestled—and even prevailed over!—is not just a man but God (*'ĕlōhîm*). This is such a startling twist that we might think that instead of translating *'ĕlōhîm* as God it more properly means "otherworldly being," as it does when the diviner brings back Samuel from the dead. If this is true then Jacob wasn't wrestling God but perhaps a dead person come up from the grave, or perhaps a messenger God sent to earth? Genesis 32:30 precludes that interpretation: "So Jacob called the place Peniel, saying, 'For I have seen God face to face, and yet my life is preserved.'" Jacob is dismayed. The sun comes up, he glimpses the person he was fighting, and he sees the face of God. Out of all that, Jacob is most struck by the fact that he is still alive. After all, in Exodus 33:20 God tells Moses: "No one shall see me and live." Jacob has not only seen God but extracted a blessing from him. Jacob wrestled God in human form.

This account has perplexed religious folks for millennia, including at least one Hebrew prophet. It seems that Hosea was confused by the fact that the narrator of the Exodus story called Jacob's assailant a man while the combatant identified himself as God. Perhaps Hosea, like many contemporary theologians, was also leery of associating God with the human form. In either case, Hosea split the difference and called the person Jacob wrestled an angel (*mal'āk*).[58] Angels are mediating beings. They belong to the divine realm in the sense that they mainly reside in heaven, but they are not full-fledged gods. Rather, they do the bidding of God. They are God's personal assistants. In the Bible their primary function is to convey messages from God to humanity.[59]

Some scholars believe this is why Hosea used this term.[60] The prophet made a rather sophisticated choice to represent the individual Jacob met. This person gave Jacob a message. It was sent by God and received by a human. Therefore, the prophet designated the being conveying this message by its technical term, an angel. While this argument makes logical, if somewhat tenuous, sense, it does not acknowledge that the person Jacob

---

58. Hos. 12:4 according to English versification; 12:5 Hebrew.
59. Samuel A. Meier, "Angel I," in *Dictionary of Deities and Demons in the Bible*, 2nd ed., ed. Karel van der Toorn, Bob Becking, and Pieter W. van der Horst (Leiden: Brill, 1999), 45–50.
60. "In that these human representations of the divine are often associated with the communication of a message, the term *mal'akh*, 'angel,' is frequently used for such mysterious manifestations (Hosea 12:4)." Marvin R. Wilson, *Exploring Our Hebraic Heritage: A Christian Theology of Roots and Renewal* (Grand Rapids: Eerdmans, 2014), 229.

wrestles identifies himself as God and then Jacob affirms this in the toponym he coins, Peniel, which translates literally as "The Face of God."[61] The Genesis narrative gives no indication that anyone other than a humanlike God is at play. Like many modern translators Hosea probably had a hesitation that made it difficult for him to believe that Jacob could wrestle a physical man who turned out to be God, so he altered the story to bring it in line with his instincts.[62] There is another option, too. Perhaps there was more than one way of telling this story, and Hosea drew from the one that he knew or preferred. After all, there was not a codified canon at the time of Hosea. It is impossible to know what sacred stories Hosea was aware of and what forms they were in during his life.

We will consider one more passage which implies that God takes concrete human form. This passage is simultaneously clear and opaque. Genesis 1:27 says, "God created humanity in God's own image, in the divine image God created them, male and female God created them" (my trans.). It seems pretty straightforward that if God created humans in the divine image then God must look like a human. And yet, an entire cottage industry began in the early years of Christianity (and is still in existence to this day) which denies this very fact. Commentators propose a myriad of alternative interpretations so they can argue that this passage does not imply that God has a humanlike form.

At issue is the image of God. More specifically: What is it? On the surface this seems easy. Ask any child, what does it mean that God created humans in God's own image? Almost every child will answer: It means that we look like God. But as we have seen, theologians do not read the Bible like children. They come up with sophisticated reasons for why the most obvious interpretation is not the right one, why the surface reading of the text is the wrong reading, why the most common definition of a word is not the one employed. Commentators offer a myriad of definitions for the image of God that are designed to make this phrase abstract, to deny it a physical component. These are the most common definitions theologians give for the image of God: it is the capability for logic and reasoning, or a capacity for relationship, or an ability to subdue other creatures, or a hierarchy of authority, or moral conscience, or personality.[63] All of these explanations share a common thread.

---

61. John E. Anderson, *Jacob and the Divine Trickster: A Theology of Deception and YHWH's Fidelity to the Ancestral Promise in the Jacob Cycle* (Siphrut 5; Winona Lake, IN: Eisenbrauns, 2011), 134 n. 9.

62. Hosea was not alone in this. Jewish and early Christian interpreters followed his lead. James L. Kugel, *The Bible as It Was* (Cambridge: Belknap Press of Harvard University Press, 1997), 224–36.

63. G. A. Jónsson, *The Image of God: Genesis 1.26–28 in a Century of Old Testament Research* (Coniectanea Biblica: Old Testament Series 26; Stockholm: Almqvist & Wiksell, 1988).

They assume that whatever the image of God is, it is not an actual image or material appearance. Rather, it is something that differentiates humans from the rest of creation, most particularly other animals. Most theologians go about understanding what the image of God is by locating the ability or capacity that humans have and animals do not. That difference, they say, is the image of God.

On paper, this sounds reasonable, although somewhat unnecessary. We all know what an image is. It is something that has shape, something that we see with our eyes. But the quest to determine the sine qua non of humanity—the thing that makes humans human and separates them from all other forms of life—is a worthy goal. On some level it even makes sense to apply this essential human characteristic to Genesis 1:27.[64] Yet every one of the attempts to define this essential difference has failed. Empathy? Bonobos display it.[65] Language? Even trees communicate with each other and plants have memories.[66] A sense of curiosity? Octopuses are inquisitive, playful, and mischievous.[67] Hierarchy of authority? Heard of the term "alpha male"? An ability to have a relationship with God? Animals have vibrant religious lives.[68] A sense of right and wrong? My dogs slink off in shame when they are caught doing something they know is bad.[69] Consciousness? If we define consciousness as the ability to process external information, then rocks must be seen as conscious because the constant and nonrandom jiggling of their chemical bonds

---

64. Of course, theologians don't speak this way. They assert that Gen. 1:27 *reveals* the essential nature of humanity. See, for instance, Javier R. Alanís, "God," in *Handbook of Latina/o Theologies*, ed. Edwin David Aponte and Miguel A. De La Torre (St. Louis: Chalice, 2006), 12.

65. Frans de Waal, *The Bonobo and the Atheist: In Search of Humanism among the Primates* (New York: Norton, 2014), and de Waal, *Are We Smart Enough to Know How Smart Animals Are?* (New York: Norton, 2016).

66. On the communication of trees, see Peter Wohlleben, *The Hidden Life of Trees: What They Feel, How They Communicate*, trans. Jane Billinghurst (Vancouver: Greystone Books, 2016), and for the memory of plants, see Stefano Mancuso, *The Revolutionary Genius of Plants: A New Understanding of Plant Intelligence and Behavior* (New York: Atria, 2018), 1–15.

67. Peter Godfrey-Smith, *Other Minds: The Octopus, the Sea, and the Deep Origins of Consciousness* (New York: Farrar, Straus & Giroux, 2016).

68. Douglas John Hall argues for the relational model of the image of God in *Imagining God: Dominion as Stewardship* (Grand Rapids: Eerdmans, 1986), 98–112. Donovan O. Schaefer demonstrates that relationships are primarily driven by affects and that animals practice religion through the display of their emotions. *Religious Affects: Animality, Evolution, and Power* (Durham, NC: Duke University Press, 2015).

69. In this discussion my aim is not, as Roger Scruton has described it, to contribute to the "charm of disenchantment . . . that comes from wiping away the appearance of human distinctiveness" (*The Face of God* [London: Continuum, 2012], 28). My goal is to honestly evaluate the various proposals people offer to identify the one feature that differentiates humans from animals and suggest that this line of thinking may not be ultimately productive. The biblical story seems to suggest that humans look different from other animals because they take the appearance of God, not because they have a certain ability that other forms of life do not possess.

resulting from the gravitational and electromagnetic signals they receive from other objects mirrors the sequence of mental states in the human brain.[70]

Perhaps it is time to reconsider the clear and obvious meaning of the phrase "image of God"? Perhaps the thing that differentiates humans from other animal species is exactly what Genesis flatly says: humans resemble the shape of God's body? This interpretation is, grammatically, the easiest one to support. This alone is reason enough to accept it, but there is an even better reason.

The Hebrew word that is translated as "image" in Genesis 1:27 appears a few chapters later in Genesis 5:1–3:

> This is the list of the descendants of Adam. When God created humankind, he made them in the likeness of God. Male and female he created them, and he blessed them and named them "Humankind" when they were created.
> When Adam had lived one hundred thirty years, he became the father of a son in his likeness, according to his image, and named him Seth.

This passage explicitly links God's creation of humankind with the creation of a baby from a human pair. God creates humans in his own likeness, and when Adam fathers a son, this son is in Adam's likeness in accordance to his image. Seth physically resembles his father, Adam.[71] He is a chip off the old block. He carries on his body the appearance of his father. This is what happens when humans give birth—they produce beings that look like them, that take their form. Adam did not spawn an iguana. According to the authors of Genesis, this is the way God designed human reproduction to work because this is the way that God created humans. Human generation is derivative. It points back to that very first act of God creating humans in the divine image. God made humans chips off the old block. We look like the divine because we are God's offspring.

---

70. "Of course, the rock doesn't exert itself as a result of all this 'thinking.' Why should it? Its existence, unlike ours, doesn't depend on the struggle to survive and self-replicate. It is indifferent to the prospect of being pulverized. If you are poetically inclined, you might think of the rock as a purely contemplative being. And you might draw the moral that the universe is, and always has been, saturated with mind, even though we snobbish Darwinian-replicating latecomers are too blinkered to notice." Jim Holt, *When Einstein Walked with Gödel* (New York: Farrar, Straus & Giroux, 2018), 296. Note also that in Gen. 4, "Earth is not dumb matter, an inanimate object with no capacity for feeling and sentiment, but a spirited and vulnerable living being who experiences the terrible and catastrophic loss of Abel's death." Mark I. Wallace, *When God Was a Bird: Christianity, Animism, and the Re-Enchantment of the World* (New York: Fordham University Press, 2019), 148. In a similar way, American Indigenous peoples have long recognized the ground as a person who speaks. Vine Deloria Jr., *God Is Red: A Native View of Religion*, 3rd ed. (Golden, CO: Fulcrum, 2003), 80–81.

71. M. Stol, *Birth in Babylonia and the Bible: Its Mediterranean Setting* (Cuneiform Monographs 14; Groningen: Styx, 2000), 150.

Maybe it does not need to be said, but I will write it anyway for the sake of clarity: if humans resemble the physical structure of God, then it only stands to reason that God resembles the physical structure of humanity. Old Testament theologian Theodorus Vriezen said it quite well: "The fact that man was created in God's image also presupposes that to some extent God is thought of as being human in shape."[72] If you want to discover what God looks like, glance at the mirror.

GENDER AND SEX

Not only did the authors of the Old Testament think of God as having human form, they thought of God as a being marked for sex.[73] Most readers already know that Scripture uses masculine pronouns to refer to God.[74] More discerning readers are familiar with the handful of passages that employ feminine analogies to describe God's nature.[75] For instance, the image of a female giving birth is used to describe God's relationship with the Israelites. Biblical writers use the picture of a maternal bond to underscore God's frustration when the Israelites do not respect their relationship with the divine (Deut. 32:18; Isa. 42:14; 49:15; 66:13). Hosea says that God will lash out at Israel's enemies like a mother bear robbed of her cubs (13:8), and the Deuteronomist portrays God as a mother bird who cares for her chicks (Deut. 32:11–12). Psalms imagine God as a midwife and use birthing terminology to describe the divine.[76] God's wisdom is personified in the first chapters of Proverbs as a woman. Not only is the Hebrew word for wisdom feminine but Proverbs 8 personifies divinely originating discernment as Lady Wisdom.

Feminist theologians point out that in Jewish and Christian tradition the divine presence in the tabernacle/temple is often understood in feminine terms

---

72. Theodorus Christiaan Vriezen, *An Outline of Old Testament Theology*, trans. S. Neuijen (Newton, MA: Branford, 1958), 172.

73. The authors of the Hebrew Bible never talk about God's physical sexual features, though, in contrast to Ugaritic sources which explicitly describe Baal's penis. Amy C. Merrill Willis, "Heavenly Bodies: God and the Body in the Visions of Daniel," in *Bodies, Embodiment, and Theology of the Hebrew Bible*, ed. S. Tamar Kamionkowski and Wonil Kim (New York: T&T Clark, 2010), 17.

74. As Delores S. Williams notes, the Bible is thoroughly masculine. "The Bible is a male story populated by human males, divine males, divine male emissaries and human women mostly servicing male goals, whether social, political, cultural or religious." *Sisters in the Wilderness: The Challenge of Womanist God-Talk* (Maryknoll, NY: Orbis Books, 2013), 166.

75. For a list and treatment of many of these, see Virginia Ramey Mollenkott, *The Divine Feminine: The Biblical Imagery of God as Female* (New York: Crossroad, 1984).

76. Judy Fentress-Williams and Melody D. Knowles, "Affirming and Contradicting Gender Stereotypes," in *The Hebrew Bible: Feminist Intersectional Perspectives*, ed. Gale A. Yee (Minneapolis: Fortress, 2018), 152.

as well. The Hebrew word šĕkînâ is used in the Old Testament to describe the divine presence, and this word is grammatically feminine.[77] There is a danger in making too big an implication from the etymology of a term because the use of a particular word in a particular context can be very different from its grammatical construction. Authors can also use a word in a new way that diverges from the pattern of how it was used in the past.[78] Nonetheless, the use of a feminine word to indicate the very presence of God is worthy of note.

Even though the authors of the Bible occasionally use feminine analogies to describe God, God remains decidedly male in the minds of Scripture's authors.[79] The masculine pronoun is almost always used to refer to God. The same goes for verb conjugations. The only times feminine forms are used are within analogies. Perhaps this is because the Bible, at this point, reflects the male-dominated, patriarchal culture of the ancient Near East.[80] Men dominated the home, palace, and temple, so it should come as no surprise that the (male) writers of Scripture would project their place in the world onto God.[81] If men were at the top of earth's hierarchy, then a male god must be at the top of heaven's. In this understanding, the language used to depict God functions like a mirror.[82] Instead of revealing otherworldly realities, it reflects the patterns embedded within human society. We should note, however, that depictions of God as a male father—the most dominant and pervasive image of God in Christian understanding[83]—are rare within the Old Testament. The Old Testament refers to God as a father only seventeen times in contrast to its seven thousand uses of the Tetragrammaton (YHWH) and twenty-six hundred uses of 'ĕlōhîm (God).[84]

Scholars have pointed out the rich history of feminine representations of the divine within various religious systems, including Christianity and

77. Elizabeth A. Johnson, *She Who Is: The Mystery of God in Feminist Theological Discourse* (New York: Crossroad, 1994), 85.

78. James Barr, *The Semantics of Biblical Language* (Oxford: Oxford University Press, 1961), 89–160.

79. For most of the history of Christian reflection about God, God has remained male in the eyes of theologians as well. Elaine L. Graham, *Making the Difference: Gender, Personhood and Theology* (London: Bloomsbury, 2016), 52.

80. Mary E. Mills, *Images of God in the Old Testament* (London: Cassell, 1998), 75.

81. There are scholars who argue that the Bible includes women-authored texts as well as male-authored ones, for instance, Athalya Brenner and Fokkelien van Dijk-Hemmes, *On Gendering Texts: Female and Male Voices in the Hebrew Bible* (Leiden: Brill, 1996). And if we think religiously legitimated misogyny and patriarchy were only passed on in the past, we are badly mistaken. Stephanie M. Crumpton, *A Womanist Pastoral Theology against Intimate and Cultural Violence* (New York: Palgrave Macmillan, 2014), 93–123.

82. Ann Weatherall, *Gender, Language and Discourse* (Women and Psychology Series; New York: Routledge, 2002), 156.

83. For example, the Nicene Creed begins, "We believe in one God, the Father Almighty. . . ."

84. Reinhard Feldmeier and Hermann Spieckermann, *God of the Living: A Biblical Theology*, trans. Mark A. Biddle (Waco, TX: Baylor University Press, 2011), 52.

Judaism.[85] It was common in the medieval ages for Christians to think about God as a mother. Julian of Norwich (1342–ca. 1416), for example, thought God's motherhood is displayed in three ways: giving birth to the first creation, taking on human nature in the incarnation, and diffusing God's grace outward to restore the world.[86]

Even if the Bible is in many ways a representation of the gendered perceptions of ancient culture, it does not mean that the religions which adopt it as a sacred text blindly assimilated its views on gender. That is to say, just because the Bible is a sexist book, it does not necessarily mean that the religions it inspired are sexist as well. Julian of Norwich's image of a mother god is not the only representation of God as a woman. Furthermore, many contemporary theologians note the presence of the divine feminine within the history of religious discourse and argue that we should refer to God as *she*. God has been called *he* for thousands of years, and since, these theologians tell us, God is not gendered, why not add some balance and call God *she*? This is a way, we are told, to fight back against patriarchy. Certainly, patriarchal forms of religious thought have caused much pain and oppression, and we should work to counter their malignant effects. Perhaps calling God *she* is one way to do so. This practice may, however, unwittingly contribute to a flawed understanding of God. If we continue to use a binary system to think about God—if we think of the divine merely in terms of two modes, masculine or feminine—our understanding of God will remain stunted and impoverished.

For instance, in her discussion of gender and God, the brilliant theologian Elizabeth Johnson identifies a legitimate problem but offers a less than satisfactory diagnosis and solution:

> Predicating personality of God, however, immediately involves us in questions of sex and gender, for all the persons we know are either male or female. The mystery of God is properly understood as neither male nor female but transcends both in an unimaginable way.[87]

Johnson rightly points out one of the many difficult questions that arise when we think of God as a person instead of as an idea or a philosophical premise, but there are at least two major problems with her discussion. Most

---

85. Rosemary Radford Ruether, *Goddesses and the Divine Feminine: A Western Religious History* (Berkeley: University of California Press, 2005).

86. Julian of Norwich, *Revelations of Divine Love*, trans. Barry Windeatt (Oxford World Classics; Oxford: Oxford University Press, 2015), xxx–xxxi. A canticle inspired by Julian's vision of God's motherhood, "A Song of True Motherhood," is included in a volume of supplemental liturgies of the Episcopal Church, *Enriching Our Worship*, vol. 5, *Liturgies and Prayers relating to Childbearing, Childbirth, and Loss* (New York: Church Publishing, 2009), 49. It begins, "God chose to be our mother in all things."

87. Johnson, *She Who Is*, 55. See also Elizabeth Johnson, "Naming God She: The Theological Implications," *Boardman Lectureship in Christian Ethics* 5 (2000).

troubling to me is her statement that "all the persons we know are either male or female." It may be that we *assume* all the persons we know are either male or female but, statistically, this is likely false. Estimates vary, but possibly one in a hundred of the persons populating this planet do not conform to either sex.[88] Some individuals are born with both male and female genitalia, others have underdeveloped sexual organs, and others identify as queer and feel that their gender does not match the physical sex they were born with. A strictly binary understanding of sex and gender fails to properly reflect the realities of the world we live in.

The second problem with Johnson's explanation of the nature of God is her assertion that God transcends sex and gender "in an unimaginable way." Johnson is not alone in this opinion. This is the standard answer to the question of God's gender that theologians have supplied since Christianity and Judaism were born. There is support for this belief. Even though many of God's body parts are mentioned in the Bible (for example, God's face, hands, and hair) there is no mention of God's sexual organs.[89] Since God does not appear to have sexual organs, the logic goes, God is not a sexual being. And yet, there are romantic metaphors that biblical authors associate with God. God gives birth to the Hebrews (Deut: 32:18), and there is Song of Songs, which Jewish and Christian interpreters often regard as an allegory of God's love toward Israel (as is the book of Hosea[90]). The love in Song of Songs is profoundly and explicitly sexual, but as we have seen in other cases, there is the predictable response that labels these passages as anthropomorphic. God giving birth to the Hebrews is a metaphor, the thinking goes, and as such it does not tell us anything meaningful about God's physical construction. As one scholar observed: "God is not a sexual male, and therefore even the erotic metaphor of passion reveals a lack of physicality. God is not imagined in erotic terms and sexuality was simply not part of the divine order."[91] On the surface, these assertions appear to be well-founded. Furthermore, it is rather odd, to my mind at least, to think of God as a sexual being. Yet some

---

88. Melanie Blackless et al., "How Sexually Dimorphic Are We? Review and Synthesis," *American Journal of Human Biology* 12 (2000): 151–66. A couple of physicians who read this section of my manuscript doubted the veracity of this statistic. They did not have research at hand but said they felt that the gender-nonconforming population was far less than 1 in 100. Part of this depends upon how one defines gender conformance. I am not a medical professional, merely a humble writer and theologian, and am content to merely pass along the research I encountered.

89. Smith, *How Human Is God?*, 56. Smith also says that God's sexual activity is never mentioned in the Bible but contradicts this statement one page later with a discussion of Eve procreating with God in Gen. 4:1.

90. Jon D. Levenson, *The Love of God: Divine Gift, Human Gratitude, and Mutual Faithfulness in Judaism* (Princeton: Princeton University Press, 2016), 96–97.

91. Tikva Frymer-Kensky, *In the Wake of the Goddess: Women, Culture and the Biblical Transformation of Pagan Myth* (New York: Free Press, 1992), 189.

of the writers of the Bible believed that the reason why humans are gendered beings is because God is too.

Behind Genesis 1:27 is an understanding that God does not transcend gender but concretely embodies it. God created humankind in the divine image. God created humans *male and female*. Gender is as much a part of the divine nature as it is part of humanity's. Many scholars rightly point out that God is not *either* male *or* female.[92] If God were, we would have to say that only one gender, predictably the masculine one, fully matches God's image. If we went this route we would arrive at a highly disturbing answer to Dorothy Sayers's provocative question: Are women human?[93] If men more fully embody the image of God than women (i.e., if God is male, men are more like God than women), we would have to conclude that women are, in Sayers's words, "human-not-quite-human." That is, if what it means to be human is that people bear the image of God, and if women do not bear this image as fully as men, then they are less human than men. Most theologians circumvent this problem by asserting that God is above gender or asexual. They remove gender from God entirely. I think it is more productive to conclude that God embodies all genders simultaneously. We should, therefore, understand the God of the Old Testament as intersex.

Before we get too far in this discussion I should define what intersex is. "Intersex" is a term used to describe people who do not fit the medical definitions of male or female.[94] There are many conditions that the term intersex includes, but all of them, in some way or another, result in the ambiguous sex of an individual.[95] Intersex describes people who simultaneously exhibit the features of male and female genitalia, individuals whose genitalia is ambiguous, persons who lack genitalia, people whose chromosomes deviate from the

---

92. So many scholars point this out that an exhaustive list is hardly possible. I will mention one scholar, picked almost at random, to illustrate the point. "God is not male, nor is he male and female—he transcends sexuality." Robin Routledge, *Old Testament Theology: A Thematic Approach* (Downers Grove, IL: InterVarsity, 2008), 105.

93. Dorothy L. Sayers, *Are Women Human?* (Grand Rapids: Eerdmans, 1971).

94. Megan K. DeFranza, *Sex Difference in Christian Theology: Male, Female, and Intersex in the Image of God* (Grand Rapids: Eerdmans, 2015), 23. I should note that the American Psychological Association reports, "Many experts and persons with intersex conditions have recently recommended adopting the term *disorders of sex development* (DSD). They feel that this term is more accurate and less stigmatizing than the term intersex." "Answers to Your Questions about Individuals with Intersex Conditions," American Psychological Association, 2006, https://www.apa.org/topics/lgbtq/intersex.pdf. I use the term "intersex" with the utmost respect and have no intention of stigmatizing anyone. I also want to avoid the connotation that people who do not line up with a binary scheme of sex and gender are necessarily "disordered." This is particularly important given the theological discussion in this chapter. Therefore, I will cautiously continue to use the word "intersex."

95. For a detailed description of these conditions, see DeFranza, *Sex Difference in Christian Theology*, 25–44.

XX or XY pattern, and individuals who undergo a naturally occurring sex change at puberty. It is difficult to chart out all the different sexes a person could have, but some scholars estimate there are hundreds of possibilities.[96] And, according to some of the Bible's earliest commentators, Adam was created as a person with one of these possibilities.

Genesis Rabbah is a compilation of Jewish interpretations of the book of Genesis. It reached its more or less present form between the end of the fourth century CE and beginning of the fifth. According to historian Jacob Neusner, Genesis Rabbah "presents the first complete and systematic Judaic commentary to the book of Genesis."[97] Genesis Rabbah is not an obscure or avant-garde piece of speculation. It is the earliest synthesis of traditional Jewish thought regarding the book of Genesis that we have. The commentators in Genesis Rabbah had the highest respect for Scripture and for God. They tried to understand the biblical picture of God as precisely and faithfully as they could. This is important to remember, because some of their observations may be quite shocking to us. If they are, they are shocking merely because the ideas are new to us and they challenge our prejudices and preconceptions, not because there is anything purposely provocative or sensational about them. These are interpretations from traditionalist and observant clerics, not speculative and firebrand extremists. The rabbis who contributed to Genesis Rabbah believed that because God inspired the writing of the Bible, all the little details that make up Scripture are interpretatively significant. They sought to understand the nature of God in light of a close study of Scripture's every word. One of these close readings resulted in an idea that probably will seem very odd to you, if not downright crazy.

Within early Judaism it was not uncommon for interpreters to conclude that God did not create Adam a male. Second-century rabbi Jeremiah ben Eleazar explains, "When the Holy One, blessed be he, came to create the first man, he made him androgynous, as it is said, 'Male and female created he them and called their name man' (Gen 5:2)."[98] Rabbi ben Eleazar did not pull out of thin air his conclusion that Adam was androgynous. He noticed that Genesis 1:27 and 5:2 say that God created humankind male and female. But according to Genesis 2, Adam was created before Eve. Rabbi ben Eleazar believed that Adam must have fully embodied what it means to be human, that is, Adam did not become fully human once Eve was made. Along with many other commentators, Rabbi ben Eleazar assumed that for Adam to be

---

96. J. David Hester, "Intersexes and the End of Gender: Corporeal Ethics and Postgender Bodies," *Journal of Gender Studies* 13:3 (November 2004): 219.

97. Jacob Neusner, *Genesis Rabbah: The Judaic Commentary to the Book of Genesis; A New American Translation*, vol. 1 (Brown Judaic Studies 104; Atlanta: Scholars Press, 1985), ix.

98. Genesis Rabbah 8.1; Neusner, *Genesis Rabbah*, 73.

fully human, Adam must have been *both* male and female. The rabbi termed this androgyny but we could say that God created Adam as an intersex being. Exactly how Adam embodied the male *and* female sex was not completely understood. There were theories, though.

Another commentator, Rabbi Samuel bar Nahman, thought that God created Adam like conjoined twins: half of Adam was male and the other half female. God made Eve by splitting Adam in two: "When the Holy One, blessed be he, created the first man, he created him with two faces, then sawed him into two and made a back on one side and a back on the other."[99] Rabbi bar Nahman ingeniously solved the problem of Adam being simultaneously male and female, but someone objected to the rabbi's hypothesis by pointing out that Eve was made from one of Adam's ribs. The rabbi responded that the word used for rib in Genesis is from the same Hebrew root that is used to indicate the second side of the tabernacle in Exodus 26:20.[100] God did not form Eve from one of Adam's ribs, Rabbi bar Nahman said, but from one of his sides. Those objecting did not rejoin the debate. Apparently, they conceded Rabbi bar Nahman's point.

Early Christian interpreters also had complex understandings of Adam's gender. The great fourth-century scholar Gregory of Nyssa influenced Christian understandings of the Trinity, and his ideas helped form one of Christianity's most important documents, the Niceno-Constantinopolitan Creed. He believed that the differentiation of sex within humanity was a curse, a result of the fall. According to Gregory, Adam and Eve were not sexually different at their creation. Like his Jewish colleagues, he tried to make sense of the passages in Genesis 1 and 5 that speak of God creating humanity as male *and* female. Sex difference, for Gregory, only came into being after the first humans sinned. Furthermore, Gregory thought that after death humans revert to their pre-fall condition as both male *and* female. Glorified humans are sexually integrated beings similar to angels.[101]

Even if theories of an androgynous Adam and a sexually integrated, post-death humanity seem strange, the fact remains that for the author of Genesis 1 the image of God is connected to humans as gendered beings: "So God created humankind in his image, in the image of God he created them; male and female he created them" (Gen. 1:27). It is not only ancient theologians who took this seriously. For Karl Barth, the great twentieth-century theologian, this connection was crucial to his understanding of the image of God.

---

99. Genesis Rabbah 8.1; Neusner, *Genesis Rabbah*, 73.

100. Wilda C. Gafney, *Womanist Midrash: A Reintroduction to the Women of the Torah and the Throne* (Louisville: Westminster John Knox, 2017), 21.

101. Gregory of Nyssa, *On the Making of Man*, trans. William Moore and Henry Austin Wilson (Edinburgh: T&T Clark, 1892), §17.2–4.

He believed that every person needs another to be fully human. For Barth, the male and female sexes complement each other and together make up the image of God:

> It belongs to every human being to be male or female. It also belongs to every human being to be male and female: male in this or that near or distant relationship to the female, and female in a similar relationship to the male. Man is human, and therefore fellow-human, as he is male or female, male and female.[102]

Confusingly, Barth never makes this discussion practical. What exactly does it mean for a male to be female within a distant relationship? He doesn't make this clear. Barth was brilliant, but I do not think he is particularly helpful at this point.

But Barth was onto something. He respected the portrait of God and humanity the book of Genesis provides. He should have looked at another Old Testament passage, though. In Isaiah 56 the prophet looks forward to a time when people who were excluded from full communal life in Israel would be integrated into society. The prophet specifically mentions two types of people who were excluded in his day: foreigners and eunuchs. Neither were welcome to worship at the temple. Most relevant to our discussion, though, are the eunuchs. Deuteronomy 23:1 bars castrated individuals from the assembly of Israel. Deuteronomy makes no distinction between those who willfully underwent castration and those who suffered an accident or were castrated by their parents when they were children.[103] Whatever the cause, the loss or absence of their sexual organs excluded them from public life. In addition, Leviticus 21:20 includes crushed testicles among a list of so-called blemishes that prohibited one from joining the priesthood. And yet, Isaiah 56 looks past these stipulations and imagines a time when full communal membership would not be contingent upon the condition of one's genitalia:

> Do not let the foreigner joined to the LORD say,
>   "The LORD will surely separate me from his people";
> and do not let the eunuch say,
>   "I am just a dry tree."

---

102. Karl Barth, *Church Dogmatics*, III/4, *The Doctrine of Creation*, trans. A. T. Mackey et al., ed. G. W. Bromiley and T. F. Torrance (London: T&T Clark, 1961), §54.

103. There were economic opportunities for castrated men within the ancient Near East. Castrated men were in charge of royal harems and were highly paid singers. It is probable that like Italian opera performers, many of the professional singers in the ancient world were castrated by their families when they were children. Colm Tóibín has a fascinating discussion of Italian castration practices which, I suspect, have many parallels to ancient life. "Ravishing," *London Review of Books* 37:19 (October 8, 2015): 13–16.

> For thus says the LORD:
> To the eunuchs who keep my sabbaths,
>   who choose the things that please me
>   and hold fast my covenant,
> I will give, in my house and within my walls,
>   a monument and a name
>   better than sons and daughters;
> I will give them an everlasting name
>   that shall not be cut off.
>
> Isa. 56:3–5

In Christian tradition, Isaiah's prophetic vision was fulfilled in Acts 8 when the evangelist Philip baptized a eunuch from Ethiopia. This act was not only "the first recorded Christian ministry to a non-Semite" but also a tangible demonstration that individuals who do not conform to binary gender expectations are to be included within the people of God.[104] In this one Ethiopian eunuch both classes of exclusion that Isaiah 56 references—being a foreigner and being a eunuch—are dismissed. The day that the prophet of Isaiah 56 looked forward to had come. Everyone, regardless of their nationality or sex, is included within the people of God.[105]

We should highlight something about this passage that often goes unnoticed. The Ethiopian eunuch is included in the kingdom of God, but there is no indication that he is healed. In this story he remains a eunuch. Many people within the New Testament experience physical healing but this person is not one of them. The reason why he is included in the community of God is not because *the eunuch's* genitalia have regrown and this person is transformed into an "unblemished" and gender-conforming state. Rather, it is the *community* that has been healed. Instead of excluding people because of their sex and gender, the community, according to Isaiah 56 and Acts 8, now must accept intersex and gender-nonconforming folks.[106]

Historically, Christian communities have resisted this interpretation, if they thought of it at all. More often, Acts 8 is understood as a classic example of colonial evangelism. The eunuch is taught how to properly see the world and undergoes a ritual to reflect his conversion. The main beneficiary of this encounter is the eunuch, not Philip. In light of this, contemporary theologian Willie Jennings reflects on how churches put this mentality

---

104. The quotation is from Tom Bissell, *Apostle: Travels among the Tombs of the Twelve* (New York: Pantheon, 2016), 93.

105. I do not discuss it, because it is off topic, but the baptism of this Ethiopian has profound consequences for how Christians regard and treat "strangers." One place to begin piecing together these consequences is Zygmunt Bauman's *Strangers at Our Door* (London: Polity, 2016).

106. Susannah Cornwall, "The *Kenosis* of Unambiguous Sex in the Body of Christ: Intersex, Theology, and Existing 'for the Other,'" *Theology and Sexuality* 14:2 (January 2008): 196.

into practice: "We have more often than not sought to eradicate the differences we perceive in those new and strange to us through soul killing and life draining forms of assimilation."[107] As we have seen, the main focus of this passage is not that the eunuch conforms to the Christian community's expectations but that the community is transformed into an accepting one. Remember, the eunuch was not healed but was accepted into the community. The rules governing communal membership have changed. Eunuchs are now accepted. This rule change is the healing the community experienced. Therefore, while the meeting of the eunuch and Philip was undoubtedly mutually beneficial, perhaps we should understand Philip as one who changed the most. In this exchange Philip was moved by the Spirit to be generous and inclusive rather than exclusionary and tense.[108] Like Philip we can learn to "see difference as an invitation to change, transform, and expand our identities into the ways of life of other peoples."[109] We can experience healing when we embrace people who are different from us. This is all the more important when we consider the fact that our interpersonal differences are never going away.

Acts 8 gives reason to believe that in biblical imagination, intersex individuals will remain as they are with their unique sex in their postdeath existence. The book of Revelation provides support to this idea. Revelation 7:9 indicates that differences that are essential to a person's identity will remain in place after death. Tribal affiliation, nationality, even the languages one speaks seem to endure in glorified existence: "After this I looked, and there was a great multitude that no one could count, from every nation, from all tribes and peoples and languages, standing before the throne and before the Lamb." The vision of Revelation 7 is of heavenly reality. The setting is the throne of God, not the present world. The people who stand in front of the divine throne are different from one another. They are from various nations and tribes, and they speak disparate languages. These differences remain and are discernible in heaven. Yet these differences no longer divide humanity into competing factions, nor do they produce exclusionary responses.[110] All the people before the throne are united into the same community even though their profound differences remain.

Susannah Cornwall uses this passage to argue that just as a person's national or linguistic heritage will not be erased in heaven, neither will their sexual and gender identities be changed or "healed":

---

107. Willie James Jennings, *Acts* (Louisville: Westminster John Knox, 2017), 87.
108. Pádraig Ó Tuama, *In the Shelter: Finding a Home in the World* (London: Hodder & Stoughton, 2015), 148.
109. Jennings, *Acts*, 88.
110. DeFranza, *Sex Difference in Christian Theology*, 183.

> It is conceivable that other instances of physical impairment, and physical atypicality, will also persist in the human bodies of the general resurrection.... The resurrected Jesus, with his impaired hands and feet, is God's revelation of a new humanity—"underscoring the reality that full personhood is fully compatible with the experience of disability." The wounds of the impaired Jesus are not to be vilified, nor to be pitied; they are marks of life experience, and signposts to a new kind of life.[111]

Cornwall is not alone in thinking that a person's sex will not be washed away in their existence after death. There is a fairly deep history of theological reflection imagining that sexual intercourse will be part of heavenly reality.[112] After all, in the Genesis narrative God creates humans as sexual beings with sexual desire and it is good for them to satisfy this desire. Why would this be obliterated in the future if that is how humans were created to be?

Sex and gender are important markers of human identity, perhaps the most deeply felt of all. Could it be that the reason why these physical and social aspects of human experience would endure after the resurrection is because they are central features of the divine image that God bestowed upon humanity and, concomitantly, reflect the central features of the very essence of who God is?

I think it is best to avoid thinking of God in primarily male or female terms. Nor should we picture the divine as an ungendered being. Rather, we should follow the example of Isaiah 42:13–14, which fuses together male and female language to describe God:

> The LORD goes forth like a soldier,
>   like a warrior he stirs up his fury;
> he cries out, he shouts aloud,
>   he shows himself mighty against his foes:
> "For a long time I have held my peace,
>   I have kept still and restrained myself;
> now I will cry out like a woman in labor,
>   I will gasp and pant."[113]

---

111. Cornwall, "*Kenosis* of Unambiguous Sex," 195. She quotes Nancy L. Eiesland, *The Disabled God: Toward a Liberatory Theology of Disability* (Nashville: Abingdon Press, 1994), 100.

112. We are most certainly in the realm of speculation here but Patricia Beattie Jung raises the point that biblical authors often speak of heaven as a place of feasting. Would digestion and elimination also go along with heavenly food and drink as it does now? If we believe digestion and elimination are a part of heavenly reality, then it seems to follow that various forms of sexual play and intercourse would be present as well. Jung, *Sex on Earth as It Is in Heaven* (Albany: State University of New York Press, 2017), 111–18.

113. I modified the punctuation of the NRSV to more clearly distinguish the prophet's voice from God's. For a very helpful study of this passage, see Claudia Bergmann, "'Like a Warrior' and 'Like a Woman Giving Birth': Expressing Divine Immanence and Transcendence in Isaiah 42:10–17," in *Bodies, Embodiment, and Theology of the Hebrew Bible*, ed. S. Tamar Kamionkowski and Wonil Kim (New York: T&T Clark, 2010), 38–56.

The prophet uses masculine terms to describe God: God is a warrior, God is a he who goes out to fight. But God's self-description in this passage is that of a woman in labor crying out in pain. Neither description is right or wrong or more accurate than the other. In one moment God is male and in another female.[114] This is because, we could imagine after the writers of Scripture, God embodies the entire gender spectrum.[115] God is not he or she or it. God is all of these simultaneously. God does not conform to the bifurcated gender understanding that permeates our culture. But neither is God "above it all" as an ungendered, asexual being. God is intersex, a being that embodies the fullness of humanity within the divine person. God has a localized presence and an embodied form that is profoundly human in appearance. If someone were to ask us what God looks like, we could sweep our arm across the horizon and say, "God looks like all of us."[116]

---

114. Jürgen Moltmann attempts to capture this in his phrase "God is a motherly father." "The Motherly Father: Is Trinitarian Patripassianism Replacing Theological Patriarchalism?," in *God as Father?*, ed. Johannes Metz et al. (Edinburgh: T&T Clark, 1981), 83. While this is a good start, the phrase assumes a binary view of gender and also makes God's motherly aspect a modifier while the primary gender of God remains masculine.

115. This understanding was not exclusive to ancient Israel. It was fairly common in the ancient world for people to picture creating deities as embodying both male and female forms. See, for instance, Nicolas Wyatt, *The Mythic Mind: Essays on Cosmology and Religion in Ugaritic and Old Testament Literature* (London: Equinox, 2005), 238–55.

116. Thinking about God's body in terms of gender is only the beginning. There are many more dimensions of embodiment we should consider. As Kelly Brown Douglas describes J. Deotis Roberts's theological vision, "Roberts argued that if the universal Christ came to all people in their particular historical context, then all people had a right to define Christ through their particular experience and image Christ in their own likeness." *The Black Christ* (Maryknoll, NY: Orbis Books, 1994), 61. Anthony B. Pinn helpfully cautions that anytime we think of an embodied person (and god) there are potential dangers as well as generative possibilities. *Embodiment and the New Shape of Black Theological Thought* (New York: New York University Press, 2010), 62.

4

God's Mind

In contemporary North American context it is common to understand that the brain and its related parts provide the biological capacity for the mind to emerge,[1] but the dominant view in the ancient world was that the head was a mere storage container for semen.[2] Many ancients believed the cranium functioned like a water tower. It held seminal fluid which flowed down through the spinal column and went out the body at ejaculation.[3] This seems odd to me, but to an ancient person who might have seen brain matter leaking out of fractured skulls on the battlefield, it apparently made complete sense. Ancient peoples located the seat of the mind further down in the human body, in the upper chest, inside the heart. Emotions, particularly deeply felt ones like empathy and disgust, were thought to reside even lower still, inside the bowels.

---

1. If it is even right for us to speak of the mind as distinct from the physical workings of the body. I will tentatively follow the assumption that the mind is distinct because this is the predominant assumption of the culture that I am writing within. However, many contemporary societies believe that the mind is not separable from the body, or the mind and body are far more connected than European and North American cultures typically assume. For example, many within Ghanaian society are not concerned with hard distinctions between mind and nonmind. John Dulin, "Vulnerable Minds, Bodily Thoughts, and Sensory Experiences: Local Theory of Mind and Spiritual Experience in Ghana," in "Mind and Spirit: A Comparative Theory," ed. T. M. Luhrmann, special issue, *Journal of the Royal Anthropological Institute* 26:S1 (2020): 61–76. I am in no way trying to privilege Euro–North American perspectives or make them normative. I am merely trying to write within my own context and the context in which this book will first appear.

2. Both men and women were thought to have forms of sperm. Pieter W. van der Horst, "Sarah's Seminal Emission: Hebrews 11:11 in the Light of Ancient Embryology," in *A Feminist Companion to the Hebrew Bible in the New Testament*, ed. Athalya Brenner (Sheffield: Sheffield Academic, 1996), 117–20.

3. Troy W. Martin, "Paul's Argument from Nature for the Veil in 1 Corinthians 11:13–15: A Testicle instead of a Head Covering," *Journal of Biblical Literature* 123:1 (2004): 75–84.

In the ancient world, emotions and thought were seen as deeply integrated with the body. The ways people feel and think about the world were interwoven into the patterns of the human body. For ancient peoples, one could not cleanly divide a person into a center of abstract thought on one side and a material body on the other. More and more scientists are returning to an understanding of an integrated and holistic human experience, but it was not always this way within European-inspired tradition—particularly when it comes to theological reflection. For a long time theologians and philosophers believed humans were bifurcated beings. A person's mind, which was encompassed in the soul, was thought to be distinct from the body and would continue to exist even after a person's material substance ceased living.[4] A modern iteration of this very old line of thought took shape in the transhumanist movement, which believes the human mind can be uploaded to a computer network and freed of the constraints of the finiteness the body imposes.[5] In any event, the mind is a complicated topic. Humans cannot even agree where it is located: inside the brain, inside the heart, or within a computer network. Before we think about God's mind, we need to examine more closely what a mind really is.

WHAT IS A MIND?

According to the philosopher René Descartes, the essence of the mind is the awareness that we are alive and inhabiting a particular place. The mind, according to him, could be equated with consciousness.[6] In fact, Descartes did not think that bodies are essential to the human condition at all. If there were a way to disconnect consciousness from a body, like separating the germ from a husk of wheat, this human being would continue to exist as a disembodied mind.[7]

It is common for biblical scholars to reject this kind of thinking.[8] Many scholars insist that the authors of the Hebrew Bible reflected the common

---

4. Most thinkers have imagined the soul as residing inside the body; however, Celtic tradition pictures the body encased by the soul. John O'Donohue, *Anam Cara: A Book of Celtic Wisdom* (New York: HarperCollins, 1997), 168–69.

5. A classic book on this topic is Ray Kurzweil, *The Singularity Is Near: When Humans Transcend Biology* (New York: Viking, 2005).

6. A myriad of questions rise from this, including, Do we experience a unified flow of consciousness or do we sense a series of pictures that flash before us like the frames of a moving piece of film? I do not have space to pursue these issues; if you are interested in them, a good place to start is Oliver Sacks, *The River of Consciousness* (New York: Knopf, 2017), 161–84.

7. Anthony Kenny, *The Metaphysics of Mind* (Oxford: Clarendon, 1989), 1.

8. As with every issue, there are scholars who argue the opposite. For instance, John W. Cooper outlines a biblical case for traditional mind-body, or soul-body, dualism in *Body, Soul and Life Everlasting: Biblical Anthropology and the Monism-Dualism Debates* (Grand Rapids: Eerdmans, 1989).

understanding throughout the ancient world that humans are unitary creatures. That is, they believed mind and body, or body and soul, were thoroughly integrated and were not separable. For instance, the great Old Testament theologian Walther Eichrodt denied that the Hebrew Bible had any understanding of a soul that would continue to exist after a person had died. When a person dies, their vitality disappears as their physical body begins the process of becoming once again the dust it originally was. Eichrodt was adamant about this. He asserts, "It is the distinguishing feature of Israelite as of all other primitive thinking that it makes no difference between spiritual principle and physical manifestation."[9]

For the moment, let's overlook Eichrodt's description of Israelite thinking as "primitive" and focus on his claim that Israelites and their contemporaries made no distinction between a spiritual or nonphysical principle and the physical thing that represents it. Eichrodt provided an example of what he meant. Oftentimes the authors of the Hebrew Bible used the word "blood" to stand in for a person's life. For instance, "to shed someone's blood" means "to kill someone." Eichrodt takes this to mean that to the Hebrew mind the physical blood pumping through someone's veins is identical to and inseparable from a person's life. Now, it is true that if a person's veins are empty that person is not able to live. But Eichrodt is saying more than this. He asserts that ancient people, Israelites included, were unable to conceptualize a person's life apart from their blood. Blood and life were one and the same concept to them.

What Eichrodt is really saying is that Israelites did not understand metonymy. Metonymy is a rhetorical act in which a speaker refers to a part of something in order to indicate the entire thing. It's like a beatnik referring to a banker as a "suit." The beatnik uses the banker's dress as a stand-in for the entire person. We assume the beatnik is able to differentiate an article of clothing from the person who wears it. Eichrodt apparently did not think the same about ancient Israelites.

Scholars now understand that ancient perceptions were more varied. They understand that the authors of the Hebrew Bible were able to and did employ rhetorical devices like metonymy.[10] Furthermore, new discoveries seem to indicate that many people in the ancient Mediterranean believed the human

---

9. Walther Eichrodt, *Theology of the Old Testament*, vol. 2, trans. J. A. Baker (Philadelphia: Westminster, 1967), 136.

10. Scholars also are now more careful to study ancient texts within their cultural settings and, as much as is possible, refrain from interpreting ancient documents in light of modern assumptions. Matthew J. Suriano has an excellent discussion of this as he explores the ways in which *nepeš* functions in the Hebrew Bible. *A History of Death in the Hebrew Bible* (New York: Oxford University Press, 2018), 131–248.

body housed an animating force which formed the real core of who that person was. In other words, they differentiated a person's physical body from an aspect of the person that was capable of surviving death. They termed this animating force "breath" (*nepeš*), which many translations render as "soul."[11] They seemingly anticipated Descartes's mind-body dualism, yet as we will see in a moment, their thought patterns were more nuanced on this point than Descartes's.

The discovery that was, perhaps, most responsible for complicating our understanding of ancient perspectives of the mind is an inscription from the ancient town of Sam'al, now Zincirli, Turkey. In July 2008 a team of archaeologists from the University of Chicago found a stele that was commissioned around 735 BCE by a royal servant named Katumuwa. In the inscription Katumuwa directs his descendants to place offerings of meat at the base of the stele each year in order to remember him after he dies. Katumuwa seems to indicate that his soul (*nbš*)[12] will reside inside the stele, because he directs his descendants to provide "a ram for my soul, which is in this stele."[13] Katumuwa believes that his vitality, his conscious self, will live on after he is dead. It will no longer be housed within his body but within a piece of carved stone. It is significant that Katumuwa did not believe that his soul, once free of his body, would float free as an intangible spirit. Even after he died his soul would continue to be embodied. The body would take different form, from living flesh to cold stone, but the soul would continue to be encased in matter.

As many biblical scholars have noted, the concept in the Hebrew Bible that a vitality (*nepeš*) flows through a person's body does not directly equate with the modern idea of a soul that is completely separate from the body. However, I do not think the ancient and modern concepts are as dissimilar as many scholars claim. Some scholars go out of their way to stress that the vitality (*nepeš*) was not immortal and did not transcend death.[14] Once a person's blood ceased to flow or their breath was cut off, their vitality ceased to be. To be sure, a good many people in the ancient world probably believed

---

11. I agree with Eichrodt that "soul" is not the best translation for *nepeš*; however, I would not go as far as he did and call it "dangerous" (*Theology of the Old Testament*, 2:135).

12. The inscription reads *nbš*, which most scholars believe is cognate to Hebrew *npš*. For a discussion of this, see my review of Michael Coogan's anthology, "Has Michael Coogan Seized His Opportunity?," in *Marginalia Review of Books*, January 29, 2013, https://marginalia.lareviewofbooks.org/a-reader-of-ancient-near-eastern-texts/.

13. This inscription was first published by Dennis Pardee, "A New Aramaic Inscription from Zincirli," *Bulletin of the American Schools of Oriental Research* 356 (2009): 51–71. For a detailed treatment of this issue that includes a history of scholarship on this topic, see Richard C. Steiner, *Disembodied Souls: The Nefesh in Israel and Kindred Spirits in the Ancient Near East* (Atlanta: SBL Press, 2015). This translation is from Steiner, *Disembodied Souls*, 129.

14. For instance, Christopher D. Stanley, *The Hebrew Bible: A Comparative Approach* (Minneapolis: Fortress, 2010), 175–77.

this. Yet, some ancient people like Katumuwa seem to have thought that their vitality would obtain a new house after death. In the case of Katumuwa, it was a stele; others believed the body would be reconstituted at the end of days and their vitality would rejoin it.[15] Perhaps the differences between the Pharisees, who believed in a life after death, and the Sadducees, who did not, reflect a development of two approaches to the soul that existed in various forms for a long time prior to the first century BCE?

Whatever the case may be about ancient perceptions regarding the eternal or finite nature of the soul, almost all ancient peoples, like most humans today, believed that a living person had two main facets of conscious life. We refer to these facets as our mental and emotional life. As I mentioned above, in ancient understanding these facets were regarded as heart and bowel life. The next chapter will discuss the emotional/bowel life of God. The rest of this chapter will focus on the mental/heart life of God.

Old Testament theologian Rolf Knierim identified at least five possible connotations that are implied when biblical authors use the word "heart" (lēb).[16] We could think of these as the various functions or capacities these authors believed the mind has:

1. The heart/mind was thought of as the place from which *understanding* came. In the Hebrew Bible, understanding was the ability to make good decisions, that is, to choose rightly between available options. If someone does this well, they are regarded as wise. For instance, a wise commander on the battlefield was able to discern the strategy that had the highest chance of success. The wisest person in biblical tradition, Solomon, asked God to give him a heart that was highly calibrated and attuned to making wise decisions. Solomon puts it this way: "Give to your servant a heart that listens [lēb šōmēaʻ] to the court cases your people bring so that I might discern between good and bad because who is able to adjudicate these onerous folks who are your people?" (1 Kgs. 3:9, my trans.).

2. Knierim says, "The heart is the place of *sensitivity* and *emotion*."[17] I think I understand what Knierim meant by this, but I do not think this is the best way to phrase it. Knierim provides Psalm 104:15 in support of this claim that the heart is the place of emotion, but quotes only the first half of it: God gives "wine to gladden the human heart." This verse seems to indicate the human heart is the place of emotion, but if we read the entire sentence that mentions the heart we will see that this approach may be a bit misleading:

---

15. Jon D. Levenson and Kevin J. Madigan, *Resurrection: The Power of God for Christians and Jews* (New Haven: Yale University Press, 2008), 24–41.

16. Rolf P. Knierim, *The Task of Old Testament Theology: Substance, Method and Cases* (Grand Rapids: Eerdmans, 1995), 280.

17. Knierim, *Task of Old Testament Theology*, 280, italics in original.

> [God is the one] causing grass to sprout for cattle
> and plants for working animals,
> bringing food up from the earth
> and wine which gladdens the human heart [ləbab ʾĕnôš],
> brightening the face with oil
> and with food he sustains the human heart [ləbab ʾĕnôš].[18]

In this section, the first half says that God will provide sustenance for animals. The next half says that God will give humans not only food that sustains life but also wine and oil that bring enjoyment and relief from some of life's challenges. The structure of the last two lines gives us a window into some of the functions the psalmist believed the human heart has. The first half of this passage begins with food and the last line ends with it. The two phrases in the middle mention luxuries, wine and oil. We could arrange the structure of the passage as A B B′ A′.

The significance of this, to my mind, is that the human heart needs food to sustain its life. Humans are dependent creatures just as cows are. The psalmist says that God is responsible for the sustenance of all sentient life. This is the poet's main point. Secondarily, he says that wine can lift a person's heart above its concern for mere survival just as the face takes on a better appearance when it is cleansed and moisturized with oil. Yet I do not think the psalmist is saying that the heart, or mind in our understanding, is the central seat of deep emotion. Rather, wine can temporarily blunt a racing mind and push aside anxieties about the future. Wine does not gladden someone on an existential level. Ancients saw a link between the heart and bowels, between our mental processes and emotions. They understood that humans are interconnected beings and emotions cannot be cleanly and definitively separated from a person's thought life. Nonetheless, in the ancient world, just as today, most people made a distinction between the emotional life of the mind/heart and the deeper emotional life of the heart/bowels. Our expression "gut-level response" indicates this distinction as well. We understand that the mind experiences emotion but there are other more primal feelings that seem to come from other parts of our bodies or are more deeply rooted within us than the thoughts that stream through our minds. Most of the authors of the Hebrew Bible had this understanding as well.[19]

---

18. For the most part, I follow Mitchell Dahood's reading of this passage in *Psalms III: 101–150* (Anchor Bible; Garden City, NY: Doubleday, 1970), 40–42.

19. Hans-Joachim Kraus says that "in the ancient world the 'kidneys' were regarded as the seat of secret feelings." *Theology of the Psalms*, trans. Keith Crim (Minneapolis: Augsburg, 1986), 145. ("Secret feelings" is a translation of "geheimer Gefühlsbewegungen" in the original German edition, *Theologie der Psalmen* [Biblischer Kommentar Altes Testament 15.3; Neukirchen-Vluyn: Neukirchener Verlag, 1979], 182.) This is not the most helpful framing of

3. Knierim's third attribute of the heart is the place of *desire, longing*, and *will*. This is reflected in Psalm 21:2 (3 Heb.), in which David is attributed as praising God: "You have given [the king] his heart's desire, and have not withheld the request of his lips." In another example, Isaiah of Jerusalem describes his interpretation of the Assyrian conquest of the Levant. He says that God sent the Assyrians to punish the Judeans and cause them to repent, but the Assyrians were not aware that they were tools of Israel's god. This is how Isaiah frames it: "But this is not what [Assyria] intends, nor does he have this in mind [ləbābô]; but it is in his heart [bilbābô] to destroy, and to cut off nations not a few" (10:7). The mind/heart directs a person's plans and intentions. It decides what that person wants and constructs strategies to acquire these things.

4. The mind/heart is the source of *language*. Someone who has a finely tuned mind will be able to speak with skill and persuasion. "A wise heart [lēb ḥākām] hones a person's mouth and heaps persuasion onto his or her lips" (Prov. 16:23, my trans.). Speaking well and with persuasion does not come easily. A person must consciously look for a stable basis for their thoughts. They should base their ideas and actions on reality instead of prejudice. As Proverbs 15:14 puts it: "The mind [lēb] of one who has understanding seeks knowledge, but the mouths of fools feed on folly." By itself, knowledge is not sufficient for living well. It must be combined with a mind that will process knowledge properly and use it to guide the movements of a person's body. Proverbs 6 gives us a picture of this from a negative perspective, and it also reveals the complexity of ancient thought regarding a person's vitality: "A person committing adultery lacks heart [lēb]; the person doing it destroys their vitality [napšô]" (Prov. 6:32, my trans.). In her comments on this verse, Amy Plantinga Pauw notes that the "result of such misdirected passions is self-destruction."[20] Of course, a person's life is not literally destroyed, but the nature of how they live and feel will likely suffer greatly, particularly if their actions are discovered. If a person's mind makes poor decisions, the rest of their existence will experience hardship. In ancient understanding, a person's vitality (nepeš) not only lives on after someone dies but a person's soul can also, in some sense, die or be destroyed in this life while their body continues to live.

5. The final characteristic Knierim lists is that the heart is the place of *conscience*. He cites Psalm 51:10 (12 Heb.) in support: "Create in me, O God, a clean heart [lēb ṭāhôr] and a spirit within me that is secure and fresh" (my trans.). I suppose we could say that this verse speaks of a conscience that

---

the role of emotions, but possibly Kraus meant something like deep-seated and above/below consciousness?

20. *Proverbs and Ecclesiastes* (Belief: A Theological Commentary; Louisville: Westminster John Knox, 2015), 46.

corrects a person's way of life, but I think it might be better to understand the use of "heart" here as conforming with Knierim's third characteristic, *desire, longing*, and *will*. The person in this verse is not asking for a heart that constantly produces feelings of guilt or reminders to correct course. The person wants a mind that is cleansed of unhelpful desires and that is rebooted in a state that is steadfast in a desire for a new trajectory for their life.[21]

MIND-BODY CONNECTION

We should not see these capacities of the mind as independent from the rest of the human body. Human beings are deeply interconnected. The mind directs the body, and the body influences the mind. This relationship flows in both directions. This has profound implications for how we imagine God's mind, since, as we discovered in the previous chapter, many of the authors of the Hebrew Bible believed that God has a body.

Most of us imagine that our conscious selves are in control of our bodies. Our mind directs our hands to grasp an object and we command our legs to run. This is partially true. However, in many cases our bodies decide to act before our minds tell them to. Research physiologist Benjamin Libet created an experiment to test the relationship between our conscious sense of agency, our mental choice to do something, and the body's neurological events to make the body move.[22] Libet placed electrodes on his subjects' scalps and told them they could flick their wrists whenever they wanted. The electrodes monitored the subjects' brain activity and Libet designed a special, extra-large clock that allowed the subjects to report reactions in fractions of a second.

The flick of a wrist might seem to happen all at once as a single action, but there are 500 to 1,000 milliseconds (0.5 to 1 second) of brain activity leading up to the physical movement of a person's hand. Immediately before the flick—50 milliseconds, to be precise—the motor cortex in the brain sends a signal down the motor nerves to the wrist. When the signal reaches the wrist, the muscles in the hand move. Before this signal is sent, though, there are several hundred (up to 800) milliseconds of brain activity that scientists call *readiness potential* in which the brain plans for the upcoming movements. The intriguing part of this for our discussion is that Libet showed that it takes 350 milliseconds *after* the brain enters readiness potential for us to become

---

21. The same can be said for the only other reference Knierim lists for the fifth characteristic, Ezek. 11:19.

22. "Unconscious Cerebral Initiative and the Role of Conscious Will in Voluntary Action," *Behavioral and Brain Sciences* 8 (1985): 529–66, and "The Neural Time-Factor in Perception, Volition, and Free Will," *Revue de Métaphysique et de Morale* 2 (1992): 255–72.

conscious of the urge to move. In other words, when we reach for a coffee cup, our subconscious brain has already set into motion a whole series of processes *before* our minds become conscious of a desire to grasp the cup. We are able to shut down the readiness potential and prevent our arm from extending, but only if we stop the process 200 milliseconds before the motor cortex sends the signal for our muscles to move.[23] After this threshold has been passed, our mind is powerless to stop the process the brain initiated. This is a point of no return at which body movement will happen regardless of what our conscious mind desires.[24]

This discovery set off a vigorous debate on the question of free will. Some argued that humans do not have free will, since our conscious minds come to know of voluntary movements only after the brain has initiated them. Others said that we do indeed have free will because there is a window of time, between 350 milliseconds after the brain enters readiness potential and 200 milliseconds before the motor cortex sends the message, in which our conscious minds can veto an action.[25] I am not interested in entering this debate, but this debate and the research underneath it demonstrate how interconnected our conscious mind/heart is with our body. Even something as simple as a voluntary hand motion is initiated by the subconscious brain and vetoed or not by the conscious mind. More interesting for us still is that while the body seems to be able to act on its own—the brain can initiate an act, prepare for it, and send a message to the part of the body it wants to move—the mind cannot do this. The mind can prevent the body from acting once the body has decided to move, but only within a small window of time. We will see in the next chapter that the mind's independence is further constrained by emotion, but for now we should consider one other way in which the mind is restricted by embodiment.

It should be fairly obvious that we are dependent upon our bodies to think. Not only do our bodies keep the brain alive, but as we have seen in chapter 1, the body mediates every sensation the brain uses to think and make conclusions. This, of course, means that there are limits to what we can know. We are finite beings and therefore have limited understanding. Likely none of this is new information to you. However, our bodies influence our thinking in other, and in some cases very strange, ways.

---

23. Matthias Schultze-Kraft et al., "The Point of No Return in Vetoing Self-Initiated Movements," *Proceedings of the National Academy of Sciences of the United States of America* 113:4 (January 26, 2016): 1080–85.
24. This paragraph summarizes, but also supplements, Shaun Gallagher, *How the Body Shapes the Mind* (Oxford: Clarendon, 2005), 237–38.
25. William R. Klemm, "Free Will Debates: Simple Experiments Are Not So Simple," *Advances in Cognitive Psychology* 6 (2010): 47–65.

Body position and posture have a dramatic effect on our minds. When someone slouches in a chair instead of sitting up, they think about questions less carefully and have less resilience when questions become difficult. Crossed arms make a person more stubborn. Researchers reported that people who crossed their arms while trying to solve anagram puzzles worked on them twice as long as people whose arms were at their sides. The folks with uncrossed arms were also more successful at solving the puzzles.[26] The mere act of crossing one's arms has a strong effect on the outcome of mental tasks.

The state of one's body has a large influence on a person's thought life, too. Minds can be clouded, blunted, or influenced by chemical substances. Lack of sleep can lengthen the time it takes the brain to perform calculations. Breathing in deep sighs can make a person feel sad or scared. One study showed that performance on standardized tests was correlated to the quality and depth of a person's normal breathing pattern.[27] People make better choices when they have a strong desire to pee. Apparently, the concentration and attentiveness required to prevent an accident focuses other cognitive operations. The self-control we must have over our bodies to keep ourselves dry also helps to restrain impulses that could lead to poor decisions.[28]

It should be very clear by now that our bodies radically shape the ways in which we think, process information, and react to the world around us. Is the same true for God? It seems that many biblical authors assumed so. The previous chapter noted that many ancient Israelites believed that God has a body and that human shape and sex reflect God's own contour and intersex embodiment. As we examine various passages from the Hebrew Bible that have to do with God's mind, we will discover that they present a deity whose body constrains the divine mind in much the same ways that the human body constrains us.

THINGS GOD DOESN'T KNOW

One of the ways the human body is constrained has to do with the knowledge we can possess. There are certain things we cannot know. And humans are not able to exhaustively understand the information we do have. Many passages in the Hebrew Bible reflect a similar view of God. There is a significant

---

26. Guy Claxton, *Intelligence in the Flesh: Why Your Mind Needs Your Body Much More Than It Thinks* (New Haven: Yale University Press, 2015), 156.

27. U. Tan, M. Okuyan, and A. Akgun, "Sex Differences in Verbal and Spatial Ability Reconsidered in Relation to Body Size, Lung Volume and Sex Hormones," *Journal of Perceptual and Motor Skills* 3:2 (1996): 1347–60.

28. Mirjam Tuk, Debra Trampe, and Luk Warlop, "Inhibitory Spillover: Increased Urination Urgency Facilitates Impulse Control in Unrelated Domains," *Psychological Science* 22 (2011): 627–33.

difference, though, between human and divine limitations, which I will discuss at the end of this section. For now, let's investigate some of the types of things that God does not know.

Future Choices an Individual Will Make

According to Jewish tradition, the binding of Isaac is the last of ten tests Abraham went through.[29] The great medieval Jewish interpreter Rashi compared Abraham's last test—God's command that Abraham sacrifice his son Isaac— to Job's afflictions. Rashi said that in both cases the tests arose from a confrontation between God and Satan. Satan entered a gathering of the divine beings (messengers, seraphim, and the like)[30] and questioned Job's piety (Job 1–2). He attributed Job's obedience to his wealth and well-being. Take that away from him, Satan said, and Job would walk away from God. God set up a test to prove Satan wrong. God told Satan he could afflict Job's body, kill his children, and take away his money. Satan went about doing these very things, and he and God then watched to see how Job would respond. Would Job continue to trust in God, as God said he would, or would Job curse God and resign himself to a meaningless death?

In the case of Abraham, Rashi imaged that Satan snuck into a divine banquet and openly questioned Abraham's obedience. Satan said that Abraham had not offered an appropriate sacrifice to God in return for all of the blessings God gave him. Abraham had made offerings but they were rather paltry, not the ram or bull God was due. God told Satan that Abraham's motives were pure and that he was fully capable of offering the kind of sacrifice Satan outlined. In fact, God said, Abraham was so faithful that if God directed Abraham to sacrifice his own son, he would. God then tested Abraham with this very request.[31]

---

29. Pirke Avot 5.4: "Ten trials tested Abraham our father, and he stood up to them all—so as to make known the love of Abraham our father." William Berkson and Menachem Fisch, *Pirke Avot: Timeless Wisdom for Modern Life* (Philadelphia: Jewish Publication Society, 2010), 205. The precise enumeration of these tests varies a bit from commentator to commentator. See, for instance, the differences between the lists compiled by Maimonides and Martin Buber, in Louis Arthur Berman, *The Akedah: The Binding of Isaac* (Northvale, NJ: Aronson, 1997), 34–37.

30. For discussions of the divine council, see Simon B. Parker, "Council," in *Dictionary of Deities and Demons in the Bible*, 2nd ed., ed. Karel van der Toorn, Bob Becking, and Willem van der Horst (Leiden: Brill, 1999), 203–6; Robert P. Gordon, "Standing in the Council: When Prophets Encounter God," in *The God of Israel*, ed. Robert P. Gordon (Cambridge: Cambridge University Press, 2007), 190–204; and Ellen White, *Yahweh's Council: Its Structure and Membership* (Tübingen: Mohr Siebeck, 2014).

31. Compare Rashi's discussion with Babylonian Talmud tractate Sanhedrin 89b. Also worthy of comparison is Erich Auerbach's analysis of Gen. 22 in light of book 19 of Homer's *Odyssey*, "Odysseus' Scar," in *Mimesis: The Representation of Reality in Western Literature* (Garden City, NY: Doubleday Anchor, 1957), 1–20.

But what does it mean for God to test someone? Genesis 22:1 explicitly says that this is what God did. God commanded Abraham to kill his son as a way to test (*nissâ*) Abraham's faithfulness. Some contemporary commentators say the point of this testing was not for God to see what Abraham would decide, but to give Abraham the opportunity "to demonstrate a truth that can be observed, in contrast to a truth that is only asserted."[32] That is, God gave Abraham a situation in which he could realize the full potential of his trust in God. No longer would Abraham's piety be a theoretical matter; it would be shown and enacted in the real world.[33] Underlying this interpretation is the assumption that God knows everything, even the future choices people make. It goes like this: We know that God already knows what Abraham will decide, so what can it mean for God to test someone?[34] Answer: It must mean that divine "testing" is not really a testing but a forum for humans to enact their faith. This logic is similar to what we saw John Calvin do when he argued that biblical assertions that God changed God's mind mean the opposite of what they say. However, if we get rid of the assumption that God knows future choices and attempt to discern what this passage reveals about God, we come to a different conclusion. Furthermore, it seems to me that for a test to be genuine, its outcome must be unknown to the participants, even if one of the participants is God.[35] Otherwise, a test is not really a test.

---

32. Bill T. Arnold, *Genesis* (New Cambridge Bible Commentary; Cambridge: Cambridge University Press, 2009), 202.

33. James McKeown, *Genesis* (Two Horizons Old Testament Commentary; Grand Rapids: Eerdmans, 2008), 116–17. Miguel A. De La Torre helpfully points out that perhaps the word "test" is not accurate here. "If [a trial] comes from God, we call it a test; but if it comes from anywhere else (i.e., Satan, demons, other humans, society), we call it a temptation." *Genesis* (Belief: A Theological Commentary on the Bible; Louisville: Westminster John Knox, 2011), 215. Traditionally, theologians disagree with De La Torre, but for the most part their disagreement is supported solely by their assertion that God would not tempt someone. Joseph Blenkinsopp, *Abraham: The Story of a Life* (Grand Rapids: Eerdmans, 2015), 143. I agree with De La Torre, but for the sake of continuity I will continue to translate *nissâ* as "to test" since it occurs in other passages we will examine that do not have a connotation of temptation.

34. There is another dimension to this. Theologians want to avoid the conclusion that God would lead someone into sin. However, there is a link between testing and the Lord's Prayer asking that God "lead us not into temptation" (Matt. 6:13; Luke 11:4). Walter Brueggemann, *Genesis* (Interpretation; Atlanta: John Knox, 1982), 190–91.

35. Walter Moberly, *The Bible, Theology, and Faith: A Study of Abraham and Jesus* (Cambridge: Cambridge University Press, 2000), 97–107. However, Terence E. Fretheim's note that the test is set within a relational context is important (*Abraham: Trials of Family and Faith* [Columbia: University of South Carolina Press, 2007], 133). Fretheim says that God did not know the outcome of the test until Abraham made a decision, but Abraham's vantage point was a bit different. Abraham also would not know the full outcome of the situation until it was complete, yet he could nonetheless assume good would come of it. Abraham could base this assumption upon the previous interactions he had with God. However, we should keep in mind that Abraham had no idea this was a test. That is a note the narrator gives to us readers. Abraham, poor soul, did not get this memo. Jon D. Levenson, *Inheriting Abraham: The Legacy of the Patriarch in Judaism, Christianity, and Islam* (Princeton: Princeton University Press, 2012), 67. Because of this, I side

This is how the word "to test" (*nissâ*) is used in other parts of the Bible. For instance, in Exodus 17 the people are locked in a bitter dispute. They are in the wilderness, fresh from walking through Re(e)d Sea and watching Pharaoh's army drown. The people are thirsty. God has sent manna and quail for them to eat, but they lack water. Some of the Hebrews think this signals that God is no longer present with them. They argue that if God were still in their midst they would have ample sources of water. Others argue against them, saying that God is still faithful even though they do not have everything they want at that moment. This argument becomes a full-fledged legal dispute. Exodus 17:7 terms it a *rîb*, a formal dispute between two parties that centers on a point of law.[36] We could think of this case as an argument over canon law. It is a communal dispute regarding the nature of the society's religious life. The case is adjudicated with a test. If God provides them with water, God is still with them.[37] If the people do not receive water, then God has brought the people out of Egypt and into the wilderness only to abandon them and let them die.[38] Or, God is simply unable to provide for them in that way. Either way, the test would determine which side of the dispute is correct.

In Exodus 17 the Hebrews do get water. The outcome of the test settles the dispute in favor of those who kept their trust in God. It should be clear that the test in Exodus 17 was a legitimate test. The Hebrew people who conducted the test did not know what the outcome would be. Certainly, both sides of this dispute *hoped* the test would conclude in their favor, but they did not *know* if it would until its end. And the outcome of the test brought resolution to the dispute. Once God provided water, everyone

---

with Moberly when he says that since this is a real test "there is no reason to suppose that the test will have a benign outcome" (97).

36. Pietro Bovati, *Re-Establishing Justice: Legal Terms, Concepts and Procedures in the Hebrew Bible*, trans. Michael J. Smith (Sheffield: Sheffield University Press, 1994), 30.

37. Franz-Josef Helfmeyer, "nissâ," in *Theological Dictionary of the Old Testament*, vol. 9, ed. G. Johannes Botterweck, Helmer Ringgren, and Heinz-Josef Fabry, trans. David E. Green (Grand Rapids: Eerdmans, 1998), 446.

38. Terence E. Fretheim notes the coercive nature of this test. The people are forcing God's hand and making God act in order to clear the divine name. Fretheim characterizes this as an impious act, an "attempt to turn faith into sight." *Exodus* (Interpretation; Louisville: John Knox, 1991), 189; see also J. H. Korn, ΠΕΙΡΑΣΜΟΣ: *Die Versuchung des Gläubigen in der griechischen Bible* (Beiträge zur Wissenschaft vom Alten und Neuen Testament 72; Stuttgart: Kohlhammer, 1937), 76. John Goldingay takes this a step further and provides two different rationales for tests in *Old Testament Theology*, vol. 1, *Israel's Gospel* (Downers Grove, IL: IVP Academic, 2003), 469. God tests people not to come to know something but because God is being respectful toward individuals by not prying into their inner thoughts but letting people choose to bring them to the surface. When people test God, however, it is because they do not trust God in the face of ample evidence. Perhaps this test in Exod. 17 was impious, as so many commentators conclude. On the other hand, water is a basic need and the people had seen God provide for them in the past only to be cut off from further provision. In that light, the people's doubts seem legitimate.

knew that God was still present. Those who had argued that God was absent admitted they were wrong.

If we bring this definition of *test* (*nissâ*) to Genesis 22, and there is no good reason why we should not, it becomes clear that God did not know what Abraham would decide until Abraham reached for the knife he would use to kill his son. God created a test to learn the extent of Abraham's trust. Like the Hebrews of Exodus 17, God hoped for a certain outcome and likely had a good hunch about what that outcome would be, but until the test concluded God did not know what Abraham would do. From this it seems reasonable to conclude that God does not know the choices individuals will make in the future. Again, God may have a high-confidence guess as to what humans will choose, but God does not have *knowledge* of it until the choice is made.[39]

The Character of a People

Another thing God does not know is the character of a people. Since God does not know the future choices an individual will make, God obviously cannot know the future choices of a collection of people. Choices made over time build and demonstrate a person's character. An accumulation of choices reveals the inner qualities a person has. And just as individuals have character, so do societies. God knows the decisions individuals and communities made in the past, and this can be a basis for God to gauge the present and future character of a people or group. But what happens if there is not a sufficient track record? What if a group of people drastically change their ways of life? Will their character change as well?

The exodus story presents this very situation. God freed the Hebrew people from slavery in Egypt. God brought the people out of that land, promised to give them a new place to live, and gave to this people a set of teachings to help them better understand how to move through the world in beneficial ways. God did not bring them into this new land immediately. God needed to learn if the people were ready, if they would live in accord with the teaching God gave them. Deuteronomy 8:2 puts it this way: "Remember the long way that the LORD your God has led you these forty years in the wilderness,

---

39. This is not a new insight. Philosophers since at least Aristotle believed that God could not know the impossible (which includes future decisions), as did biblical interpreters such as medieval Jewish commentator Gersonides. Seymour Feldman, "Levi ben Gershom / Gersonides," in *Hebrew Bible/Old Testament: The History of Its Interpretation*, vol. 2, *From the Renaissance to the Enlightenment*, ed. Magne Sæbø (Göttingen: Vandenhoeck & Ruprecht, 2008), 70. However, the idea that there is nothing God does not know has dominated European theological discourse even though this understanding contradicts biblical texts.

in order to afflict you, testing you to know what was in your heart, whether or not you would keep his commandments."[40]

Here again God tests (*nissâ*) humans. This passage could not be more clear about the test's purpose, "to know what was in your heart."[41] God wanted to discover the people's character, to learn the condition of the people's inmost desire. The last phrase of this verse provides even more specificity. God wanted to know if the people would observe the commandments God gave them.[42] If we read along with the grammar and narrative flow of this passage, it is clear that God did not know if the people were willing to live in accord with divine instruction. Therefore, God delayed their entrance into the land so there would be an appropriate amount of time to test the people's desire. Just as with an individual, God does not know the collective choice of a nation until that choice is made.

THE GOINGS-ON OF EARTH

In addition to not knowing the future decisions individuals and communities will make, God also does not know the details of events that happen far away from God. This makes sense when we picture God as an embodied being. One of the limitations of having a body is that the knowledge one has is limited to the sensations one's body is able to detect. If we understand God in this way, a straightforward reading of the story of the tower of Babel makes perfect sense.

Genesis 11 tells of a time when humanity speaks a single language. Apparently, this causes humans to overestimate their place within the hierarchy of the universe.[43] These folks are no longer content to spread out over the earth and fill it, as God instructed (Gen. 1:28). Apparently, they want to congregate together and centralize their power. Nor are they willing to live together in diversity, embracing the variety of ways humans live and act

---

40. I have slightly modified the NRSV according to Robert Alter's observation that the word the NRSV translates as "humble" is more suitably translated as "afflict." *The Five Books of Moses: A Translation with Commentary* (New York: Norton, 2004), 921.

41. The infinitive *lāda'at* ("to know") indicates purpose. E. Kautzsch and A. E. Cowley, eds., *Gesenius' Hebrew Grammar* (Oxford: Clarendon, 1910), §114f.

42. Intriguingly, we do not know what the results of this test revealed. Patrick D. Miller, *Deuteronomy* (Interpretation; Louisville: John Knox, 1990), 116.

43. The theme of humans overestimating themselves is repeated all through the Bible. Richard Feldmeier, *Power, Service, Humility: A New Testament Ethic*, trans. Brian McNeil (Waco, TX: Baylor University Press, 2014), 1.

(Gen. 10:32).[44] Instead, they want to be uniform. They come together in a single place and build a large city with a tower whose top was "in the heavens" (11:4). At this point God exits heaven and goes down to earth to see what is going on. This is exactly how the Genesis account frames it. Genesis 11:5 says: "The LORD came down to see the city and the tower, which mortals had built."

We could respond to a text like this in various ways. We could say that the statement that God "came down to see the city" is metaphorical and does not really mean that God had to travel from heaven to earth to discover what was going on. We could be like Augustine and say that God never moved position but the biblical writers said God did because that is the only way feeble human minds could understand this. In fact, God is always everywhere all the time and knows everything that happens. The authors of the Bible merely told a white lie to help us understand the story. Or, we could say that God is always everywhere all the time, but God is also more intensively present at some places at certain times. This divine movement from heaven to earth signified one of those times.[45] That is to say, God knew all about the tower of Babel because God is all-knowing and everywhere, but God was mystically more present in Babel at that moment than God was in other places.

It seems better to me that we simply read what the text says: "The LORD came down to see the city and the tower, which mortals had built." In Genesis 11 God physically moves, God "came down," in order "to see." In order to learn what was going on in Babel, God had to physically move. God had to put God's body in a position where God could see with God's eyes. The description of the actions God took in order to investigate the new construction in Babel is almost identical to the human act of looking at a piece of art. One does not merely gaze at a picture with one's eyes. The poet and essayist Jean-Louis Chretien notes: "It is not with one's eyes but rather with all one's being that one looks upon a picture."[46] In order to look at a picture, a person must move their feet to get in position. Once in front of a painting a person might walk toward it to study a detail or move back to grasp the entire canvas. A person becomes silent to focus the mind. One's heart may slow if the work is serene or perhaps it speeds up if it recalls intense emotions. It is important

---

44. Rolf Rendtorff, *The Canonical Hebrew Bible: A Theology of the Old Testament*, trans. David E. Orton (Leiden: Deo, 2005), 19.

45. Terence E. Fretheim does not reference this particular passage but he constructs this type of theology. *God and World in the Old Testament: A Relational Theology of Creation* (Nashville: Abingdon, 2005), 25.

46. *Hand to Hand: Listening to the Work of Art*, trans. Stephen E. Lewis (New York: Fordham University Press, 2003), 18.

for us to notice that in order to learn by sight, oftentimes one must move. The implication of Genesis 11 is that if God did not leave heaven and go to earth, God would not be able to see the city and the tower. At least, that is how the author of Genesis 11 frames it.

What happens when there are multiple places on earth that God wants to investigate at the same time? If God has a body, God cannot be in two places at the same time, so God sends helpers to spy out locations and report back what they see. One example of this is embedded in a vision the prophet Zechariah experiences (1:7–17). In this vision, the prophet sees four horsemen. One horsemen is the leader and the other three "patrol the earth" and report back the state of things they encounter.[47] Presumably, the captain would then assemble a report to give to God. Many other accounts in the Bible also depict divine messengers acting in God's place.

Perhaps the most entertaining account demonstrating the embodied knowledge of God is Deuteronomy 23:12–14. This account contains instructions for the Hebrews as they journey through the wilderness:

> You shall have a designated area outside the camp to which you shall go. With your utensils you shall have a trowel; when you relieve yourself outside, you shall dig a hole with it and then cover up your excrement. Because the LORD your God travels along with your camp, to save you and to hand over your enemies to you, therefore your camp must be holy, so that he may not see anything indecent among you and turn away from you.

This passage instructs the people to go outside the camp when they feel the urge to eliminate. Why? Many interpreters point to the hygienic aspects of defecating in designated places away from where people live.[48] One does not want to pollute the water supply or attract bugs and disease by defecating close to where one lives. Certainly this is true, but the passage makes no mention of hygiene. The passage does give a specific reason for the command: so that God will not see the people with their trousers down.[49] Again, the implication

---

47. Even though most commentators assume that the horses have riders or are attached to chariots (cf. 6:1–3), this is never specified within this passage, and some interpreters picture the horses themselves scouting the earth and verbally giving their report. Marvin A. Sweeney, *The Twelve Prophets* (Berit Olam; Collegeville, MN: Liturgical Press, 2000), 578. If this interpretation is accurate, this account would gain a flavor of magic realism that is present within biblical literature (for instance, see the talking donkey in Num. 22); however, it seems preferable to assume the horses have riders.

48. Oded Borowski, *Daily Life in Biblical Times* (Atlanta: SBL, 2003), 79–80.

49. Edward Ullendorff provides a better translation of the first line of the passage. He understands the Hebrew word *yad*, translated by the NRSV as "area," in its common use as a euphemism: the "exposure of your pudenda shall be outside the camp." "The Bawdy Bible," *Bulletin of the School of Oriental and African Studies* 42:3 (1979): 442.

here is that God lives inside the camp, and God does not want to watch people relieving themselves. If the people go out of the camp to defecate, then God will not see their naked backsides.[50] This is a far different understanding of God from one that assumes God is everywhere all the time.

If we use our imaginations, there might also be another reason why the people are forbidden to defecate in the camp. The NRSV translates the beginning of verse 14 as "Because the LORD your God travels along with your camp. . . ."[51] This is not a bad rendering, but it does obscure the literal idea of what is said. A more literal translation of the Hebrew would be "Because the LORD your God walks around [*mithallēk*] in the middle of your camp. . . ." Again, at this point there is a cottage industry of biblical interpretation which claims that this text means the opposite of what it says. One commentator seems to dismiss the idea that God actually walked through the camp. Instead, he says that this passage expresses a "spiritual or religious reality."[52] And yet, the passage clearly says that God walks around the camp. Perhaps, in addition to not seeing people naked, God did not want to step in a pile of human feces, and so God commanded the people to do their business away from the area where God lived and walked?

The point that is relevant for our discussion is that this passage indicates that if the people *went out* of the camp to relieve themselves, God would not see them. That is, God could not see something that was not near where God was. In still other words, this passage pictures God as an embodied being who walked around the Hebrew camp and did not see things that happened outside of it.

THE WAYS GOD LEARNS

Because God does not know everything, God learns and comes to know things as humans do. There are several ways in which the authors of the Hebrew Bible believed God learns. All of these ways assume that God learns through God's body. The same embodiedness that constrains God's knowledge also facilitates God's acquisition of information.

---

50. Curiously, rabbinic commentators understood the command to bury excrement only applied when one was in a military camp. Otherwise, this stipulation was not in force. David I. Shyovitz, *A Remembrance of His Wonders: Nature and the Supernatural in Medieval Ashkenaz* (Philadelphia: University of Pennsylvania Press, 2017), 184.

51. This is verse 15 in the Hebrew Bible.

52. Peter C. Craigie, *The Book of Deuteronomy* (New International Commentary on the Old Testament; Grand Rapids: Eerdmans, 1976), 300.

Through the Divine Body

Across the ancient Mediterranean world, sight was the most important way people came to know something.[53] In Indo-European, the word "to know" was formed from the root *weid*, which also means "to see." As I have mentioned before, etymology can lead us astray when we use it to understand the meanings of words in different languages. There is even more danger in using the history of word meanings to prove metaphilosophical points about ancient cultures. However, with these risks in mind, I do think the linguistic link between sight and knowledge reflects an assumption throughout the ancient world (as well as the modern) that seeing is knowing.[54] If ancient peoples wanted to learn something, they had to go out into the world and look. This included looking into the heavens to discern the will of the gods that was embedded in the placement of the stars. In more pedestrian situations, they would send spies into enemy territory to chart troop movements. Regardless of the type, most knowledge came from sight. This also applied to God. Even though it is never explicitly mentioned in the Hebrew Bible, it seems likely that many ancient Israelites pictured God as having eyes.[55]

Divine body parts other than eyes are mentioned in the Bible. The most curious example, and one that has caused amusing speculation, is the mention of God's "backside" in Exodus 33:23. Moses asks to see God's glory. God agrees but tells Moses it is too much for him to see the divine face. If he did, he would die. God tells Moses he can see his back (*'ăḥorāy*). What precisely Moses saw is a matter of considerable debate. Some say God's "backside" was just that, the back of God's torso. However, others, including me, think it refers to God's buttocks. The face is the most individual and signifying feature of a person's body. In many ways, a face *is* the person. It projects one's personality into the world. The buttocks is, perhaps, a person's most humble body part. It is the place out of which waste is expelled. God seems to be saying to Moses: You cannot handle my most radiant feature, so I will show you the most lackluster part of me.

Psalm 18 lists other parts of God's body: ears, nostrils, a mouth, and feet. It is not much of a stretch to add eyes to this list. The features listed in Psalm 18 aid God's ability to know. With ears God heard the cry of the Hebrews as they

---

53. Kimberly Dawn Russaw, "Wisdom in the Garden: The Woman of Genesis 3 and Alice Walker's *Sophia*," in *I Found God in Me: A Womanist Biblical Hermeneutics Reader*, ed. Mitzi J. Smith (Eugene, OR: Cascade, 2015), 230.

54. Paul S. Fiddes, *Seeing the World and Knowing God: Hebrew Wisdom and Christian Doctrine in a Late-Modern Context* (Oxford: Oxford University Press, 2013), 167–74.

55. Zech. 2:8 does mention the "apple of God's eye," but this seems to be an idiom that indicates something valuable.

suffered under Pharaoh in Egypt. The people's cry moved God to look at their plight. It was after learning of their mistreatment through sound and sight that God appointed Moses to deliver them. God explains this to Moses at the burning bush: "I have observed the misery of my people who are in Egypt; I have heard their cry on account of their taskmasters. . . . The cry of the Israelites has now come to me; I have also seen how the Egyptians oppress them" (Exod. 3:7, 9). God hears a cry that piques God's interest and then God must *look* in order to learn more. And, as we saw in Genesis 11, because God's sight is restricted God travels to new places to spy out what is going on. For instance, in Genesis 3:8 God walks (*mithallēk*) in the garden of Eden. If God walks, God must use legs and feet. All of this points to the idea that God, like humans, learns through God's body. As we saw in the passage from Zechariah 1, when God's body limits the extent to which God can know something, such as not letting God be in all places at once, God sends messengers to spy out a place and report back what they saw. These messengers can be thought of as extensions of God's body. They function as God's eyes when God either does not care to leave the heavenly temple or is unable to be at a particular location.

Tests

In addition to using the divine body to learn, God also constructs tests to understand the inner disposition of human individuals and communities. We saw examples of these tests in the stories of Abraham and the wilderness wanderings. In each of these instances, God set up a test designed to give a yes-or-no result. Does Abraham fully trust me or not? If he does, he will attempt to sacrifice his son. If he does not, he won't. These tests are similar to the use of two stones in the priestly repertoire, the Urim and Thummim (Exod. 28:30 and Lev. 8:8).[56] Based on models of yes-or-no queries from Mesopotamia, Israelite priests posed a yes-or-no question to God and then cast the Urim and Thummim. The priests used these dice-like objects to discern the answer of binary questions.[57]

God puts similar tests to humans. They take the form of binary questions, but they do not involve divination objects such as the sheep livers used in

---

56. For a detailed study of the Urim and Thummim, and one that slightly deviates from my analysis, see Cornelis Van Dam, *The Urim and Thummim: A Means of Revelation in Ancient Israel* (Winona Lake, IN: Eisenbrauns, 1997).

57. In some cases the question could be, Is a certain prophecy legitimate? At other times the questions may have inquired about the outcome of a specific event in the future, e.g., Will we win the upcoming battle? For studies of yes-or-no queries from Mesopotamia, see Ivan Starr, *Queries to the Sun God: Divination and Politics in Sargonid Assyria* (State Archives of Assyria 4; Helsinki: Helsinki University Press, 1990), and W. G. Lambert, *Babylonian Oracle Questions* (Winona Lake, IN: Eisenbrauns, 2007).

Mesopotamia or the Urim and Thummim in the Hebrew Bible. God places humans into situations that are designed to reveal a clear yes or no to specific queries God has. The implication of these biblical accounts is that if God did not administer these tests, the results would not be available to the divine mind. God must learn the result of these queries; God does not automatically know the answers.

Questions

In Genesis 3, after God travels down to Eden and walks through the garden, God asks Adam and Eve a series of questions. "Where are you?" (v. 9), "Who told you that you were naked?" (v. 11a), "Have you eaten from the tree of which I commanded you not to eat?" (v. 11b), and "What is this that you have done?" (v. 13). Of course, someone could argue that this is merely a Socratic encounter where God teaches the first humans a point by asking them leading questions. God's questions, these interpreters might say, were not asked so that God could learn something but so that Adam and Eve could. Other commentators frame this as a courtroom proceeding.[58] The questions are veiled charges of wrongdoing; they are not designed to help God learn something God does not know.

Perhaps these ways of viewing God's questions to Adam and Eve are legitimate. However, could they not simply be questions? If read in the most straightforward manner, that is what they seem to be. God visits the garden in the temperate time of day and looks for the humans. God does not find them, so God calls out, asking where they are. When they reveal themselves, God knows something is not right, so God asks them questions. That seems to be the natural flow of the story. The only reason we would read against the grain of it and posit alternative interpretations of the function of the questions is if we have decided before even reading the account that God does not learn by asking questions because God knows everything already.

How God's Knowledge Works

In contrast to classical, Eurocentric theologies which assume that God knows everything that is possible to know, many Old Testament authors picture the divine mind as constrained by God's body. God is, nonetheless, a supernatural being—a being that is above nature. Like the dead prophet Samuel whom the diviner at Endor conjured up for Saul, God is able to transverse

---

58. John H. Sailhamer, "Genesis," in *The Expositor's Bible Commentary: Genesis–Leviticus*, ed. Tremper Longman III and David Garland (Grand Rapids: Zondervan, 2008), 89.

boundaries that mortal humans cannot. God can leave the heavenly plane and come to earth. God can seemingly go anywhere on earth or send messengers to those places. God has the ability to learn anything about the happenings of the universe.[59] This is not to say, though, that God knows everything.

We looked at passages in which God did not. Before God left heaven and came down to Babel, God did not know the details of the tower the humans constructed. God learned from the screams of the ground that there was something profoundly wrong between Cain and Abel. God asks Cain, "Where is your brother Abel?" Cain responds with defiance and disdain. If we read between the lines, God connects the dots and assumes Cain was the one who shed Abel's blood that soaked into the dirt (Gen. 4:1–16). Before this investigation, though, what did God know? The text does not explicitly say, but it seems to imply that God knew enough to be alarmed but not enough to know exactly what took place. God had to move God's body to investigate further.

It seems clear that God does not know things that take place at a distance. The inner life of a human also is a mystery to God. Until a person reveals themselves by answering questions or acting within a test that God administers, God may have a hunch as to the person's disposition, but God does not know it. Even biblical passages which seem to indicate that God knows the thoughts of a person, upon deeper reflection, fit the paradigm of God's bodily limited knowledge. For instance, Jeremiah 17:9–10:

> The heart is devious above all else;
>   it is perverse—
>   who can understand it?
> I the LORD test [$ḥoqēr$] the mind
>   and search [$boḥēn$] the heart,
> to give to all according to their ways,
>   according to the fruit of their doings.

Jeremiah depicts God as saying that God knows a general fact about the human mind—it is devious and difficult to figure out—and that God is able to discern the character of a person through testing and searching. This passage does not say how God tests the mind and searches the heart to understand the nature of a person. Many commentators assume that God magically intuits the depths of humanity.[60] It is almost as if the divine functions like an MRI for the emotions. God scans a person's psychological makeup and constructs a map of their inner

---

59. Cf. John Goldingay, *Old Testament Theology*, vol. 2, *Israel's Faith* (Downers Grove, IL: IVP Academic, 2006), 102.

60. For example, Louis Stulman, *Jeremiah* (Abingdon Old Testament Commentaries; Nashville: Abingdon, 2005), 170.

life. If we dispense with this assumption, perhaps it is more plausible to imagine that God goes about understanding a person through watching a person's behavior, asking them questions, and/or arranging a test? In other words, God learns in exactly the ways the biblical authors say God learns.

CHANGES IN GOD'S MIND

Descartes admitted it would be possible for God to change God's mind if the nature of God were changeable. He compares this to a king deciding to change a law that same king put into place. That kind of thing happens fairly often in human society. But Descartes believed that God is immutable, that God always remains the same and does not change. Therefore, the philosopher argued, God's mind never wavers or backtracks.[61] Historically, most Eurocentric theologians believed this as well.[62] Indeed, dissenting from this perspective and asserting that God can change God's mind was the stance that offended traditional theologians more than almost any other.[63] People were deemed heretics and killed for saying that God could change God's mind.

A good representative of the classical position (minus the call to kill the heretics) is contemporary scholar Thomas Weinandy. He admits that there are biblical passages that make it seem as though the divine mind changes, such as Exodus 32:12–14; 1 Samuel 15; and Jonah 3:10. On the other hand, there are verses that deny God's mind changes at all: Numbers 23:19; Psalm 110:4; and Jeremiah 4:28. Weinandy regards these conflicting pictures of God as a "dilemma." Weinandy believes the Bible presents only one, unitary picture of God. The contradictory passages should be harmonized so they say the same things. He recommends creating "an interpretive or hermeneutical tool for bringing consistency to them."[64] The tool Weinandy comes up with is similar to the approach of John Calvin that I discussed in chapter 1. Weinandy claims that when the Bible seems to say that God's mind changed, it actually means the opposite:

---

61. David Cunning, "Descartes' Modal Metaphysics," *Stanford Encyclopedia of Philosophy* (Spring 2018), ed. Edward N. Zalta, https://plato.stanford.edu/archives/spr2018/entries/descartes-modal/.

62. Grace Ji-Sun Kim and Susan M. Shaw helpfully point out that the theologies that emphasize divine immutability are most often male-dominated theologies centered on hierarchical power. *Intersectional Theology: An Introductory Guide* (Minneapolis: Fortress, 2018), 66–67.

63. Jörg Jeremias, *Die Reue Gottes: Aspekte alttestamentlicher Gottesvorstellung* (Neukirchen-Vluyn: Neukirchener Verlag, 1975), 9. Historian Jaroslav Pelikan says that "the impassability of God was a basic presupposition of all [institutional] Christological doctrine." *The Emergence of the Catholic Tradition* (Chicago: University of Chicago Press, 1971), 270.

64. Thomas G. Weinandy, OFM, *Does God Suffer?* (Notre Dame: University of Notre Dame Press, 2000), 60.

> In a sense, God is said to "change his mind" precisely because, as Wholly Other, "he does not change his mind." The interpretive tool here is the same as that articulated throughout. The very language that is used, being "sorry," "relenting," "repenting," and "changing" of mind seeks to express Yahweh's answerable and unalterable love which is expressed in his compassion, mercy and forgiveness, and equally, that he is adamant in his demand for justice and goodness.[65]

It never ceases to astonish me that theologians are able to get away with this kind of rhetoric. In what other discipline can someone say, "In a sense, Y is said to be X precisely because, according to my ad hoc assumption, X means the very opposite of what X means"? In any case, Weinandy says that when it appears God changes God's mind, God's mind doesn't change at all. What has happened is that humans have changed their behavior, which then results in an alternative response from God. In my judgment, this interpretation is impossible to square with the narrative flow of many biblical texts.

Not every author of Scripture believes that God's mind can change.[66] Some seem to think that God's essential being is somewhat static, but others believe that God's mind changes as any thoughtful human being's would.[67] As I have mentioned before, I do not think contradictory portraits of God are a problem. In my view, there is no dilemma here. Like light, God's characteristics are multiple and contradictory. We should read biblical texts on their own terms and let them communicate what they communicate instead of baselessly pronouncing that they mean the opposite of what they say. If we read biblical passages straightforwardly, we will discover that in many accounts God radically changes course and in some cases God admits that God's way of interacting with the world was wrong.

The narrator of the book of Genesis tells the reader something intriguing in Genesis 8:21. At this point of the story, Noah has survived the great flood God brought upon the world to punish it for evils, human and angelic.[68] The waters have subsided and Noah has exited the ark. He has built

---

65. Weinandy, *Does God Suffer?*, 61.

66. As you will discover in my treatment of 1 Sam. 15, I do not see this situation as clear-cut as Eric A. Seibert does when he says, "While one passage speaks of God as the kind of being whose mind cannot change, another clearly states that 'God changed his mind' (1 Sam. 15:29; Jonah 3:10)." *Disturbing Divine Behavior: Troubling Old Testament Images of God* (Minneapolis: Fortress, 2009), 172–73. I agree with Seibert's idea that biblical passages conflict, but 1 Sam. 15 is not as straightforward as he thinks it is.

67. As Rowan Williams has shown, an ability to have remorse and to change one's mind is a sign of maturity. *Lost Icons: Reflections on Cultural Bereavement* (Edinburgh: T&T Clark, 2000), 95–138.

68. The account of the Nephilim, which the narrator of Genesis describes as divine beings, "sons of God," in Gen. 6:1–4 immediately precedes God's judgment of humanity in 6:5–8. The flood seems to be a response to the Nephilim just as much as it was a judgment against humans. In fact, if we read between the lines, as did many early Jewish interpreters, we would conclude that

an altar and offered sacrifices to God. The narrator tells us, "And when the LORD smelled the pleasing odor, the LORD said in his heart, 'I will never again curse the ground because of humankind'" (8:21a). With this statement, God changes the way God has related to creation since Eden. After Adam and Eve ate the fruit of the forbidden tree, God cursed the ground. With the flood, God cursed the ground again by destroying everything that lived on top of it. But in Genesis 8:21 God says that "the divine policy of injuring the Earth because of humans—operative since Eden—has now been reversed."[69]

This is an entirely new way of interacting with humanity and the greater universe. The pattern of how God acts in relation to the world changed in the most fundamental of ways. It cannot be explained as a mere response to something humans did. That is, God did not act out of a static condition and the only reason the world seemed to change is because humans altered course.[70] Humanity keeps on sinning after the flood, as we learn from the rest of Genesis and the Bible at large. Humans remain fundamentally the same after Genesis 8. God does not. God will no longer punish the ground for what humans do. God decides to deal with humanity's continued waywardness in a new way. Humanity, in the most essential of ways, remains static. It is God who alters course.

Some commentators try to explain this passage a different way. They say God does not change the divine mind but merely has "regret" or sorrow at the bad choices of humanity. This interpretation has the same weakness as other attempts to downplay the humanlike behavior God exhibits in Scripture: it argues against the clear meaning of the words in the text. In this case, the word for "change of mind" is *nḥm*. In an extensive analysis of this term, one scholar says, "The only element common to all meanings of *nḥm* appears to be the attempt to influence a situation: by changing the course of events, rejecting an obligation, or refraining from an action."[71] The verb *nḥm* signals a break from the past, a change from a previous way of acting. It is not merely to have some sort of abstract, psychological feeling. Feelings may certainly be involved, but *nḥm* most fundamentally indicates a purposeful and conscious change of mind.

God sent the flood as a response to male angels mating with human women. James L. Kugel, *The Bible as It Was* (Cambridge: Belknap Press of Harvard University Press, 1997), 107–12.

69. Norman Habel, *An Inconvenient Text: Is a Green Reading of the Bible Possible?* (Adelaide: ATF, 2009), 82.

70. For instance, this is how Bruce K. Waltke explains God's change of mind. *An Old Testament Theology* (Grand Rapids: Zondervan, 2007), 285 n. 4, and Bruce K. Waltke with Cathi J. Fredricks, *Genesis: A Commentary* (Grand Rapids: Zondervan, 2001), 118–19.

71. Heinz-Josef Fabry, "nḥm" in *Theological Dictionary of the Old Testament*, ed. G. J. Botterweck et al., trans. David E. Green (Grand Rapids: Eerdmans, 1998), 9:342.

Many theologians try to argue against this. They point to two verses to prove that the divine mind does not change: Numbers 23:19 and 1 Samuel 15:29. Both passages convey the same message even though they are worded slightly differently. Numbers 23:19 is set within a poetic oracle and contrasts the trustworthiness of God against the fickleness of humankind. Balak, the king of Moab, hires a prophet named Balaam to curse the people of Israel. Balaam builds an altar and offers sacrifices to Yahweh. In return, God gives Balaam an oracle that blesses Israel. Balak becomes angry at Balaam and sends him to a different place to offer sacrifices, hoping that this will cause Balaam to curse instead of bless Israel. Once again, Balaam receives an oracle of blessing. Within this second oracle are a couple of statements regarding God's trustworthiness:

> God is not a human being, that he should lie,
>   or a mortal, that he should change his mind.
> Has he promised, and will he not do it?
>   Has he spoken, and will he not fulfill it?

In the other verse, 1 Samuel 15:29, the prophet Samuel tells King Saul that God has decided to take the kingdom away from Saul because Saul did not fully obey God. Saul pleads with Samuel and tries to persuade him to petition God to relent and let him remain king. Samuel responds that God's mind is made up:

> Moreover the Glory of Israel will not recant or change his mind; for he is not a mortal, that he should change his mind [nḥm].

Both of these passages compare the divine mind to a human one. Both passages say that God's mind will not change as a human mind might. However, neither verse accomplishes what traditional commentators want them to. Neither statement makes a categorical judgment against the divine mind ever changing. Rather, they present two qualifications as to what kind of change takes place within the divine mind.[72]

The first phrase in Numbers indicates that God does not lie. This assertion is set within a poetic structure that is synonymously parallel:

> A (God is not a human being)
> B (that he should lie)
> A′ (or a mortal)
> B′ (that he should change his mind)

---

72. R. W. L. Moberly, "'God Is Not a Human That He Should Repent' (Numbers 23:19 and 1 Samuel 15:29)," in *God in the Fray: A Tribute to Walter Brueggemann*, ed. Tod Linafelt and Timothy K. Beal (Minneapolis: Fortress, 1998), 112–23.

Some interpreters assume that it is out of the question for God to lie (however, God does cause lying in the Hebrew Bible[73]) and so the phrase about God not lying is used to strengthen the assertion that God will not change God's mind. This is a somewhat convoluted way of thinking, and if the assumption about God not lying is set aside, it is clear that both phrases, B and B', refer to the same essential thing. Balaam's use of this statement is to underscore the point that God has determined how God will react to this situation and there is no use in trying to persuade God otherwise. In a sense, this is saying that God is stubborn and intractable in this particular situation. Samuel has this same rhetorical goal in 1 Samuel 15:29. In both cases, a prophet responds to a particular circumstance and presents God's response to a particular individual's objection to God's decision.[74] The prophets are saying, *In this decision*, God's mind is firmly made up.

The second qualification these verses offer is that when God changes God's mind, God does so in a way that is somehow different from how humans go about it. These passages do not explain this explicitly, but they may imply that humans are fickle and they lie for selfish reasons. The prophets say that *in these situations*, God will not act like that. The divine mind is set.

We should note one other feature of the 1 Samuel account. The statement in 1 Samuel 15:29 that God will not change God's mind about taking the kingdom away from Saul is set within two other statements which assert that God changed God's mind about wanting Saul to be king.[75] In 1 Samuel 15:11 God tells Samuel, "I regret [*niḥamtî*] that I made Saul king, for he has turned back from following me, and has not carried out my commands." Apparently, God thought there was a good chance that Saul would obey God's commands, but he did not. Because of this, God has a change of mind about entrusting Saul with the responsibility of leading Israel. In other words, God appointed Saul as king but Saul made decisions that caused God to remove Saul from the throne and put someone else in his place. God's mind changed. The account of Samuel and Saul's encounter ends with another statement that God regretted ever making Saul king: "And the LORD was sorry [*niḥām*] that he had made Saul king over Israel" (1 Sam. 15:35).

Even though the NRSV translates the word that describes God's change of mind differently in these passages—"regret," "change his mind," and "sorry," respectively—each passage uses the same Hebrew word, *nḥm*. Therefore, one

---

73. The prophet Micaiah tells the kings of Israel and Judah, "So you see, the LORD has put a lying spirit [*šeqer*] in the mouth of all these your prophets; the LORD has decreed disaster for you" (1 Kgs. 22:23).

74. John Sanders, *The God Who Risks: A Theology of Divine Providence*, 2nd ed. (Downers Grove, IL: InterVarsity, 2007), 74.

75. Sanders, *God Who Risks*, 75.

thing 1 Samuel 15:29 *cannot* mean is that God's mind never changes. This is because on either side of this statement are two other verses (15:11, 35) that say that God changed God's mind about Saul being king! First Samuel 15 must, then, mean that God regretted choosing Saul to lead Israel, so God decided to change course. God would take the kingdom away from Saul and give it to someone else. In this decision to remove Saul from power, God would not be dissuaded. God had firmly decided, and Saul would not be able to persuade God not to do this even though a human might be persuaded (or bribed) to back down.

First Samuel 15 reveals another thing about God's mind. In this case, God changed God's mind because of new information. Presumably, when God first chose Saul to be king, God had high hopes that Saul would be obedient. When it turned out that Saul was not, God shifted course. God learned something new about the interior condition of Saul's nature. God had no way of knowing for certain if Saul would be a good king when God selected him. As with Abraham and the Hebrews who wandered the wilderness, God had an idea of what their future behavior might be, but until Saul revealed his character through tests, questions, or a combination of circumstance and time, God did not know what his future decisions would be. Saul did not turn out as God hoped or expected. So God changed course and removed Saul from the throne. As we will see in the next chapter, new information is not the only thing that can cause God's mind to change.

5

God's Emotions

Charles Darwin famously synthesized some of the foundational ways that natural selection influences biological evolution. He had the idea that genetic mutations which better enable a species to survive the rough-and-tumble natural world eventually take over a species' gene pool. The organism's traits that are better adapted to survive come to dominate the genetic makeup of the entire group. Darwin's theory quickly became the universal understanding of evolutionary development and influenced almost every field of thought from economics to history. Darwin endured fierce controversy in his day, but he is now considered a saint of science and is interred at Westminster Abbey beside British monarchs, Rudyard Kipling, and Stephen Hawking.[1]

Darwin shaped the field of biology more than, perhaps, any other person. Yet Darwin did not spend his scholarly life focused solely on the material development of organisms. He thought quite a lot about the emotional lives of animals, humans in particular. His theory of emotion, although almost totally unheard of in popular culture, has had an equally large influence on contemporary assumptions about human behavior as his theory of natural selection has had on biology.

---

1. Darwin's theory of natural selection still dominates popular thought even though his actual theory was more complicated and multidimensional than it is often portrayed. For instance, Darwin believed that beauty, in addition to pure material survival, also played a role in natural selection. Richard O. Prum, *The Evolution of Beauty: How Darwin's Forgotten Theory of Mate Choice Shapes the Animal World—and Us* (New York: Doubleday, 2017), and Michael J. Ryan, *A Taste for the Beautiful: The Evolution of Attraction* (Princeton: Princeton University Press, 2018).

WHAT IS EMOTION?

Darwin published *The Expression of the Emotions in Man and Animals* in 1872. He originally intended it as a section in his book on the theory of natural selection and human development, *The Descent of Man*, which was published in 1871. However, Darwin's description of emotion became so large that its almost five hundred pages required its own binding. Darwin's understanding of emotion followed a train of thought that began with Plato. Like the Greek philosopher, Darwin viewed emotions as universal. He believed that every human experiences the same feelings as everyone else because the categories for sensing emotion are embedded within humans at birth. When outside circumstances or internal imaginations trigger these embedded categories, emotions stir inside us. Emotions are always present in our inner life. We bump around from one feeling to the next as we move through the world. We are servants, even prisoners to a certain extent, of these categories of emotion that rule our lives.

Our emotions do not stay locked inside our heads, though. They are also expressed outwardly through our bodies. That is to say, we signal to those around us what we are feeling inside our minds. People cry when they are sad and smile when they are happy. Darwin took these ancient assumptions and merged them with his theory of evolution. The categories humans have for emotions are not implanted by the gods, Darwin thought, in contrast to Plato, but they arise as adaptations to help our species survive.

Darwin also created a hierarchy of emotion. He thought that base emotions which are necessary for biological survival—hunger, thirst, fear, and sexual impulses—evolved first. These base emotions were supposedly hardwired into the stem of the brain and composed the so-called limbic system. As animals evolved, they developed additional emotional passions, like anger and sadness. Finally, humanity alone developed the ability to transcend reptilian impulses when they developed the capacity to keep emotional passions in check through rational thought. People are able to get control of their emotions by reasoning with themselves. A person who is afraid can examine their situation with a sense of rational distance and decide whether their fear is founded or not. Emotions influence us to a great extent but we can, using our minds, transcend them.

Emotions, in Darwin's view, are received. That is, humans have no control over the emotions we experience.[2] Feelings are brought out of us by events. We see a person suffering an illness, and our innate categories cause us to feel

---

2. John Black, "Darwin in the World of Emotions," *Journal of the Royal Society of Medicine* 95:6 (June 2002): 311–13.

sadness and compassion. We cannot change our emotions because they are triggered by the circumstances we are in and they are produced by the categories we are born with. All we can do is apply rational strategies that will allow us to cope with our passions and mitigate their harmful effects.

Darwin's theory of emotion was immensely influential.[3] Pretty much every aspect of life assumes it now. *Sesame Street* and the blockbuster movie *Inside Out* teach children that emotions are concrete entities which are inside of us and which burst out into the world through our facial expressions; companies like Affectiva and Realeyes help corporations analyze customers' feelings by studying their expressions via webcams; NBA teams evaluate potential draft picks in similar ways; and the "American legal system assumes that emotions are part of an inherent animal nature and cause us to perform foolish and even violent acts unless we control them with our rational thoughts."[4]

It is becoming increasingly clear to cognitive researchers that Darwin's update of Plato's theory of emotion is wrong. Emotional categories are not innate. They are not hardwired into us by the hand of God, nor are they woven into our brains by our genetic code. Emotional categories are not given to us at birth; rather, they are constructed over time. The cultures that surround us, the environments we grow up in, and the patterns of life we adopt form our emotional lives. Like our vision and perception of color, emotions are not universal. Each culture, and even each person, experiences different emotions. We feel emotions with different intensities and qualities. Some of us have access to emotions that others do not. And, even though humans have *similar* feelings, there is no emotion that is felt *universally* by all people. Even powerful emotions like fear are not ubiquitous.[5]

To take one example, the !Kung, a people indigenous to the Kalahari Desert, do not have the concept of fear as it is understood in European-related cultures. The !Kung use the term *kua* to describe the feelings *and* the actions surrounding rituals and events that encompass awe, fear, and respect. *Kua* is not merely an inner feeling, but the simultaneous inner experience along with the ritualized bodily expression of this emotion. For instance, a new bride is expected to feel and ritually act with *kua* when she is first alone with

---

3. Contemporary researchers who closely follow Darwin's approach include Silvan S. Tomkins, *Affect Imagery Consciousness: The Complete Edition*, ed. Bertram P. Karon (New York: Springer, 2008). While Darwin used pictures of facial expressions to prove his theory, Tomkins built a camera capable of capturing 10,000 frames per second in order to analyze facial expressions in a more detailed way than Darwin could.

4. Lisa Feldman Barrett, *How Emotions Are Made: The Secret Life of the Brain* (Boston: Houghton Mifflin Harcourt, 2017), xii.

5. Darwin believed that fear is one of the clearest examples of universal emotion, and some contemporary researchers agree with him, such as Jaak Panksepp, *Affective Neuroscience: The Foundations of Human and Animal Emotions* (New York: Oxford University Press, 1998), 47.

her husband. Even if the woman has been a man's lover before marriage, the woman will still be expected to feel and act with *kua* on their marriage night.[6] A !Kung woman is expected to be reticent to engage in sex on her wedding night and feign apprehension even if she has a long sexual history with her partner. Sometimes the bride will run away into the bush at sunset in order to ritually enact *kua*. She will return the next morning once her actions have made her feelings of *kua* (even if feigned) known to the tribe.

Aristotle defined fear very differently. He said that we feel fear when we believe that we will experience something painful in the future.[7] We fret about hypotheticals and lose sleep over outcomes that may or may not happen. There may be some overlap between the ways the !Kung and European-influenced cultures understand fear, but they are fundamentally different emotional categories. For the !Kung, *kua* is based upon concrete rituals, not abstract hypotheticals.

Not only are emotions felt and expressed differently across cultures, but the same person can experience different emotions at different points in their life. We normally think of the death of a loved one as a sad event. No doubt it often is, but sadness can be felt in different ways or mixed with additional feelings. What if that loved one also abused you and never asked for your forgiveness? You might feel relief and happiness at their death in addition to sadness. How about the idea that sadness makes a person cry? Not everyone cries when they are sad. Sometimes sadness exhibits as rage or off-color jokes. Sometimes people cry when they are sad, but we also cry when feeling extreme joy.

Psychologists now believe that emotions are *created* in the brain. Our brains are constantly engaged in a process of receiving information from the body's sensory systems and then predicting the body's future energy needs. The neurons in your brain communicate with one another trying to guess what is going on in the world around you and then figuring out how to keep your body safe and alive.[8] If your ears sense a buzzing sound, your brain must predict whether this sound indicates a swarm of killer bees about to descend on you or electronic spa music designed to help you relax. If the brain predicts an imminent attack by killer bees, it will signal the pituitary and adrenal glands to release a series of hormones that will increase your blood pressure and sugar levels while suppressing your immune system to create a burst of energy so you can have a chance of escaping the swarm. On the other hand, if the brain interprets the buzzing sound as relaxing music, the brain will reduce

---

6. Marjorie Shostak, *Nisa: The Life and Words of a !Kung Woman* (London: Earthscan, 1990), 147.

7. David Konstan, *The Emotions of the Ancient Greeks: Studies in Aristotle and Greek Literature* (Toronto: University of Toronto Press, 2006), 130.

8. Barrett, *How Emotions Are Made*, 59.

the body's rate of metabolism, stress hormones will return to normal levels which will help the immune system come more fully online, and the digestive systems will function more efficiently. These are vastly different responses all built around the brain's prediction of what is happening around it. Emotions are part of the brain's predictive processing.

Emotions are to the body what imagination is to the mind. Imagination supplements and enhances the mind's ability to solve problems and navigate the world. Imagination is particularly helpful when a person's rational thinking processes are stuck. Our rational selves tend to think of the world through binary categories. Things are good or bad, ugly or beautiful. This can lead to intellectual stagnation. We can end up seeing only one solution to a problem or begin to believe that there is no solution at all. Imagination, on the other hand, is more welcoming to paradox, contradiction, and different ways of thinking. One strength imagination has over rational analysis is that the imagination can view a situation in new and previously unconsidered ways. It has the potential to help the mind break through logjams and open up additional interpretations of situations that were thought to be dead ends.[9]

Emotion functions in a similar way. The brain can sense if the body is content or in a state of unease. Beyond this binary categorization, though, it must scramble to understand what is happening, and about to happen, to the body. Like imagination to the mind, emotions help the body systems interpret the world in a more complex way. The brain may sense a shadow coming toward you. On the face of it, it could be anything. A cloud bringing some welcome cool. A bird flying overhead. A boulder about to squash your head. The body might recognize the shape of the shadow and its movement as something dangerous. This would cause an immediate feeling of panic. Your brain does not yet consciously know what the shadow's shape and movement specifically mean, but because the body feels panic the brain kicks into gear and makes you run. A few seconds later you realize that the shadow was caused by a hungry bear who considered you a convenient snack. Thankfully, your emotional self had a suspicion the shadow was dangerous before your mind had time to identify what it was. Emotions aid the brain as it interprets and predicts the world around the body.

It is important to highlight that there is no part of the brain that is responsible for producing emotions. Every region that psychologists and brain scientists have claimed is home to emotion (such as the amygdala) does not, in fact, react to emotion. These parts of the brain are components of the brain's interoceptive network that makes predictions and regulates the body's budget

---

9. John O'Donohue, *Beauty: The Invisible Embrace* (New York: Harper Perennial, 2005), 138–39.

of chemicals and physical activities.[10] All parts of the brain communicate with each other in constantly morphing webs of interconnected neurons. Neurons link together into clusters and trade information. Moments later the cluster that was just formed dissolves as neurons create new links and communicate with different parts of the brain. The associations between neurons are constantly shifting and new information-sharing clusters are in a constant state of creation and disintegration. There is no one, stable part of the brain that is delegated with the task of producing emotion. Emotion arises out of the total working of the brain as neurons from all parts connect with each other and trade information.

One of the purposes of all this communication is to categorize the reports the body's sensory systems send the brain. The brain uses these categorizations to adjust the way the body budgets its resources in order to keep the body safe and thriving. The categories the brain uses to classify sensations are based on goals, primarily the goals of avoiding danger and operating bodily functions as efficiently as possible. Humans use a goal-based system of classification to recognize almost everything around us. These goals also change and adapt. They are not fixed inside of us. For example, when you see a car you know it is a car because it is an object that is used to take people from one part of town to another. You do not classify a car as *an object that has four doors and four wheels*. The benefit of a goal-based classification system is that it is more flexible than characteristic-based classifications. A car may be painted red or gold, it may have two doors or four, it may be low to the ground or high, it could have a roof or it could not. None of these things ultimately matters for your categorization of that object as a car. You are able to recognize a car as a car no matter if it has two seats or eight. The object fulfills the particular goal or purpose of a car, so that is what it is.[11] It gets you from one part of town to another, so it is a car.

Emotions aid the categorization process by helping the brain explain what it experiences. Say your brain senses an accelerating heart rate. It must figure out why the heart is beating faster so it can distribute resources effectively and keep the body safe. Is the heart beating for a pleasant reason (such as sexual arousal) or because there is an incoming threat (the bullying boss is walking toward you)? Emotions help the brain sort this out. If you feel attraction to the person walking down the hall the brain will respond far differently than if it needs to brace your body for confrontation. From this example we see the three functions of emotions: (1) they assist the brain in interpreting the information it receives and help the brain create meaning from it, (2) this meaning

---

10. Barrett, *How Emotions Are Made*, 69.
11. Lawrence W. Barsalou, "Ideals, Central Tendency, and Frequency of Instantiation as Determinants of Graded Structure in Categories," *Journal of Experimental Psychology: Learning, Memory, and Cognition* 11:4 (1985): 629–54.

primarily takes the form of categorizations that are used to prescribe action the brain should take, and (3) this action is done for the purpose of regulating the body's resources to keep the body efficient and safe.

Emotions are connected to the human body. They are born when the brain receives information from the sensory systems embedded in the body, and emotions help the brain allocate resources to the body in the most efficient way. In fact, it is impossible to contemplate emotion without a body. They simply would not exist. It is a biological impossibility. This is one of the reasons why theologians traditionally assert that God is unemotional and unaffected by what transpires on earth. The great contemporary Catholic theologian Herbert McCabe said, "Whatever the consciousness of the creator may be, it cannot be that of an experiencer confronted by what he experiences."[12] McCabe dismisses the biblical accounts of God's emotional life as mere metaphors that do not have grounding in reality. This is because, McCabe asserts, God has no body: "Animal passions cannot be attributed to what is not material."[13] Since God is an immaterial, disembodied spirit, God cannot experience the emotions that fill physical, human life.

This view of a disembodied God who is wholly different from creation and does not experience things embodied creatures do works well when we think of God in a primordial state. Before anything else existed, it is possible to think of God as unemotional. After all, there would be no external stimulus or threats to God's well-being for God to manage. God would rest in God's self with nothing to influence God in any way. In this context, we can imagine God as the unchanging foundation of consciousness, unmoved, always remaining the same and not experiencing anything other than God's own self.

However, as philosopher Keith Ward notes, this view of God "neglects the way in which that primordial nature turns towards a created world in its expressive nature and relates to the world in suffering, compassion, and cooperating power."[14] If God is unemotional, what would move God to create the world? If God did not have an affective desire to appreciate the beauty of something God has made, why would God make a waterfall? And, if God did not want the company of other beings capable of relationship, what would move God to make the universe, which seems programmed to produce sentient life?[15]

---

12. *The McCabe Reader*, ed. Brian Davies and Paul Kucharski (London: Bloomsbury T&T Clark, 2016), 73.
13. *McCabe Reader*, 75.
14. *The Christian Idea of God: A Philosophical Foundation for Faith* (Cambridge: Cambridge University Press, 2017), 133.
15. Pierre Teilhard de Chardin, *The Phenomenon of Man*, trans. Bernard Wall (New York: Harper Perennial, 2008).

The view of God as unemotional and removed from experiences also contradicts the many portions of the Old Testament that portray God as embodied, having a mind that is changeable, and experiencing fluctuating emotions. We will study a few of the passages that portray God's emotional life, beginning with some descriptions of God's love.

LOVE

Contemporary theologians often say that the book of Deuteronomy is the most important section of the Hebrew Bible for constructing a theology of God. Peruse the index of any volume of Old Testament theology, and Deuteronomy will likely be the most-cited biblical book. Theologians point to the fact that Deuteronomy is the culmination and summation of the Pentateuch. It tells the story of humanity from its beginning in the garden of Eden to the new collection of humans, the Hebrews, on the brink of entering the new Eden, the land of Israel. Deuteronomy summarizes the way of life this people should have once they enter the land. Christian theologians also point out that Jesus referenced the Pentateuch more than any other section of the Old Testament. Since Deuteronomy is the Pentateuch's pinnacle, they argue, Deuteronomy must be its most significant piece.[16] Whether or not we want to get into the business of ranking the significance of biblical books, we can probably agree that Deuteronomy is vital for Jewish and Christian theological reflection and religious practice.

Within Jewish liturgy, Deuteronomy 6:4–9 is recited each morning and evening. In rabbinic thought, repeating this passage as a prayer is a way of recognizing God's kingship over the earth.[17] This was an incredibly prescient observation for the rabbis to make, because it was not until the twentieth century that scholars discovered the book of Deuteronomy reflects the structure of an ancient Near Eastern treaty. Not only does Deuteronomy reflect the structure of an ancient treaty, but it also explicitly frames God's relationship with Israel in covenantal terms: "Know therefore that the LORD your God is God, the faithful God who maintains covenant loyalty [ḥesed] with those who love him and keep his commandments, to a thousand generations" (Deut. 7:9).

This verse is significant for our consideration of divine emotion because an important stipulation of ancient Near Eastern treaties was that the kings signing them must love each other. This love primarily took the form of being

---

16. R. Norman Whybray, *Introduction to the Pentateuch* (Grand Rapids: Eerdmans, 1995), 1.
17. Jon D. Levenson, *The Love of God: Divine Gift, Human Gratitude, and Mutual Faithfulness in Judaism* (Princeton: Princeton University Press, 2016), 1–2.

loyal and living up to the terms specified in the covenant.[18] If a king did not adhere to the stipulations of an agreement, he could be accused of not loving the other king who was involved in the treaty. Many scholars have concluded from this that love in the ancient world was primarily about service instead of feeling. Emotion, if it existed at all within a framework of love, did not matter very much. Love was thought to be obedience, not an emotional disposition. To be sure, kings who begrudgingly entered into covenants with more powerful kings to avoid war, blockade, or siege likely did not have warm and fuzzy feelings toward their treaty partners. This is not to say, though, that every covenant was devoid of positive emotional dimensions.

Marriages were, and often still are, covenants in which each party has obligations to the other. And even though in the ancient world marriages were usually arranged and created to strengthen interfamily relationships and to secure lines of inheritance, there are many examples of marriages that had intense emotional connection.[19] Emotional dimensions of love were routinely felt within relationships that, like treaties, were structured around loyalty and service. In every marriage there are expectations, whether they are explicitly laid out or not. Most people enter marriage expecting their spouse to refrain from forming erotic attachments to other people. People entering marriage might expect their spouse to share the responsibility, as they are able, to help with household chores. Even though marriages, like treaties, have stipulations, we do not say that because a marriage has stipulations then emotions must be absent from it. Furthermore, treaties and marriages were not the only relationships in the ancient world that involved covenants. Friendships could entail covenantal agreements as well.

The most prominent friendship in the Bible is between David and Jonathan. David and Jonathan initially bond over their shared passion for killing Philistines. David volunteers to fight the Philistines' champion, Goliath, and presents his severed head to the Israelite king, Saul. Jonathan, Saul's son, sees this and immediately feels a sense of love toward David (1 Sam. 18:1). Jonathan had led his own military expeditions that killed a good number of Philistines (1 Sam. 14), and he apparently thought he and David shared an affinity in this. Almost as soon as they meet, Jonathan makes a covenant with David (1 Sam. 18:3). David and Jonathan must have been aware that Jonathan's

---

18. William L. Moran, "The Ancient Near Eastern Background of the Love of God in Deuteronomy," *Catholic Biblical Quarterly* 25 (1963): 77–80.

19. For instance, Jacob loved/lusted after Rachel so ardently he agreed to work for seven years for her father in exchange for her hand in marriage. There are examples like this all over the ancient Near East. In light of this, Karen Nemet-Nejat says, "Like people the world over and throughout time, ancient Mesopotamians fell deeply in love." *Daily Life in Ancient Mesopotamia* (Westport, CT: Greenwood, 1998), 132.

father was jealous of David, and this presented a great danger to their friendship. They swear to stick by each other regardless of what King Saul might do to break them apart.

The Philistines eventually kill Jonathan, and when David learns of his friend's death he composes a song, which he teaches to the people of Judah. Its second-to-last line is: "I am distressed for you, my brother Jonathan; greatly beloved were you to me; your love to me was wonderful, passing the love of women" (2 Sam. 1:26). Because of the last phrase, some commentators speculate that David and Jonathan had a sexual relationship.[20] David and Jonathan's friendship, they believe, was an erotic one. While men sometimes did have sex with other men in the ancient world, the scholars who propose an erotic framework for David and Jonathan seem to misunderstand the nature of friendship in the premodern world. They approach friendship from a binary assumption—it is either platonic or sexual. Those might be the most common categories operative today, but they are far from the only types of friendship that existed in years past.

Historian Keith Thomas describes friendships in early modern England (1530–1780) that seem to reflect very well the kind of relationship David and Jonathan had. Marriages in early modern England were arranged. Marriage was primarily thought of in Aristotelian terms: an amiable relationship that centered on utility and reproduction. In the medieval period the highest form of friendship was not between husband and wife but between males who were partners in war. While a man might develop a cordiality with his wife, his truest and deepest friends would be other males.[21] In fact, when the idea of friendship started to change in the late 1800s and men and women expected the marriage relationship to fulfill their desires for both political and economic utility as well as intimate friendship, people started to demand legal divorce when they were unable to achieve all of these goals in one person.[22]

Friendships between same-sex persons in early modern England were considered to be the summit of all relationships. Philosophers even thought that same-sex friendship was "the best thing in the world." These kinds of friendships were not casual acquaintances who provided people with diversion and

---

20. For example, Tim Horner, *David Loved Jonathan* (Philadelphia: Westminster, 1978); Silvia Schroer and Thomas Staubli, "Saul, David and Jonathan—The Story of a Triangle? A Contribution to the Issue of Homosexuality in the First Testament," trans. Barbara and Martin Rumscheidt, in *Samuel and Kings: A Feminist Companion to the Bible*, ed. Athalya Brenner (Sheffield: Sheffield Academic, 2000), 22–36; Steven Greenberg, *Wrestling with God and Men: Homosexuality in the Jewish Tradition* (Madison: University of Wisconsin Press, 2004), 99–102; and James E. Harding, *The Love of David and Jonathan: Ideology, Text, Reception* (New York: Routledge, 2014).

21. Keith Thomas, *The Ends of Life: Roads to Fulfillment in Early Modern England* (Oxford: Oxford University Press, 2009), 214.

22. Thomas, *Ends of Life*, 217.

entertainment. They were regarded as "spiritual unions" between two people. The people in them were expected to tell each other their innermost thoughts without reserving anything, even if it was unpleasant to hear. Male friends shared their lives together, and it was not uncommon for men to choose to be buried next to their male best friends instead of their wives.[23]

Some of these friendships may have involved sex. The vast majority did not. In most cases, two people intertwined their lives in a deeply emotional but not erotic way. The kind of friendships males had in the medieval and early modern periods were probably similar to the way 1 and 2 Samuel portray David and Jonathan's relationship. It is a form of friendship that few of us in the contemporary world even understand. The depth of emotion in David and Jonathan's relationship is important for our discussion because out of their friendship came a covenant. Every friendship involves obligations, whether they are vocalized or not. For instance, one cannot repeatedly and publicly denigrate someone and expect to remain friends.

But David and Jonathan make their obligations toward each other explicit. They create a formal covenant that has an almost liturgical formulation. Jonathan's father, King Saul, has tried to kill David. David runs away and secretly meets up with Jonathan. Jonathan agrees to watch his father in the coming days and try to find out if Saul is still intent on killing David. Jonathan swears that he will be loyal to David no matter what happens and he will do everything in his power to protect him. At the end of their agreement we read this:

> Thus Jonathan made a covenant with the house of David, saying, "May the LORD seek out the enemies of David." Jonathan made David swear again by his love for him; for he loved him as he loved his own life.
> Jonathan said to him, ". . . As for the matter about which you and I have spoken, the LORD is witness between you and me forever."
> (1 Sam. 20:16–18a, 23)[24]

The covenant between David and Jonathan was not a transactional arrangement. It was not a covenant intended to accomplish an abstract goal. Nor did it merely *involve* emotions. The covenant was *born out of* the affection David and Jonathan shared. Emotion was not an inconsequential corollary to this agreement. The agreement was put into place in order to protect the love

---

23. Thomas, *Ends of Life*, 195–97.
24. Some of the pronouns in this passage are ambiguous. It is sometimes unclear who in particular is doing the loving. Yet, as A. Graeme Auld observes, "given the reciprocal nature of true love, the ambiguity does not matter." *I & II Samuel* (Old Testament Library; Louisville: Westminster John Knox, 2011), 242.

David and Jonathan already had. The covenant was designed to make sure their love endured.

Similarly, God made covenants with many people: Noah and all of humanity (Gen. 9), Abraham and his descendants (Gen. 12–17), and Moses and the Hebrew people (Exod. 19–24), for instance.[25] Like David and Jonathan's, each of these covenants was put into place because God *already* loved the people God covenanted with. God brought the Hebrew people out of Egypt *and then* God covenanted with Moses on Mount Sinai. God's love and care for the Hebrews were present before God led the people out of Egypt. God's love for the Hebrews motivated God to save them, and this act of salvation came *before* God outlined the instructions within the Sinai covenant that specified how the Hebrews were to live once they arrived in the land of Canaan.[26] God called Abraham out from Ur to go to Canaan *before* God made a covenant with him. God brought Noah through the catastrophic flood *and then* God made a covenant with Noah and the animals.

Even before all of this, though, God created the world. This act of love supports all the agreements God subsequently makes with humans and the universe.[27] Without God's creative activity there would obviously be no need for God to make covenants, because nothing besides God would exist. There would be no creation, though, if God did not first desire it.[28] And desire is

---

25. Moshe Weinfeld provides some specificity to these covenants. He says that they are not all of an identical type. The Sinai covenant with Moses was a treaty that was an inducement to future loyalty, and the covenant with Abraham was a grant that rewarded loyalty and good deeds that had already been performed. Weinfeld, "The Covenant of Grant in the Old Testament and in the Ancient Near East," *Journal of the American Oriental Society* 90 (1970): 185. Nonetheless, while these covenants may have been weighted toward the past or the future, all of them involve both time frames. Abraham's relationship with God would extend into the future even though he showed faithfulness in the past. God had led the Hebrews out of Egypt in the past and makes a covenant to guide their behavior in the future.

26. This sequence is remembered in Jewish and Christian baptism. The convert goes under baptismal waters to signify walking through the Re(e)d Sea as they escape from bondage and also making a new crossing of the Jordan River as they enter a new pattern of life in the New Edenic land. In baptism an individual is united with the creation of Israel. Charles P. Price and Louis Weil, *Liturgy for Living*, rev. ed. (Harrisburg, PA: Morehouse, 2000), 66–68.

27. Karl Barth believed that creation was the external basis for covenant (Stanley Hauerwas, "The End Is the Beginning: Creation and Apocalyptic," in *Approaching the End: Eschatological Reflections on Church, Politics, and Life* [Grand Rapids: Eerdmans, 2013], 3–21), and for New Testament writers such as Luke, creation and redemption go together. Luke mentions creation when he speaks of redemption. As Hans Conzelman observed, "Wherever the Creation is mentioned (Acts xiv and xvii), it is with reference solely to the Word of God that is to be proclaimed, to God's commands and to the offer of salvation" (*The Theology of St. Luke*, trans. Geoffrey Buswell [New York: Harper & Row, 1961], 150). These two things, commands and offers of salvation, are subsets of biblical covenants. The covenants in the Bible either explicitly or implicitly include them. That is, covenants contain directions on how the divine-human relationship is to go forward and they provide remedies for when the divine-human relationship is strained.

28. Keith Ward, *Religion and Creation* (Oxford: Oxford University Press, 1996), 185.

part of what it means to love. For how can you truly love something if you have no desire for it?[29]

Divine covenants involve both God's universal love for all creation and the particular love God has for God's covenant partner. Just because God makes a covenant with Noah and the other life-forms on Earth, it does not mean that God does not love parts of creation outside our solar system. Every act of God's love involves universal and particular dimensions.

For instance, Psalm 145:8–9 describes God's love in universal terms:

> The LORD is gracious and merciful [raḥûm],
>   slow to anger and abounding in steadfast love [gədol-ḥāsed].
> The LORD is good to all,
>   and his compassion [raḥămāyw] is over all that he has made.

These two lines are centered upon God's ḥesed, the divine love that scholars often characterize as a loyalty which causes someone to adhere to covenant stipulations. Yet on either side of this loyalty-based love there are expressions of God's deep, bodily love for all creation. In this passage the NRSV translates the words based on the Hebrew root rḥm in different ways but they refer to the same thing. Rḥm is a love that is compassionate and merciful. The noun form of the word, which was in all likelihood the original form from which the verbal usage was derived, refers to a womb. The verbal and adjectival uses of the word create a metaphor that is linked to the original physical referent. As Phyllis Trible explains:

> [The] metaphor lies in the semantic movement from a physical organ of the female body to a psychic mode of being. It journeys from the concrete to the abstract. "Womb" is a vehicle; "compassion," the tenor. To the responsive imagination, this metaphor suggests the meaning of love as selfless participation in life.[30]

The semantic movement Trible highlights is crucial for us to note. As I explained before, there are dangers in overemphasizing the etymologies of words; however, we cannot escape the fact that rḥm-love is tied to the body. It reflects one of the most intense forms of love there is. This is the kind of love that the psalmist claims God has for creation. It is a love that flows out from

---

29. Hegel believed that relationships require both desire and love. Thom Brooks, *Hegel's Political Philosophy: A Systematic Reading of the Philosophy of Right*, 2nd ed. (Edinburgh: Edinburgh University Press, 2013), 61–67. Love and desire have some distinct patterns of meaning but they also overlap quite a lot. Simone Weil had a similar belief. She thought that since humans are created out of God's love, they are also products of God's desire. *Waiting on God*, trans. E. Craufurd (London: Fontana, 1959), 168. For a fuller treatment of the philosophical components of divine love and creation, see Paul S. Fiddes, "Creation out of Love," in *The Work of Love: Creation as Kenosis*, ed. John Polkinghorne (Grand Rapids: Eerdmans, 2001), 167–91.

30. *God and the Rhetoric of Sexuality* (Philadelphia: Fortress, 1978), 33.

the core of God's body. In other words, it is a particular iteration of love. It is God's unique way of embodying compassion toward the creatures God created. It is not an allegiance to an abstract idea of loyalty.

There are other types of love attributed to God, too. In the course of outlining the foundation of the Sinai covenant, the narrator of Deuteronomy 10:14–15 says, "Although heaven and the heaven of heavens belong to the LORD your God, the earth with all that is in it, yet the LORD set his heart in love [ʾahăbâ] on your ancestors alone and chose you, their descendants after them, out of all the peoples." Even though everything in the universe belongs to God and God loves everything, God gave a particular iteration of God's love to the Hebrew people.[31] The narrator says that because of this, the Hebrew people have an obligation to obey the teachings God gave them.

We should not think that the particular iteration of God's love toward the Hebrew people spoken of in Deuteronomy 10 was somehow more intense or of a better quality than God's love for other groups of people. The descendants of Abraham were loved and chosen for a particular task. According to the Genesis narratives, Abraham and his offspring were selected by God so that they would become vehicles of God's blessing to the rest of humanity.[32] They were not shown this form of God's love because they were better than anyone else, nor because they experienced God's love and others did not. There was a particular purpose God had for the Hebrews, but this was set within and was intended to demonstrate God's universal love.

In theological imagination, the pinnacle of obedience is the emulation of God. Since God loved Israel, the Israelites must love those around them. Even more, while Israel must have universal love toward all, they must have a particular iteration of this love for the vulnerable. Deuteronomy 10:17–19 makes this clear:

> For the LORD your God is God of gods and Lord of lords, the great God, mighty and awesome, who is not partial and takes no bribe, who executes justice for the orphan and the widow, and who loves [ʾōhēb] the strangers, providing them food and clothing. You shall also love [waʾăhabtem] the stranger, for you were strangers in the land of Egypt.

The love God has for strangers, and that the Hebrews should in turn have for strangers as well, is a type of love that has emotion at its core.[33] The verb

---

31. For an excellent discussion on the particularity of God's love, see Jonathan Sacks, *Not in God's Name: Confronting Religious Violence* (New York: Schocken, 2015), 189–206.

32. Benjamin J. Noonan, "Abraham, Blessing, and the Nations: A Reexamination of the Niphal and Hitpael of drb in the Patriarchal Narratives," *Hebrew Studies* 51 (2010): 73–93.

33. The call for the Hebrews to love the stranger is so central to the ethic of biblical narratives that Richard Kearney says, "You either welcome or refuse the stranger. Monotheism is the

for love that is used in this passage, ʾhb, often implies a sexual union.[34] This particular connotation is not in play in Deuteronomy 10, but the fact that the semantic range of the verb includes erotic passion indicates ʾhb does have a strong emotional component. The point of the instruction in Deuteronomy 10 is that the Israelites were to serve foreigners with gladness, compassion, and genuine concern for their well-being. They were not to attend to them merely out of rote obedience. The Hebrew people were *to love* the stranger, full stop, and with all that love entails, emotion and action, both.

This is not to say that there are some forms of love that involve deep emotion and others that don't. There is a connection between the passionate love of ʾhb and the loyalty-based love of ḥsd. Jeremiah 31:3–4 demonstrates this well: "I have loved you [ʾăhabtîk] with an everlasting love [ʾahăbat ʿôlām]; therefore I have continued my faithfulness [ḥāsed] to you. Again I will build you, and you shall be built, O virgin Israel!" The first phrase of this passage uses the word with erotic connotations, ʾhb, twice, once as a verb and once as a noun. God tells the people that God loves them with a love that will not pass away. This feeling of love moves God to be faithful to the people. It is very important that we note the order here. God loves (ʾhb) the people and because of this (therefore) God says that God will continue to be loyal (ḥsd) to them.[35] Covenant loyalty is not devoid of emotion.[36] It is not adherence to an abstract ideal of behavior or expectation. God exhibits loyalty to the Hebrews because God has an existing emotional affection for them.

SADNESS

This does not mean it is easy for God to love humanity. On the contrary, the Bible often pictures God struggling to love humans.[37] Some interpreters believe this struggle comes as God's love bumps against God's wrath. God wants to love humanity, but God's sense of justice and vengeance makes God

---

history of this wager." *Anatheism: Returning to God after God* (New York: Columbia University Press, 2010), 22.

34. Richard M. Davidson, *Flame of Yahweh: Sexuality in the Old Testament* (Peabody, MA: Hendrickson, 2007), 11, and Gerhard Wallis, "ʾāhabh," in *Theological Dictionary of the Old Testament*, vol. 1, ed. G. Johannes Botterweck and Helmer Ringgren, trans. John T. Willis (Grand Rapids: Eerdmans, 1974), 107.

35. Reinhard Feldmeier and Hermann Spieckermann, *God of the Living: A Biblical Theology*, trans. Mark E. Biddle (Waco, TX: Baylor University Press, 2011), 142.

36. See also Jacqueline E. Lapsley's essay, "Feeling Our Way: Love for God in Deuteronomy," *Catholic Biblical Quarterly* 65 (2003): 350–69, which demonstrates the emotional dimensions of texts that scholars normally use to prove that love in the Hebrew Bible was primarily focused on outward performance and not inner feelings.

37. Feldmeier and Spieckermann, *God of the Living*, 138–39.

tired and causes God pain.³⁸ Some biblical authors, such as Ezekiel, seem to support this as they tend to portray God as distant from humanity and concerned most primarily with holiness and God's own reputation.³⁹ In this scheme, it might make sense to view God's sadness as rising from the conflict between love and wrath. However, other sections of the Old Testament see it quite differently.

Jeremiah, for instance, pictures God as a loving parent who is pained at seeing God's children commit self-destructive acts. In Jeremiah 31:20, God is not disturbed because humans triggered divine wrath, but because God loves humanity and experiences deep feelings of anguish for the struggles the people of Israel endure: "Is Ephraim my dear son? Is he the child I delight in? As often as I speak against him, I still remember him. Therefore I am deeply moved for him [*hāmû mēʿay*]; I will surely have mercy on him, says the LORD." The first two lines of this passage are rhetorical questions that have yes as answers. Yes, Ephraim is God's dear son; yes, Ephraim is the child God delights in. Even though God has the occasional harsh word to bring against Ephraim, God will ultimately have mercy on him. The harsh word that God has brought against Ephraim was the exile—the Assyrians conquered the northern kingdom of Israel and forcibly removed a sizable portion of its inhabitants and resettled them elsewhere. A harsh word indeed. Yet God says that God has not written off the Israelites forever. God, like a parent who disciplines their children for a time, has a softening of heart. God now relates to the people with mercy instead of anger. God's mercy is more than a cognitive decision to no longer be angry against Ephraim. God did not undergo a simple mental shift.

This passage frames God's path to mercy as a deep-seated internal struggle.⁴⁰ The NRSV translates the phrase idiomatically, "I am deeply moved for him," but the construction in Hebrew is visceral and evocative. The verb *hmh* means to growl, moan, or roar, and the noun it is used with refers to one's internal organs, including the bowels and reproductive system. The phrase indicates that God's insides are heaving. The very depth of the divine body is in tumult. God is so distressed, God experiences so much emotional turmoil at seeing Ephraim struggle in exile, that it affects God on a psychophysical level.⁴¹ God's body responds to Ephraim's suffering. God does not make a detached and purely rational judgment to reassemble the people in the land of Israel. God responds to witnessing human pain as we do,

---

38. Kazoh Kitamori, *Theology of the Pain of God* (Philadelphia: John Knox, 1965), 19–30.
39. Walter Brueggemann, *The Theology of the Book of Jeremiah* (Cambridge: Cambridge University Press, 2007), 148.
40. Brueggemann, *Theology of Jeremiah*, 126.
41. Jack R. Lundbom, *Jeremiah 21–36* (Anchor Bible 21B; New York: Doubleday, 2004), 446.

emotionally. God's very body responds as well. It is as if God has as little control over the divine body as we have over ours. God is emotionally distraught, and God's stomach seizes up.

There is another passage in Jeremiah that has to do with God's emotions. It is equally astonishing. Jeremiah 8 recounts a time when an enemy was at the nation's gates. The kingdom of Judah faces a reckoning. For a long time God tried to persuade the people to turn away from bad behaviors. The people continued them with vigor. Since nothing worked—no amount of persuasion shunted the people into a more beneficial direction—God sent a foreign army to raze Judah to the ground. There was once a time when Judah could have avoided war by repenting of their evil, but that time has passed. Once the foreign army began its march, not even God could call it back. Calamity is inevitable and the only response is sadness. Kathleen M. O'Connor summarizes the situation well: "Since the enemy cannot be turned back, there's nothing to do now but mourn, shed tears, and grieve the nation's death publicly and privately."[42] Here is how the book of Jeremiah records it:

> My joy is gone, grief is upon me,
>   my heart is sick.
> . . . .
> Is there no balm in Gilead?
>   Is there no physician there?
> Why then has the health of my poor people
>   not been restored?
> O that my head were a spring of water,
>   and my eyes a fountain of tears,
> so that I might weep day and night
>   for the slain of my poor people!
>   Jer. 8:18, 22–9:1 [8:23 Heb.]

The imagery here is intense. The speaker says their joy is gone and their heart is sick and there is nothing anyone can do to make them feel better. They imagine that their body is a fountain supplied by an ever-flowing spring so that they never run out of tears. They cry until anyone else would be unable to continue and then they cry some more. It is undeniable that whoever is saying this is deeply distressed. But who exactly is it? Who is doing all this crying?

Commentators are all over the map. The translators of the NRSV believe it is the prophet Jeremiah who mourns for his fellow citizens.[43] One prominent interpreter believes the speaker in this passage is a personified version of

---

42. "The Tears of God and Divine Character in Jeremiah 2–9," in *God in the Fray: A Tribute to Walter Brueggemann*, ed. Tod Linafelt and Timothy K. Beal (Minneapolis: Fortress, 1988), 179.
43. The NRSV titles this section "The Prophet Mourns for the People."

the city of Jerusalem, while another believes it is the inhabitants of the city.[44] Other commentators identify three voices within this text, and yet another thinks that the prophet Jeremiah personally embodies God's pain.[45] This is a confusing assortment of proposals. However, several scholars have demonstrated that the speaker is God.[46]

When we analyze the grammar of this passage it is comically obvious that God is the one speaking. The only reason to not go with this interpretation is if one assumes at the outset that God does not experience emotion. Some interpreters might be reticent to attribute the humanlike activity of crying to God, but ancient people were not.[47] In Mesopotamian tradition the gods cried every time a city fell to an enemy.[48] This was a common way for people in the ancient Mediterranean to picture their deities. So, what is the grammatical key that clearly shows God is the speaker here? At the end of Jeremiah 9:3 (9:2 in the Masoretic Text) there is a speech marker. Speech markers are very common in prophetic books, and they mark the end of direct speech and identify the person who is speaking. The speech marker reads, "—says the LORD" (*nĕʾum YHWH*). There are no other speech markers in this section except for the one at the end of 8:17, which is also "—says the LORD" (*nĕʾum YHWH*). The most likely thing to conclude from this is that everything between these markers is divine speech. The narrator explicitly says God is the one speaking.

God is the one who cries never-ending tears. God is the one who says that joy has departed the divine life and that "grief is upon me." And God is the one who says, "My heart is sick [*libbî dawwāy*]." Again, we have God's emotional anguish set in bodily terms. God's sadness is so great that God's heart beats with hardly any energy (*dwh* means "to be faint"). Of course, it is possible this is only a metaphor and the author of this passage is not intending to say that God actually has a heart. And yet, even if it is a metaphor, it must mean something. The most straightforward interpretation is that it indicates God experienced sadness so acute that it affected God's body.

---

44. Robert P. Carroll, *Jeremiah* (Old Testament Library; Philadelphia: Westminster, 1986), 255, and A. Condamin, *Le livre de Jérémie* (Paris: Gabalda, 1920), 84, respectively.

45. William L. Holladay, *Jeremiah* (Hermeneia; Philadelphia: Fortress, 1986), 1:288–89, and Terence E. Fretheim, *The Suffering God: An Old Testament Perspective* (Philadelphia: Fortress, 1987), 135, respectively.

46. O'Connor, "Tears of God," 180–81, and Walter Brueggemann, *To Pluck Up, to Tear Down: A Commentary on the Book of Jeremiah 1–25* (International Theological Commentary; Grand Rapids: Eerdmans, 1988), 88.

47. Terence E. Fretheim discusses some of the "anti-anthropomorphic" assumptions that commentators bring to this passage. "The Character of God in Jeremiah," in *What Kind of God: Collected Essays of Terence E. Fretheim*, ed. Michael J. Chan and Brent A. Strawn (Siphrut 14; Winona Lake, IN: Eisenbrauns, 2015), 295.

48. J. J. M. Roberts, "The Motif of the Weeping God in Jeremiah and Its Background in the Lament Tradition of the Ancient Near East," *Old Testament Essays* 5 (1992): 361–74.

If God was saddened by the events recorded in the Bible, we must assume that subsequent human history has not made divine sadness go away. If anything, God is sadder now than before. As Desmond Tutu put it:

> I can picture God surveying the awful wrecks that litter human history—how the earth is soaked with the blood of so many innocent who have died brutally. God has seen two World Wars in this century alone plus the Holocaust, the genocide in Cambodia and Rwanda, the awfulnesses in the Sudan, Sierra Leone, the two Congos, Northern Ireland, and the Middle East, and the excesses that have characterized Latin America. . . . I imagine God surveying it all, seeing how His children treat their sisters and brothers. God would weep as Jesus wept over the hard-hearted and unresponsive Jerusalem, where he had come to his own people and they would not receive him.[49]

Sadness must be an emotion that God feels all the time. And God feels this, biblical authors tell us, within the divine body.

HATE

The book of Job tells the story of a man who suffers some of the worst events a person could imagine. A servant comes to Job and tells him that all of his agricultural animals—oxen and donkeys—were carried off by a band of traders who lived on the edge of the desert. This was no trivial loss. Without draft animals it was doubtful Job could produce a crop the next year that could support his family. He must have wondered whether his children would starve to death in the coming months. Shortly after this, a fire burns up all of Job's possessions, including his servants. Not only did Job face the prospect of a future death, now he faced an imminent one. With no property, no shelter, and no help, Job was exposed to the elements. There was nothing to protect him. Job had absolutely nothing left apart from his family members. They would not last either. Another messenger brings the news a parent fears the most: all of Job's children were killed when a windstorm knocked down the house of Job's oldest son. Even Job himself is not spared calamity. His body breaks out in sores. As Job scratches his skin with a scrap of broken pottery, his wife stands over him and tells him: What you need to do, Job, is curse God and die.

Job does not know why he has suffered so much. His friends come along and tell him it is because he must have done something wrong and God is punishing him for it. Job rejects their assessment. He says he has done nothing that would deserve this level of calamity. Nonetheless, Job does blame

---

49. *No Future without Forgiveness* (New York: Doubleday, 1999), 124.

God for his distress. He also demands an account from God of why God brought misfortune into his life.[50] Before Job gets to the point of interrogating God, he develops a couple hypotheses to explain it. One of them is "God hates me." This phrase is set within a larger statement that frames God as a vicious animal who acts as Job's enemy: "He has torn me in his wrath, and hated me [*wayyiśṭĕmēnî*]; he has gnashed his teeth at me; my adversary sharpens his eyes against me" (Job 16:9). Amazingly, God permits Job to bring these charges.[51] God does not affirm them, but neither does God deny them. God lets Job say his piece and then tells Job that, since he is human, Job does not know everything. Job has only a limited and partial knowledge of the world and what occurs in it.

Even though God sidesteps Job's statement, it is an astonishing thing for someone to accuse God of hating them. It is even more striking that God receives that comment without batting an eye. Job attributes a wild ferocity to God's acts. Job attaches a nearly uncontrollable rage to the divine psyche. God is not divine in Job's eyes; God is not even acting like a human. God is a dangerous animal acting out of base impulses. We might be tempted to dismiss Job's description as a rash result of pique. Job was emotionally distressed and created the fictional idea that God hated him. After all, God does not deign to even address the charge. But Job is not the only character in the Bible to accuse God of hating them.

When Moses led the Hebrews out of Egypt the people faced a variety of hardships: a body of water in front of them with the pursuing Egyptian army behind them, a lack of food, and hostile inhabitants in the land God told them to enter. The people were often discouraged and they sometimes regretted leaving Egypt. In the beginning of Deuteronomy, Moses recounts one of these times the people despaired. The people are on the brink of entering the land God promised them, but here is how Moses describes what they did: "But you were unwilling to go up. You rebelled against the command of the LORD your God; you grumbled in your tents and said, 'It is because the LORD hates us [*bəśin'at YHWH 'ōtānû*] that he has brought us out of the land of Egypt, to hand us over to the Amorites to destroy us'" (1:26–27).[52]

---

50. Job is not the only biblical character to demand an accounting. Habakkuk does as well. Wilda C. M. Gafney's comments about Habakkuk's approach are also applicable to Job's: "Habakkuk boldly calls on God to account for God's conduct. Habakkuk is not entirely satisfied with what he has heard and presses God for more answers, more clarity. In womanist parlance, Habakkuk talks back to God." *Nahum, Habakkuk, Zephaniah* (Collegeville, MN: Liturgical Press, 2017), 70.

51. Marvin A. Sweeney, *Reading the Hebrew Bible after the Shoah: Engaging Holocaust Theology* (Minneapolis: Fortress, 2008), 198.

52. The original story is told in Num. 13–14. That version does not include the assertion that God hates the people. There are other differences between the accounts, but they are not

The Hebrews in the Deuteronomy passage use a different word for hate than Job (*śnʾ* vs. *śṭm*, respectively), but the meanings are similar. Hate is the antitype of love.[53] The Hebrews in Deuteronomy believe that God is not adhering to covenant stipulations. Instead of showing the Hebrews love—making good on the agreement God made with the Hebrews to protect them and bring them into the land—God has seemingly abandoned them, or worse, brought about some of the curses embedded in the covenant without sufficient cause.[54] Lest we be tempted to view the descriptions of God's hate as not having anything to do with emotion and merely indicating God's adherence or not to stipulations, remember our discussion of love in the context of agreements. If covenantal love includes emotional dimensions, so also does hate. Job and the Hebrews who escaped Egypt accuse God of displaying emotional animus toward them. They frame God's hate as something bad. This is not because they see hate by itself as something bad. Rather, they believe God hating them is bad because in their mind *they do not deserve it*. Other biblical writers believe it is fine for God to hate. For them, it is only problematic if God hates *them*. There is no moral issue when God hates other people who deserve it.

For instance, the psalmist: "Do I not hate [*ʾeśnāʾ*] those who hate you [*məśanʾeykā*], O LORD? And do I not loathe those who rise up against you? I hate them [*śānēʾtîm*] with perfect hatred [*taklît śinʾâ*]; I count them my enemies" (Ps. 139:21–22). The psalmist believes it is a good thing to respond with hatred to those who hate God. He seems to be following the ethos of Leviticus 24:19–20: "Anyone who maims another shall suffer the same injury in return: fracture for fracture, eye for eye, tooth for tooth; the injury inflicted is the injury to be suffered." The psalmist believes in equal and proportional response. One mirrors the violence someone dispenses. But I wonder if there is more to it than that. Possibly, the psalmist thinks that he is emulating God. Hating God's enemies is the right thing to do because God hates them. You might be thinking: But God does not hate people, the psalmist got it wrong! If you thought this, you might have forgotten about Malachi 1:2–3. And since God calls the people to act like God does, to love what God loves, then they should also hate what God hates.

The NRSV titles the section of Malachi 1:2–5 "Israel Preferred to Edom." This title reflects a common interpretation that biblical language of divine hate and love do not mean hate or love. Rather, the terms have to do with

---

relevant for our discussion. For a brief but helpful analysis of them, see Moshe Weinfeld, *Deuteronomy 1–11* (Anchor Bible 5; New York: Doubleday, 1991), 144–45.

53. Saul M. Olyan, *Friendship in the Hebrew Bible* (New Haven: Yale University Press, 2017), 16.

54. Andrew J. Riley, *Divine and Human Hate in the Ancient Near East: A Lexical and Contextual Analysis* (Perspectives on Hebrew Scriptures and Its Contexts; Piscataway, NJ: Gorgias, 2017), 54–56.

election. If God chooses one person or group over another, God loves them. If God does not choose one person or group, God hates them. Even though God chooses one group over the other, these commentators argue that God does not harbor any antagonist emotions toward that group. They present God as an emotionally detached person making a rational and morally justified decision.[55] Love and hate are ciphers for covenant fidelity and divine election. This is not what Malachi 1:2–3 actually says, though.[56] Here is how the NRSV translates it: "I have loved you [ʾāhabtî], says the LORD. But you say, 'How have you loved us [ʾăhabtānû]?' Is not Esau Jacob's brother? says the LORD. Yet I have loved [waʾōhab] Jacob but I have hated [śānēʾtî] Esau; I have made his hill country a desolation and his heritage a desert for jackals."

In Malachi 1:2–3 God is portrayed as the speaker. A prophet relays God's message (1:1), but the prophet merely conveys the precise words that God gave him. And what God says is that God loves Jacob, who stands in for the Israelites, and God hates Esau, who represents the Edomites. God goes on to say that the destruction of the Edomites' land—turning Edomite country into "a desolation" and "a desert for jackals"—was God's own doing. God's emotional hatred toward them made God physically demolish Edomite society. This is difficult stuff to accept. No wonder theologians have spent so much time and effort trying to prove that God's love and hate are abstract metaphors devoid of emotion.

There is a real problem in arguing this. On the surface it may seem like a relief to narcotize the idea that God hates someone. Saying that God does not actually hate makes God seem better than petty humans who drag around all kinds of unhelpful emotional baggage they heap onto the people around them. An unemotional God who does not hate seems, well, more godlike. Yet if we say that the expression "God hates X" is merely a metaphor for election—that in actuality God does not experience hate and even more certainly God does not hate *people*—then we would also have to agree that the opposite expression, "God loves X," is a metaphor too, and that in actuality God does not experience love and even more certainly God does not love *people*.[57] I doubt many folks want to say *that*. A God devoid of love doesn't seem like a god worth believing in. It also contradicts a good many biblical verses, particularly the one that shows up at televised football games, John 3:16: "For God so loved the world. . . ." We would have to say that God really didn't

---

55. For instance, see the discussion in Andrew Hill, *Malachi* (Anchor Bible 25D; New York: Doubleday, 1998), 151–52 and 166–67.

56. Mignon R. Jacobs, *The Books of Haggai and Malachi* (New International Commentary on the Old Testament; Grand Rapids: Eerdmans, 2017), 165.

57. Tremper Longman III, *Job* (Baker Commentary on Old Testament Wisdom; Grand Rapids: Baker Academic, 2012), 244.

love the world, God merely adhered to the stipulations that God previously set forth to safeguard the world. This strikes me as pretty antiseptic and not at all what John tried to convey.

There is a long tradition in theological studies that tries to prove that God does not hate people. Malachi seems to undercut that effort quite severely. But Malachi is not alone. The psalmist and the compiler of Proverbs say that God hates people as well. Here are just a few of these passages:

> The boastful will not stand before your eyes;
>   you hate all evildoers.
>
> Ps. 5:5
>
> The LORD tests the righteous and the wicked,
>   and his soul hates the lover of violence.
>
> Ps. 11:5
>
> There are six things that the LORD hates,
>   seven that are an abomination to him:
> haughty eyes, a lying tongue,
>   and hands that shed innocent blood,
> a heart that devises wicked plans,
>   feet that hurry to run to evil,
> a lying witness who testifies falsely,
>   and one who sows discord in a family.
>
> Prov. 6:16–19

Many authors of the Bible took comfort in the fact that God hates evildoers. They transferred the emotional animus they felt toward their enemies and placed that on God. It makes sense. If you believe you are right to consider someone a jerk, you might want to believe that God feels the same way. But what happens when *you* become one of *them*? When you become one of *those people*—a person with haughty eyes, someone who wags a lying tongue, or an enemy of God's people? When you go from being loved by God to being hated by God? According to the biblical authors, you feel the full weight of another of God's emotions: anger.

ANGER

A scholar counted up all the words that refer to anger in the Hebrew Bible and arrived at a total of eleven: $aʿm$, $zʿp$, $ḥmh$, $ḥrh$, $cʿs$, $ʿbrh$, $qṣf$, rgz, $rwḥ$, $zʿm$, and $ʾp$.[58] For the most part, all of these words are translated with the same English

---

58. Bruce Baloian, *Anger in the Old Testament* (New York: Lang, 1992).

word—anger/angry. We might take this to mean that ancient Israelites were extremely angry people and so they created a highly specific vocabulary to chart the astonishing breadth of their white-hot emotional life. Since most English translations render all eleven of these Hebrew words with just a single English one—anger[59]—should we conclude that modern, European-related cultures are more mellow than ancient Asiatic societies, because they only have one word for anger instead of the eleven in Classical Hebrew? I doubt it. I think this situation has two causes, neither of them related to European calmness or supposed Hebrew tempers: (1) a lack of inventiveness on the part of modern Bible translators and (2) a historical preference for word-for-word translation practices.

To the first point, just as Hebrew has many ways of expressing the idea of anger, so does English. A person can lose their cool or blow their top; they can be angry, frustrated, irked, ticked off, or agitated. I'm not trying to flatten the differences between Classical Hebrew and English. And I am not saying that there are no unique ways of expressing anger in Classical Hebrew.[60] The English and Hebrew languages have different ways of expressing ideas, and the unique expressions that belong to each language can reflect different understandings of the human experience and philosophies about life. What I am trying to show is that it is wrong to think that English speakers have a one-dimensional understanding of anger while ancient Hebrews had a variegated one. (And concomitantly that English speakers are tranquil while ancient Hebrews were hotheads.)

To the second point, there is a long and established tendency of Bible translators to favor so-called word-for-word translation practices. The thinking goes that if the source language has one word that represents an idea, the translation should use one word too. This means that if a phrase in Classical Hebrew employed the root *ḥrh*, the translator should not use a two-word expression in English. So, off the table are ticked off, pissed off, and steamed up. Three-word phrases like blow his top, all fired up, in a lather, and mad as hell are not available either. And four-word renderings like hot under the collar are definitely out of the question. One would have to translate *ḥrh* as "angry" or "mad." As you see, a word-for-word translation philosophy greatly constrains the range of options a translator has. This can make translations unnecessarily imprecise or even in some cases misleading. For this reason,

---

59. Paul A. Kruger, "Emotions in the Hebrew Bible: A Few Observations on Prospects and Challenges," *Old Testament Essays* 28:2 (2015): 412–13.

60. One of the things that makes a language beautiful is its distinctiveness. Stefano Jossa, *La piú bella del mondo: Perché amare la lingua italiana* (Turin: Einaudi, 2018), 30.

and a few others, there have always been critics of word-for-word translation approaches.

The fourth-century monk Evagrius said, "Direct word for word translation from one language to another darkens the sense and strangles it."[61] The twentieth-century Irish poet Seamus Heaney remarks on his translation of *Beowulf*: "In the course of the translation, such deviations, distortions, syncopations and extensions do occur; what I was after first and foremost was a narrative line that sounded as if it meant business and I was prepared to sacrifice other things in pursuit of this directness of utterance."[62] Something must give in translation. Heaney says there is no way to express everything represented in one language when using the code of a different one. In order to adequately convey the meanings of one phrase into another language you have to change the target language's structure or layout, use more words or fewer, and sometimes eliminate rhyme or assonance. If a translator insists on keeping the structure identical and using only one English word when there is one Hebrew word, this constraint will not allow the translator enough flexibility to represent the patterns of meaning within the Hebrew text. And yet, many translators continue to insist that it is best for this word-for-word constraint to remain in place.

In any case, to God's anger. It is common for theologians to assert that God does not get angry. For instance, Reinhard Feldmeier and Hermann Spieckermann say, "God's wrath is his reaction to injustice and defiance (see Rom 1:18), not a divine affect."[63] In this view, what humans interpret as anger is actually God's just response to an injustice. And God responds rationally and without feeling. Wrath or anger is not, as Feldmeier and Spieckermann assert, a divine emotion. This perspective smacks of Darwin's view of emotion that places rationality at the pinnacle of human activity and so-called base or reptilian emotions like anger at the bottom. God is not a base creature and so must not be motivated by base impulses. This seems to be behind Feldmeier and Spieckermann's assertion.

---

61. Evagrius is quoted by Benedicta Ward in her introduction to Norman Russell, *The Lives of the Desert Fathers* (Kalamazoo: Cistercian Publications, 1980), 7.

62. Seamus Heaney, *Beowulf* (New York: Norton, 2000), xxix.

63. *God of the Living*, 339. Patrick D. Miller has a similar interpretation: "The wrath of God, a motif indeed prominent in the prophets, is an anthropomorphism, or better, anthropopathism, for conveying the highly negative response of God to human sin and to the disobedience and wickedness of God's people or of other nations (for example, see Isa 5:25; 9:12, 17, 21; 10:5–6; 13:3; 30:27–28; Jer 4:8, 26; 7:20; 10:24–25; 12:13; 30:23–24; Hos 8:5; Ezek 5:13, etc.). It is therefore a way of speaking of divine judgment. But that judgment, whether described in terms of the wrath of God or not, is in behalf of God's righteous and just way in the world." "Slow to Anger," in *The Way of the Lord: Essays in Old Testament Theology* (Grand Rapids: Eerdmans, 2007), 271.

The Hebrew Bible paints a different picture. It presents a god who becomes angry at many of the same things that trigger human anger.[64] For instance, Isaiah 5:25: "Therefore the anger of the Lord was kindled [lit. 'YHWH's nose became hot,' *ḥārâ ʾap YHWH*] against his people, and he stretched out his hand against them and struck them; the mountains quaked, and their corpses were like refuse in the streets. For all this his anger [*ʾappô*] has not turned away, and his hand is stretched out still." Isaiah says that God is angry against the very people God pledged to protect. They are God's people, and yet God is furious at them. God is so angry blood rushed to God's face, turning it red and making it burn with heat.[65] God lashes out against the people. Isaiah says God stretched out the divine hand and killed so many people it was impossible to bury them. Corpses rotted in open fields like animal waste thrown into the streets.[66] What produced such an extreme outburst of anger? The people didn't do what God told them to do.

The verse before Isaiah 5:25 says, "Therefore, as the tongue of fire devours the stubble, and as dry grass sinks down in the flame, so their root will become rotten, and their blossom go up like dust; *for they have rejected the instruction of the Lord of hosts*, and have despised the word of the Holy One of Israel" (emphasis added). God goes on a killing spree because the people have not listened. Instead of hearing and then obeying God's instruction, they heard what God taught and then went their own way. This passage evokes an angry parent who sees their children disregarding parental instructions and doing whatever it is they please. There have been times when I have been in situations like this and my "nose has been hot," too. Anger has led me to do things I regretted and had to later apologize for. I wonder if that might be the case here in Isaiah 5. Did God ever reflect back on this time and regret turning Canaan into a killing field? Did God's emotions carry God further than God planned? Maybe the people needed a rebuke, something to wake them up to the detrimental aspects of their behavior and cause them to listen to God once more. The people needed restorative justice, but did God intend this vast, punitive destruction? Was it truly necessary for God

---

64. Jack R. Lundbom, "Burning Anger in the Old Testament," in *Theology in Language, Rhetoric, and Beyond: Essays in Old and New Testament* (Eugene, OR: Cascade, 2014), 25. The God of the Hebrew Bible is not unique in this. For instance, El in Ugaritic tradition behaved in much the same way. Mark S. Smith, *Where the Gods Are: Spatial Dimensions of Anthropomorphism in the Biblical World* (New Haven: Yale University Press, 2016), 47–52.

65. Anger is not the only emotion that is felt in a particular part of the body. A group of scientists mapped where various emotions are typically sensed within the body. Lauri Nummenmaa, Enrico Glerean, Riitta Hari, and Jari K. Hietanen, "Bodily Maps of Emotions," *Proceedings of the National Academy of Sciences of the United States of America* 111:2 (January 14, 2014): 646–51.

66. It seems to be somewhat of a trope for biblical writers to speak of corpses piled up like trash or dung. Donald C. Polaski, *Authorizing an End: The Isaiah Apocalypse and Intertextuality* (Leiden: Brill, 2001), 241.

to snuff out so many human lives that heaps of cold bodies were treated like trash? Maybe God's anger got the best of the divine mind? Maybe God's hot nose unleashed a blood lust that God would never have enacted if God had not been so irate?

Historically, most interpreters would strongly deny these questions. They would say that it absolutely was necessary for God to kill all these people and that God intended every bit of what God dispensed. God was not affected by emotion. God responded to the situation with the justice it required. That is a common traditional view. Yet even those who embrace the idea that God has an emotional life nonetheless believe that even though God is deeply related to the universe, this relation "cannot and will not compromise [God's] providential ends."[67] That is to say, God's plans will never go off course because of God's emotional involvement with creation. God always keeps divine emotion in check. God's emotional outbursts never lead God to do something God did not thoughtfully plan. If we follow the narrative of biblical stories, this contention does not hold up. It appears that God's emotions do at times carry God away. In fact, there are times when God later regrets the things God did in a state of emotional duress.

The story of Noah and the flood is, perhaps, the most prominent example of this. We looked at this story when we considered God's regret, but let's look at it again. This time we will examine the account for what it reveals about God's interaction with divine emotions. In Genesis 6, God looks at earth and concludes that it is a moral mess. Fallen angels are mating with human women and producing giants as offspring (6:1–4), and human minds are focused on committing evil (6:5).[68] God decides to bring a cataclysmic flood against the earth. The flood will cause wholesale destruction. It will kill every person and terrestrial animal as well as the birds. Untold amounts of plant life will be wiped out. God knows all of this in advance. God tells Noah to build a huge boat to avoid death. God also tells Noah to bring his family aboard along with mating pairs of animals to repopulate the earth once the waters subside.

This decision to bring an end to almost all life on planet Earth flowed out of God's sadness. As we saw earlier, Genesis 6:6 says that God was sad and regretted making humankind. This is the extent of reflection most

---

67. Gary A. Anderson, *Christian Doctrine and the Old Testament: Theology in the Service of Biblical Exegesis* (Grand Rapids: Baker, 2017), 34.

68. On the Nephilim, see P. W. Coxon, "Nephilim," in *Dictionary of Deities and Demons in the Bible*, ed. Karl van der Toorn, Bob Becking, and Pieter Willem van der Horst (Leiden: Brill, 1999), 617–20. This passage has a long and complex history of interpretation, though. For a summary of early Jewish reception of it, see Archie T. Wright, *The Origin of Evil Spirits: The Reception of Genesis 6:1–4 in Early Jewish Literature*, 2nd ed. (Tübingen: Mohr Siebeck, 2013).

commentators make. For instance, one of the outstanding contemporary Old Testament scholars, Walter Brueggemann, says, "Verse 6 shows us the deep pathos of God. God is not angered but grieved. He is not enraged but saddened. God does not stand over against but with his creation."[69] There are several problematic elements about this observation—one of them being Brueggemann's assertion that "God does not stand over against but with his creation." How can Brueggemann say this when a few verses later God wipes almost all forms of life off the earth like crumbs from a table? Brueggemann has his theological concepts mixed up. God stands with creation in incarnation (both, I would argue, in the act of creation itself and, in Christian tradition, in the birth of Jesus). The Noah story is not about incarnation, though. This pictures God as very separate from and even against creation. Someone cannot become more "over against" something than destroying that something in premeditated fashion.

Furthermore, Brueggemann says that in Genesis 6 God is not angry. Indeed, God is sad, Brueggemann readily agrees, but he is also adamant that rage was absent from God. He says this because the text of Genesis 6 never mentions God's anger. One of the things that made Brueggemann famous is his brilliant close readings of the Old Testament. He is able to read particular passages and creatively draw out interpretations of the details that are there. This is also one of his vulnerabilities. Focusing on what is written can cause someone to overlook what is in a passage but is unrecorded. Just because the narrative does not explicitly state that God was angry does not mean that God wasn't. To be sure, God was sad and remorseful, but frustration and anger often accompany these emotions, particularly when they spring from relational tensions that involve rejection. God saw the creatures God made behaving in ways that rejected the divine intention. God seems to conclude that this was also a rejection of God's very self. This triggered God's anger and wrath.

Second Isaiah seems to interpret the Noah story this way, too. He tells his stated audience, the diaspora people of God, that in coming days God will show compassion on them even though God abandoned them after the Babylonians overran Judah, destroyed the Jerusalem temple, and forcibly deported many of Judah's inhabitants (Isa. 54:7–8).[70] The prophet links wrath to the flood when he reports what God says to the Judeans: "This is like the days of Noah to me: Just as I swore that the waters of Noah would never again go over the earth, so I have sworn that *I will not be angry* with you and will not rebuke

---

69. *Genesis* (Interpretation; Atlanta: John Knox, 1982), 77.

70. Many writers refer to this as the *exilic period*, but as Jill Middlemas points out, not all Judeans experienced exile. She suggests that the term *templeless period* is more accurate. See her book *The Templeless Age: An Introduction to the History, Literature, and Theology of the "Exile"* (Louisville: Westminster John Knox, 2007).

you" (Isa. 54:9, emphasis added). Second Isaiah implies that God was angry at Noah's generation. It could be argued that Isaiah merely uses the example of Noah as an analogy. God made an oath to Noah that God would not flood the earth again and this kind of oath is recapitulated during the Babylonian exile. The point is, I can hear some folks say, that God is making an oath to not repeat destruction. That is the extent of it, they might assert. The part about being angry is not central, and even if it is, it is an instance of accommodation that describes God's rational reaction to disobedience in terms humans can understand. Perhaps. And yet, there are many similarities between the situations of Noah and the Babylonian invasion. This is precisely why Isaiah picks the Noah story as a comparison.

In both instances God withdraws protection from the people and, more than that, actively afflicts them. In both instances God returns to the earth after the destruction, sets about healing what is left, and promises to not repeat that kind of affliction. Noah's flood and the Babylonian exile are in many ways the same event. God destroys sentient life after judging humankind (and animals, according to some ancient interpreters[71]) as evil beyond repair. God destroys the kingdom of Judah after concluding that the people of God are too sinful to repent. Isaiah says the waywardness of the Judeans enraged God and caused God to hide the divine face from the people. This is how Isaiah puts it: "In overflowing wrath for a moment I hid my face from you." It is clear from Isaiah 54 that anger propelled the divine judgment of the exile. Is it not also clearly implied that divine anger propelled God to send the destructive flood in Noah's day? It is not explicitly stated in Genesis 6, but that does not mean it is not the case.

What, apart from extreme anger, would compel someone to kill almost every form of sentient life? This is genocide on a cosmic scale. Furthermore, if we take the end of the flood story into account, it becomes obvious that whatever emotion caused God to act, it made God act far more drastically than God would have in a calm emotional state. After Noah and the other passengers on the ark disembark, Noah builds an altar and makes a sacrifice to God. Here is how the Genesis narrative describes God's reaction: "And when the LORD smelled the pleasing odor, the LORD said in his heart, 'I will never again curse the ground because of humankind, for the inclination of the human heart is evil from youth; nor will I ever again destroy every living creature as I have done'" (8:21). This statement reveals that God expresses empathy for humankind.[72] After seeing the destruction that God accomplished,

---

71. James L. Kugel, *The Bible as It Was* (Cambridge: Belknap Press of Harvard University Press, 1997), 117–18.
72. Norman Habel, *An Inconvenient Text: Is a Green Reading of the Bible Possible?* (Adelaide: ATF, 2009), 81.

God realizes that humans are not able to avoid sinning. Because of this, God further realizes that it is wrong to punish the earth so severely. Humans (and animals) sin. It's what they do. Restorative justice is appropriate. Wrath-filled and widespread punitive retribution is not.

God made this after-the-fact realization once God *saw in reality* the full and real weight of what divine action had done. It is difficult not to conclude from this that the emotional state God was in when God initiated the flood exaggerated God's response, and even carried God away to the point that God later looked on divine actions with regret. It's even more complicated than that. If God regrets some of God's wrath-fueled decisions and, as Genesis 8:21 says, God promises to change the way God will act in the future, we would have to conclude that the actions God regrets were sinful acts. Of course, many theologians will claim that anything God does is free of sin because the foundational nature of God is sinless. Furthermore, they would define sin as, by definition, things that God does not do. Possibly this makes sense in the philosophic tradition coming out of ancient Greece. However, it is incompatible with the narrative of Scripture. God admits God made a mistake, and God feels badly about it. God swears to never make this mistake again. It is implied in the Genesis narrative, and more clearly shown in Isaiah 54, that this mistake was made when God was in a heightened emotional state. God was furious and lashed out. When humans do this, we call it sin. Why should we label it differently when we see God acting this way?

Another account in which God becomes angry is 2 Samuel 6. In this story the ark of the covenant is put on a cart. The cart itself is brand-new, possibly specially built exclusively for transporting the ark. A procession escorts the ark—musicians and singers along with thirty thousand fighting men. Everything is going fine until the cart hits a bump, which jostles the ark. A man named Uzzah instinctively reaches for the ark to stabilize it. As soon as his hand touches the ark, Uzzah is struck dead. The narrator of 2 Samuel attributes Uzzah's death to God. This is how the narrative reads: "When they came to the threshing floor of Nacon, Uzzah reached out his hand to the ark of God and took hold of it, for the oxen shook it. The anger of the Lord was kindled [*wayyiḥar ʾap YHWH*] against Uzzah; and God struck him there because he reached out his hand to the ark; and he died there beside the ark of God" (6:6–7).

Uzzah's death strikes many readers as odd. Uzzah seems to do something noble but is killed for it. The ark was an extremely valuable object. Not only was it made of precious materials but, depending on the tradition, it also was thought to house God or be God's movable throne. When the cart carrying the ark is jostled, Uzzah reaches for the ark to keep it from being damaged or knocked off the cart and onto the ground. In this act Uzzah seems to show care for God. Yet God responds in anger and strikes Uzzah dead.

Commentators usually justify Uzzah's death on several grounds. They often point out that the ark was supposed to be carried, not put on a cart.[73] Moving the ark from A to B was never only an act of transportation. There were highly symbolic and complex rituals associated with the ark, especially so when the ark was moved. The rituals conveyed the idea that the object was important. The more significant an object was to the religious life of ancient Israel, the more care had to be given to it.[74] When Uzzah and the other caretakers of the ark put it onto the cart, they were communicating the idea that the ark was a common object. One threw hay and broken pots into the bed of a cart, not the very resting place of God. Uzzah trivialized the ark and, by extension, the very person of God. Therefore, it is argued, God was in the right to strike Uzzah dead. If this were the case, though, it seems odd that God did not become angry when they loaded the ark onto the cart. Why didn't God kill the folks who did that? Why does the text say that God's anger was kindled when Uzzah *took hold* of the ark? Why did God tolerate the loading of the ark onto a cart if this was the reason God was angry? Why was only Uzzah held accountable? Well, interpreters say, it's very simple. It was forbidden to touch the ark. God commanded this in Numbers 4:15: "When Aaron and his sons have finished covering the sanctuary and all the furnishings of the sanctuary, as the camp sets out, after that the Kohathites shall come to carry these, but they must not touch the holy things, or they will die. These are the things of the tent of meeting that the Kohathites are to carry."

According to the stipulations for proper care of tabernacle/temple objects, the Aaronide priests first had to wrap the sacred objects with various cloths and skins. After the ark was wrapped, the Kohathites were designated to carry it.[75] They were to put poles through slots on the ark and carry it like a litter. There is no indication from the passage in 2 Samuel that the ark was wrapped before it was placed on the cart. I should stress that just because the text does not mention that the ark was not wrapped does not mean it wasn't. However, some argue that it is reasonable to assume it wasn't since the priests had already disregarded the stipulation to carry the ark instead of putting it onto a cart. So, the reasoning goes, when Uzzah took hold of the ark, he violated Numbers 4:15. He touched the actual ark when it should have had protective coverings around it. Therefore, God got mad. Perhaps this makes sense, but if the Aaronide priests had not wrapped the ark, then Uzzah and his brother Ahio should have been struck dead when they touched the ark as

---

73. David T. Lamb, *God Behaving Badly: Is the God of the Old Testament Angry, Sexist and Racist?* (Downers Grove, IL: InterVarsity, 2011), 30.
74. P. Kyle McCarter Jr., *II Samuel* (Anchor Bible 9; Garden City, NY: Doubleday, 1984), 70.
75. Baruch A. Levine, *Numbers 1–20* (Anchor Bible 4a; New York: Doubleday, 1993), 169.

they placed it onto the cart. And yet, they were not. Something else must have made God mad.

It doesn't seem to me that touching the ark *in and of itself* was what frustrated God. Again, if this were the case, then the people who loaded the ark should have been killed. Instead, Uzzah was struck dead as a result of a very particular circumstance. It was only when one of the oxen stumbled and shook the cart and then Uzzah seized (*wayyōʾḥez*) the ark that God's anger flared up. Here is how I imagine the scene: The religious leaders commission a cart or buy a ready-made one that has never transported a load. They assemble a crowd and perform a liturgy while loading the ark onto the cart. The procession travels along, the attendants carefully watching the ark, making sure it is fine. An oxen loses his footing or stumbles on a rock. The cart is severely bumped around, maybe it tips to the side, and the ark slides toward the edge. Uzzah panics and grabs the ark, yanking it back into place. All the jostling wakes God up as God is sleeping in the ark or perhaps it disturbs God as God sits atop the ark watching the scenery pass by. God's temper flares when God is jolted awake or when God's neck is strained as the ark slides across the bed of the cart and then violently returns to where it was. God looks around to determine the cause and sees Uzzah's hand gripping the ark. God turns him to dust. This scenario takes seriously biblical descriptions regarding the function of the ark as either God's dwelling place or seat.

My telling is creative and reads between the lines, but it explains the narrative quite well. Furthermore, if we interpret this account with the understandings of God we have explored so far, my telling makes even more sense—God has a body that constrains God to a certain place, this body has sensory systems that detect pain and discomfort, God has a mind that constantly scans the world around God's body and predicts the future to adjust to anticipated needs, and God has emotions that aid God's mind in the task of keeping God well-regulated and safe. We begin to see that perhaps God acted out of a heightened emotional state when God killed Uzzah. According to the stipulations in the Pentateuch, God was in the right to kill Uzzah and the rest of the helpers when they loaded the ark onto the cart. However, God was patient and merciful (see the next chapter for more on this). God could also have killed the Aaronide priests who apparently did not wrap the ark before it was handled by Uzzah and his brother. Yet God did not do this. Neither did God lash out as the ark bumped along in procession. I can't imagine that an ancient Israelite cart provided a smooth ride. God only became angry when Uzzah seized the ark to keep it from bouncing off the cart. If God acted rationally and with the same patience and mercy God had previously shown, God would have recognized that Uzzah's motives were good and deserved the same kind of mercy God had shown before. The explanation that makes the most sense is that God's emotions got the better of God. As 2 Samuel 6:7 puts it: God's nose became hot. Out of that emotional pique, God struck Uzzah dead.

WHAT DOES GOD DO FOR GOD'S AFFECTS?

Most of us, living in a world influenced by Darwin's writings on emotion, think of ourselves as beings who use rationality to manage our emotions. We can think of instances when emotions intrude into our lives—we become irritable when hungry or angry when sleepy or weepy when our bodies are tired. When this happens we either succumb to our emotions or we do something to mitigate them—we eat or sleep or rest to bring ourselves back into balance. There are other situations in which we might have unhelpful categories through which we classify the world, and this leads to emotions that cause us or the people around us pain. In response, we might see a psychotherapist to help us rearrange our mental categories so we can change or better cope with our emotions. In all of these situations we think of our emotions as secondary and the rational self as our true foundation. Emotions serve our cognitive function. They help us better understand the world and navigate through it. When our emotions become detrimental, we attempt to change them or blunt them.

It is possible that this is an accurate picture for us most of the time, yet scholar of religion Donovan O. Schaefer offers an alternative interpretation: "Rather than asking, What do affects do for us? . . . [we should ask,] What do we do for affects?"[76] Schaefer flips the traditional understanding of emotion on its head. Instead of emotion being the servant of reason, he wonders whether reason is actually the servant of emotion. There are times, possibly a good portion of a person's existence, when we make choices not to serve a well-reasoned purpose, but to satisfy our emotional desires. In other words, as Schaefer puts it, we serve our affects. We see a tearjerker film because we want to feel a cathartic release. We take a trip to an amusement park because we want to feel the thrill of a roller coaster. We call in sick to work because we want to avoid the dread of seeing our boss. We buy a house because it looks beautiful to us from the street. We make these decisions because they satisfy our emotional wants. In fact, emotional desire is the reason why we acted. Our rationality was not enhanced by emotion. Neither did our rationality act against an emotional impulse. In fact, in these examples we used our rational functions *in order to satisfy our affective desires*. In order to skip work to avoid feeling dread, our minds had to generate a plausible excuse to give to our

---

76. *Religious Affects: Animality, Evolution, and Power* (Durham, NC: Duke University Press, 2015), 119.

supervisor. Our hand had to pick up a phone or punch out a message. To go to an amusement park we might have to plan a multiday trip. Our rational mind planned the itinerary, selected the appropriate clothes for us to pack, piloted our car to the right location, and so on. Our entire body, including the mind, served the demands of our emotions. We went to the amusement park *so that our desire for a thrill would be satisfied*. Many of our decisions, mundane and extraordinary, serve our affective wants. If this is true for us, is it also true for the God in whose image we have been made?

Some of the most prominent verses in the Bible make it seem so. If we return to John 3:16, we learn the reason why God became Jesus—because God *loved* the world. God's action in sending Jesus to earth sprang from an affective desire. God served God's emotional demand of love. Divine affects, *not* the rational part of God's mind, drove God's behavior in this instance, at least in John's telling. This is not the only time God acts to satisfy divine affects.

We discussed earlier in this chapter that theologians say that God created the universe out of love. Again, this is an act that serves God's affects. I agree with this traditional understanding but I would like to go further, too. As we have seen, there is a historical understanding of God that assumes God is fundamentally simple. This is why God is often imagined as not having emotion or undergoing change. Change assumes complexity and potential to be different than one presently is. For God to remain constant, God cannot be complex. We have seen that this view of God does not match biblical pictures of the divine. Accordingly, if God is complex and open to change with respect to God's body and God's mind, it would also seem to be the case that God's affective life is complex as well. God likely has multiple and, perhaps in some cases, competing emotional desires.

As for creation, what other desires could God have had in creating the universe? Admittedly, I am speculating; however, there are at least two reasons why speculation of this sort is entirely appropriate. First, the assumption that God created the world out of love is an assumption. There are various good reasons theologians give for this assumption—none of which I contest—nonetheless, there is no biblical passage that says: God created the universe because of love.[77] Second, if we follow my suggestion that since God made humans in the divine image, we can reverse engineer our theological reflection—then we can examine the way humans operate in order to better understand God. If humans are beings who act out of complex emotional desires, it is highly probable God functions in a similar way.

---

77. See, for instance, Adrian Thatcher's discussion of the catechism of the Catholic Church, which says that "God created man out of love." *God, Sex, and Gender: An Introduction* (Malden, MA: Wiley-Blackwell, 2011), 100.

What other emotions, then, in addition to love went into God's affective desire to create? Primates of all sorts are driven to make connections and emotionally resonate with other animals.[78] It is psychologically easier to get through life when you believe that other people care about you and support you. Perhaps God was motivated to create the world and sentient life by this same desire? If this is true it would mean that, like humans and other animals, God's creative activity served God's affects. It also means that just as the idea of God gives many humans a sense of comfort and security, perhaps our existence gives God a measure of emotional peace. Scripture and tradition emphasize the anguish and suffering humanity brings God. This is to be expected. What interhuman relationship of any depth does not contain any frustration or heartache? Perhaps theologians have overemphasized the pain humanity brings God and overlooked the divine emotions that were and are placated by the presence of created sentient beings? Perhaps we have undervalued the support we give to God through our mere existence? Maybe God wanted this support and that is why we were made? Maybe God was motivated to create by self-giving love but also because God's own affects needed placating? So, like almost every human motivation, God was both selfishly and graciously motivated.

It seems that God's acts are driven by a complex set of emotions. Biblical accounts reveal that sometimes God regrets these acts. At other times God receives pleasure from God's deeds, such as God's observations in Genesis 1 that the world was very good. One divine motivation for creating the world that professional theologians resoundingly ridicule, but that is commonly held among many ordinary readers of the Bible, is that God was lonely and wanted companions. Perhaps we can agree with theologians that it is not quite right to say that God was lonely,[79] but going along with many ordinary readers of the Bible, perhaps God did create the universe out of an affective desire. Maybe, like primates who seek the companionship of other beings, God wanted to create in order to ease God's emotional life. If this is true, God served divine emotions by creating a universe that had the potential to bring a measure of ease and depth to divine emotions. I imagine that God is often glad God made that decision. I also imagine there are times when God deeply regrets it.

---

78. Frans de Waal, *Our Inner Ape: A Leading Primatologist Explains Why We Are Who We Are* (New York: Riverhead, 2005), 176.

79. I am not averse to saying this, but some formulations of the Trinity are opposed to this perspective.

6

God's Character

One of the longest-running discussions in philosophical circles concerns the definition of *character*. Aristotle framed character in light of morality. He pointed out that someone may possess educational understanding or have encyclopedic knowledge about a topic, but we would not praise that person's character because of that. Aristotle asserts that an individual's character concerns their state of mind, whether they are good-tempered or not.[1] In other words, character refers to the features of a person's mentality that produce tendencies of behavior. A shy person is a person who, when they encounter certain types of situations, such as gatherings of people they do not know, acts in a reserved manner.[2]

WHAT IS CHARACTER?

In modern popular usage, *character*, *personality*, and *temperament* are used interchangeably even though scholars make distinctions between them. For instance, philosopher Anthony Quinton distinguishes these terms in the following ways: *character* refers to the deeply rooted and enduring (but not unchangeable) habits that produce tendencies of behavior, *personality* is linked to character but is its outward expression in a person's self-presentation to the world, and *temperament* refers to broad orientations toward dispositions of optimism or pessimism, melancholy or hope.[3] Quinton is right to point out

---

1. *Nicomachean Ethics* 1.13.
2. Christian B. Miller, *Moral Character: An Empirical Theory* (Oxford: Oxford University Press, 2013), 6.
3. "Character and Will," in *From Wodehouse to Wittgenstein* (Manchester: Carcanet, 1998), 39.

the different connotations of these interrelated terms, and I have no quibble with the way he lays them out. However, as some have pointed out, we do not have access to the psychological makeup of other people. In some ways, the distinction between these terms is theoretical. What we have are people's actions. We can detect patterns in their choices or notice similarities in the ways they approach situations, but the inner workings of their mind remain hidden. It is from a person's actions that we make judgments about their character. This is the approach I would like to take with respect to God.

The Bible contains many statements regarding God's nature and character. The psalmist says that God is "merciful and gracious, slow to anger and abounding in steadfast love" (103:8). The Chronicler describes God as "gracious and merciful" (2 Chr. 30:9). In the book of Exodus, God is said to "not leave the guilty unpunished" (34:7 NIV). All of these are indicative statements that describe God's character in the abstract. Since these statements are embedded in religious Scripture, some would say that they reveal God's character as it really is. That is, these descriptions reflect the inner workings of God that are hidden from human view. For the purposes of this book, I prefer to come at this topic from a different direction. I would rather form an understanding of divine character by examining the biblical descriptions of God's actions. When we do this, we will discover a God that is, among other things, just, patient, vengeful, jealous, forgiving, and forgetting. These attributes are not always straightforward, though. The God of the Bible is complex and multifaceted. Our imagination of how these descriptors interact with divine character should be as well.

JUST

Asserting that God is just raises a difficult philosophical issue. This issue is something the ancient Greeks discussed several millennia ago, and it remains unresolved to this day. The most prominent discussion of the problem of divine justice in ancient Greece was put forward by Socrates in a conversation memorialized (or created) by Plato.[4] Socrates is at the Agora, the place in Athens where legal disputes are settled, and he bumps into a man named Euthyphro. Socrates is on trial for charges of religious impiety and Euthyphro has brought charges of homicide against his own father. In Athenian society, treating your father with anything but respect was a heinous act. Bringing homicide charges against one's father was most certainly disrespectful

---

4. For an excellent discussion of this text and the philosophical issues it raises, see Chris Emlyn-Jones and William Preddy, *Plato*, vol. 1 (Loeb Classical Library 36; Cambridge: Harvard University Press, 2017), 3–83.

regardless of their veracity. Euthyphro defends his actions by pointing out that the Greek god Zeus punished his father for unjustly treating Zeus's children. Euthyphro says that since all Greeks believe that Zeus is the most just of all the gods, it could not be wrong for Euthyphro to emulate him by dealing harshly with his own father.

Socrates detects a weak point in Euthyphro's defense. The weak point is within Greek religion itself. The translators of the Loeb edition of Plato's writings explain it this way: "Greek religion contained an implicit tension between the all-powerful, but not necessarily virtuous, gods of Greek myth in Homer and Hesiod, and the idea of deities as ideally good and just."[5] The Greeks believed the gods themselves (at least most of them) were inherently upright. Otherwise, you would have to say that goodness and justice exist apart from the gods. This, in turn, presents a host of philosophical problems. Chief among them: Are the gods the ultimate foundation of the universe or are abstract and nonconscious notions of goodness and justice ultimate? And, how can something that is nonconscious be a notion? In other words, how can an idea that is held in a mind but has no consciousness of its own logically pre-exist conscious beings? To avoid these problems, the Greeks made goodness, justice, and the gods one and the same. That is, the gods themselves were thought to embody justice and goodness. Justice and goodness are not things that are outside and apart from the gods, dictating the actions deities take. The gods *are* just and good. The gods themselves provide the definition of what is just. Therefore, Euthyphro says that since Zeus, the highest example of a divine figure in Greek religion, brought a charge against his father, then Euthyphro's action is by definition just because Zeus's action was, by definition, just.

This sounds very neat and tidy. Yet Socrates points out that the gods often act in ways that a person of any moral integrity would condemn. The gods steal from each other (sometimes for noble intentions, but not always), get drunk frequently, conspire against one another, and even fight each other (they could not kill one another, though—they are gods, after all).[6] The gods cannot be the ultimate definition of what is just or else we would have to reclassify as good a host of things humans typically acknowledge as wrong. This same conundrum is present in the stories in the Old Testament. God is often proclaimed as entirely good and just while at the same time there are narratives in which God or biblical authors admit that divine actions were not always good.

---

5. Emlyn-Jones and Preddy, *Plato*, 1:7.
6. W. H. D. Rouse, *Gods, Heroes and Men of Ancient Greece: Mythology's Great Tales of Valor and Romance* (New York: New American Library, 2001), x.

For instance, the book of Job. Virginia Woolf wrote to a friend, "I read the book of Job last night—I don't think God comes well out of it."[7] She did not elaborate why she thought this, but it might have been because in the story God enters into a wager with another divine being over whether or not Job has legitimate faith. God allows the other divine being to kill off Job's family, loot his possessions, and afflict Job's very body with terrible suffering. God then comes to answer Job's questions about all that has happened and instead of giving Job an apology or even showing him any empathy at all, God gives Job a haranguing.[8] I agree with Old Testament scholar Ellen Davis, who says the main point of the book of Job is not the subject of God's justice, but rather, the problem of human pain.[9] The book narrates a transformation in Job as he undergoes some of the greatest pain imaginable. Nonetheless, the book of Job does communicate a picture of how God acts. The picture it gives complicates the assertion that God is always just.

There was no way God could ever make right the suffering God allowed Job to experience. Ellen Davis points out that the supposedly happy ending of the book in which "the LORD gave Job twice as much as he had before" (Job 42:10) is not a happy ending at all.[10] It is true that Job acquires a new house, becomes wealthy, and has additional children to replace the ones who died. But the sons and daughters he has after his affliction are *not the same* sons and daughters he lost. Children are not replaceable widgets. The loss of one in this life is permanent. The space they held in a parent's life is never the same even if a person has additional children. We should remember, too, that God was the one who originated the wager. The loss of Job's children was not the unfortunate result of a sinister plan that an evil being made up. In Job 1 the accusing otherworldly being often transliterated as the Satan enters the divine court and God asks him where he has come from. The Satan replies: "From going to and fro on the earth, and from walking up and down on it" (1:7). Now that we have an understanding of the story, God's rejoinder is bone-chilling. God asks the Satan, "Have you considered my servant Job?" (1:8). God then gives the Satan explicit permission to inflict whatever pain he wants onto Job.[11] The only stipulation is that the Satan could not kill Job's physical body.

---

7. *The Letters of Virginia Woolf*, vol. 2, *1912–1922*, ed. Nigel Nicolson and Joanne Trautmann (New York: Harcourt Brace Jovanovich, 1976), 585.

8. Kathryn Schifferdecker, "Of Stars and Sea Monsters: Creation Theology in the Whirlwind Speeches," *Word & World* 31:4 (Fall 2011): 357–58.

9. *Getting Involved with God: Rediscovering the Old Testament* (Lanham, MD: Rowman & Littlefield, 2001), 122.

10. Davis, *Getting Involved with God*, 121–46.

11. Katherine J. Dell, "Does God Behave Unethically?," in *Ethical and Unethical in the Old Testament: God and Humans in Dialogue*, ed. Katherine Dell (New York: T&T Clark, 2010), 175.

Commenting on the affliction of Job that God willingly allowed, one Old Testament scholar had this to say: "Even the justice of God cannot be confessed."[12] That is, this scholar believes that God acted unjustly in offering Job up for affliction. This scholar, however, believes that when one reaches the end of the book and finds Job's fortunes are restored, "in the restoration of Job there is the redemption of God."[13] However, as Ellen Davis noted, what Job experiences is pseudorestoration. Job's suffering continues and will continue to the end of his life as he mourns the loss of his family. There is no redemption for God in the unnecessary killing of Job's children. Some theologians would respond to this by asserting that God was just even in God's treatment of Job because whatever God does is just. But this brings us again to the problem behind Socrates's conversation with Euthyphro. Are actions done by a god just merely because a god does them? Do we really believe that killing someone's family merely to prove a wager is just? How would we react if a human did this to another person? It is obvious. They would be sent straight to prison or worse. If we say that when God does something it is just but if humans did the exact same thing it is unjust, we empty the word "justice" of any real meaning whatsoever.

Did God regret entering into that wager and giving the Satan permission to inflict terrible and unwarranted pain onto Job? The story does not tell us. However, some biblical scholars believe the story implies it. Dirk Geeraerts sees Job's "restoration" in which he received even more wealth and children than he had before his trial as God overcompensating because God is embarrassed by the disastrous consequences of the wager God made with the Satan.[14] As we saw previously, God does experience regret over divine actions. We discussed the flood in Noah's day and we will recall it again in a moment. But for now, it is enough to remember that after Noah and his family survived the flood, God made a covenant with them. God then placed a rainbow in the sky as a "sign" of the covenant they made. God explains to Noah that the rainbow will be a reminder to God: "I will remember my covenant that is between me and you and every living creature of all flesh; and the waters shall never again become a flood to destroy all flesh" (Gen. 9:15). God's statement seems to imply that sending floodwaters to destroy all flesh was a bad idea. If it was a perfectly just thing to do, why would God promise to never do it again? If killing almost all sentient life on earth was in keeping with the character of God, why would God set a reminder to prevent God

---

12. Leo G. Perdue, *Wisdom Literature: A Theological History* (Louisville: Westminster John Knox, 2007), 126.
13. Perdue, *Wisdom Literature*, 127.
14. "Caught in a Web of Irony: Job and His Embarrassed God," in *Job 28: Cognition in Context*, ed. Ellen Van Wolde (Leiden: Brill, 2003), 53.

from repeating it? Could it be that God realized the punishment was far out of proportion to the crime?

This is not the only time when God seems to admit this. In the book of Isaiah there is a curious statement: "Speak tenderly to Jerusalem, and cry to her that she has served her term, that her penalty is paid, that she has received from the LORD's hand double for all her sins" (40:2). Perhaps as some scholars posit the phrase, "double for all her sins" is an idiom that expresses the fullness of a period of time. Or perhaps this statement should be interpreted alongside other imagery in Second Isaiah that has to do with suffering—being childless and a widow.[15] In other words, Jerusalem has suffered double because it is described with both of these tropes—being childless and a widow. This might seem a bit tendentious to you, as it does to me.

Alternatively, we could understand the phrase to mean what it says. The exile was a long and brutal experience. The people who endured it suffered twice the agony they deserved. If we interpret this passage according to its straightforward reading—and there seems to me to be no nontendentious reason not to—then here again it is implied that God went overboard when punishing a set of humans.

PATIENT

There are times when biblical authors depict God as angry and inflicting more pain on creation than most people today would consider appropriate. On the whole, though, God is remarkably patient in the pages of the Old Testament. At least, this is how God's self-description frames it. Exodus 34 records a remarkable reflection on God's patience.[16] This comes after God fashions a second set of tablets because Moses broke the first set of the so-called Ten Commandments. After Moses cuts two more slabs of stone, he goes back up the mountain to meet with God. In keeping with our discussion of the embodiment of God, the narrator says, "The LORD descended in the cloud and stood with [Moses] there" (Exod. 34:5). God then gives Moses a description of divine character that begins with these words: "The LORD, the LORD, a God merciful and gracious, slow to anger [*'erek 'appayim*], . . ." The expression translated by the NRSV as "slow to anger" more literally means "long of nose." When people get intensely angry, blood rushes to their face.

---

15. Fredrik Hägglund, *Isaiah 53 in the Light of Homecoming after Exile* (Tübingen: Mohr Siebeck, 2008), 116.

16. For an exhaustive treatment of this passage, see Matthias Franz, *Der barmherzige und gnädige Gott: Die Gnadenrede vom Sinai (Exodus 34, 6–7) und ihre Parallelen im Alten Testament und seiner Umwelt* (Stuttgart: Kohlhammer, 2003).

The face becomes warm and flush. The expression "long of nose" indicates it takes a long time for blood to reach the full extent of the divine face. It is another way of saying that the divine temper has "a long fuse." It does not mean that God never gets mad, but that the Lord is not a hothead.

The writers of the Old Testament time and again point out that God puts up with a lot of human misbehavior before God's temper flares. The way they say this is particularly intriguing. The book of Isaiah begins with an oracle of judgment against Judah and Jerusalem. The prophet quotes God as saying, "Your new moons and your appointed festivals my soul hates; they have become a burden to me, I am weary of bearing them" (Isa. 1:14). This verse reveals that even God gets emotionally worn out from putting up with delinquents. Yet it also implies that God has patiently put up with Jerusalem's offenses for a while.[17]

A remarkable story that demonstrates God's patience is Abraham's negotiation with God recounted in Genesis 18.[18] God tells Abraham that the city of Sodom is wicked and faces destruction. Abraham boldly questions God's sense of justice by responding to God:

> Will you indeed sweep away the righteous with the wicked? Suppose there are fifty righteous within the city; will you then sweep away the place and not forgive it for the fifty righteous who are in it? Far be it from you to do such a thing, to slay the righteous with the wicked, so that the righteous fare as the wicked! Far be that from you! Shall not the Judge of all the earth do what is just? (Gen. 18:23–25)

Abraham frames this response as a series of questions and admonishments, but behind them is also an accusation that God is not acting in keeping with God's own character or that God is not adhering to the demands of universal justice that even God is accountable to (we hear Socrates's voice again).[19] It seems hard to imagine that a good God would answer Abraham by saying, Of course I'm going to kill innocent people—deal with it. This is the box Abraham puts God into. If God does not agree to Abraham's terms, God would reveal the divine character as profoundly unjust. In this passage Abraham has the courage (some would say hubris) to instruct God on the ways God should act.[20] Yet God takes in stride Abraham's swipe at the uprightness of divine

---

17. Terence E. Fretheim, *The Suffering of God: An Old Testament Perspective* (Minneapolis: Fortress, 1984), 139.

18. Alan M. Dershowitz humorously (and anachronistically) labels Abraham as a lawyer in *Abraham: The World's First (But Certainly Not Last) Jewish Lawyer* (New York: Schocken, 2015).

19. Anson Laytner, *Arguing with God: A Jewish Tradition* (Lanham, MD: Rowman & Littlefield, 2004), 4.

20. Ronald Hendel, *Remembering Abraham: Culture, Memory, and History in the Hebrew Bible* (Oxford: Oxford University Press, 2005), 39.

character and tells Abraham that if fifty righteous people are found in Sodom, then the city will be spared. Abraham persists: "Suppose five of the fifty righteous are lacking? Will you destroy the whole city for lack of five?" (Gen. 18:28a). God relents and promises Abraham that he will not destroy the city if forty-five righteous people are found. Abraham keeps pressing and finally gets God to commit to sparing the city for the sake of ten righteous people.

There are many observations one could make about this passage. One of them is that God showed a great deal of patience toward a human who repeatedly and stubbornly insisted that God's plans were not appropriate for a being who cares about justice. As philosopher Eleonore Stump observes, "Any human being who was addressed by someone close to him in the way Abraham addresses God would surely feel hurt and insulted."[21] If a human being would be insulted by this behavior, it seems safe to assume God would be too. And yet, God did not strike Abraham dead, as God did to Uzzah when Uzzah touched the ark. God showed patience and restraint even through a long series of implied accusations.

One reason why God may have shown Abraham patience is because God realized that Abraham's negotiation was helping God become more of God's best self. Unlike Noah, who gave not one contrary word against God's intent to destroy the earth, Abraham did not accept at face value God's desire to destroy Sodom. Rabbinic tradition criticizes Noah for not challenging God.[22] In fact, Rabbi Judah frames Abraham's negotiation with God as a battle in which Abraham approached God in order to fight. Abraham fought for the lives of the innocent inhabitants of Sodom. We could also imagine Abraham fighting for God as well. Noah allowed God to follow a disastrous course of action, a course of action God later regretted. It was a course of action the divine reputation would never shake off. Even to this day people are understandably put off from worshiping a god who is said to have destroyed the world. Abraham refuses to let God do this. Abraham wants God to act the way a just god should. In one sense, Abraham calls God to be God. Seen in this light, Abraham's interrogation of God was not disrespectful. It came from Abraham's sense of justice as well as Abraham's love and care for God.

Jews, Christians, and Muslims all view Abraham as a prophet.[23] Genesis 20:7 gives this title to Abraham, but commentators have long noted that Abraham's

---

21. *Wandering in Darkness: Narrative and the Problem of Suffering* (Oxford: Clarendon, 2010), 286.

22. Ellen F. Davis, *Biblical Prophecy: Perspectives for Christian Theology, Discipleship, and Ministry* (Louisville: Westminster John Knox, 2014), 26–27.

23. Jon D. Levenson, *Inheriting Abraham: The Legacy of the Patriarch in Judaism, Christianity, and Islam* (Princeton: Princeton University Press, 2012), 141, and Brannon M. Wheeler, *Prophets in the Quran: An Introduction to the Quran and Muslim Exegesis* (London: Continuum, 2002), 83–108.

actions in the Genesis narrative are often prophetic. He receives instructions from God and conveys them to his family. Abraham is guided by God to depart from his home and inspire his household to undertake ambitious journeys with him. But Abraham's prophetic ministry is not only directed at the humans in his proximity. Abraham acts as a prophet even for God. Perhaps we should interpret Abraham's negotiation with God as a prophetic judgment against what God announced God would do. It is a sermon repackaged as an interrogation. Abraham encourages God to listen to God's own sense of justice.

If we interpret Genesis this way, God's patience is all the more striking. God listens to Abraham's forceful prophecy and learns from it. Instead of killing Abraham for calling God's character into question, God recognizes God's own need of help and accountability. Like a human, God also needs prophetic correction from time to time. Instead of viewing God's intentions as the unchanging standard for right and wrong, Abraham imagined God in a very humanlike way. He must have assumed that God has moments of weak character just as we do. There are times when humans do not live up to our self-descriptions and stated ideals. God sent prophets to address humanity when societies fell into unjust patterns of life. It seems that the story in Genesis 18 implies that sometimes God needs prophets to remind God of how God wishes to be. How different would the world have been if Noah had recognized this aspect of God's character? How different would the world be today if we did as well?

VENGEFUL

Vengeance takes many forms. One might think of an ad hoc group of cowboys setting out to apply some vigilante "justice" to a person they suspect has stolen a horse. A more sanitized picture of vengeance, yet one that retains the same underlying idea, is the system of "justice" that political states dispense: fines, prison terms, and executions. In both cases, the cowboy and the state, justice is actually retaliation. If someone hurts you, you should hurt them back in equal measure. In one instance, a group of people take it upon themselves to inflict pain on someone they believe has harmed them; in the other, the state appropriates the role of dispensing retaliatory violence. In both cases, the ultimate thing that is sought is not justice but vengeance.

Vengeance, along with its close cousin *revenge*, is often thought to be motivated by emotions such as hatred and anger.[24] This is what differentiates

---

24. Erich Zenger, *A God of Vengeance? Understanding the Psalms of Divine Wrath*, trans. Linda M. Maloney (Louisville: Westminster John Knox, 1996), 70–71.

vengeance from other concepts like justice and punishment. Justice is imagined as a rational response, devoid of feeling. It adheres to agreed-upon procedure and is bounded by clearly formulated stipulations. A justice system is designed to take the task of identifying and punishing a wrongdoer away from the victim so that emotions do not cloud decisions. Punishment, on the other hand, refers only to the response that is given to an act of injustice. Punishment can be emotionally charged or not. Vengeance, however, is not ambivalent. It is a kind of catharsis in which a victim releases their wrath upon a perpetrator in hopes of gaining a measure of peace or at least a sense of twisted satisfaction at the knowledge that the person who dispensed pain is now suffering as well.

Whether a person believes God dispenses vengeance or merely applies justice depends on whether or not one believes God experiences emotion. A person who thinks that God does not feel things like anger and betrayal would likely believe that God applies punishment to humans who deserve it. God does not engage in vengeance. Rather, God acts in a rational way to uphold fairness. Christian theologians have been arguing this perspective for as long as there have been Christian theologians. Origen, for example, claimed that every punishment God applies is remedial—intended to correct the behavior of wayward humans—and never vengeful.[25] That is, Origen believed that God never *gets humans back* for the suffering their disobedience inflicts upon God. Rather, God acts in a dispassionate way within a system of divine justice to dispense rewards and punishments in order to incentivize people to act rightly. In a contemporary rephrasing of Origen's thought, we could say that God is the grand economist running the central bank of moral behavior. When human actions heat up in an unethical manner, God ratchets up the punishments in order to bring people back into line. All of this is done with cold, hard, Keynesian calculus and without vindictiveness. God acts out of well-calculated assessments on what punishment a particular human needs to cause that person to recalibrate.

Many contemporary biblical scholars and theologians follow in this train. They add some nuance, though. One twist they offer is distinguishing God's action from God's attributes. Attributes are features of God's character. They describe God's fundamental nature. Justice, they would say, is a fundamental characteristic of God but judgment (and vengeance) is not. Dispensing judgment (or vengeance) is an action that is linked to the way God defines justice but it is not a divine attribute.[26] What humans perceive as judgment or vengeance is a reflection of our experience. It is how we *interpret* what God is doing, not necessarily how God actually is. Furthermore, divine judgment or

---

25. Mark S. M. Scott, *Journey Back to God: Origen on the Problem of Evil* (Oxford: Oxford University Press, 2012), 75.
26. Patrick D. Miller, "Slow to Anger," in *The Way of the Lord: Essays in Old Testament Theology* (Grand Rapids: Eerdmans, 2007), 270.

vengeance is God's response to a particular human action. Therefore, judgment should not be considered an essential characteristic of the divine person.

There is a philosophical basis for this idea, but it seems to split hairs a bit too fine. What is a person's character other than a compilation of what they do? That is, a person may *think* they are very patient and they may *want to be* long-suffering, but if they repeatedly get mad at the drop of a hat we would conclude that one of their characteristics is being short-tempered. To be sure, humans are more than the sum of their actions. However, if a person's character reflects the tendencies of their behavior, behaviors reveal a person's underlying desires and mental states. A patient person is someone who repeatedly shows patience in exasperating situations. If God acts repeatedly in vengeance, we would rightly conclude that vengeance is part of God's character. The only thing left for us, then, is to see if the biblical writers depict God as repeatedly acting with vengeance.

There is a Hebrew word, *nqm*, which many translations render as "to avenge." Furthermore, there are a variety of other words that, from the context of the passages they appear in, indicate that God dispenses retribution.[27] Perhaps none of these passages are as central to the Hebrew Bible as the lists of blessings and curses appended to Deuteronomistic covenants. God tells the people that they will be blessed with abundance and peace if they follow God's instructions, but if they disobey, God will take away the good things in their lives up to and including the ground they live on. Scholars debate whether these covenants contain the idea of retribution or whether the curses are merely a proper application of God's restorative justice.[28] This is a difficult dispute to settle because the covenant formulas do not allow us to guess at the mental state of God. Recall that the difference between justice and vengeance mostly relates to the mental state of the person giving out punishment.

There are other passages that speak of God punishing people. I propose at least two ways these texts could signal divine vengeance: (1) the authors could describe their understanding of God's emotions that drive God's actions or (2) God's actions are out of proportion with the behavior they are punishing. The latter is a tricky criteria because there will always be people who say that God's actions are by definition just and therefore never out of proportion. Not only is this response not helpful to this topic since it begs the question,

---

27. For a book-length study of *nqm* see H. G. L. Peels, *The Vengeance of God: The Meaning of the Root NQM & the Function of the NQM-Texts in the Context of Divine Revelation in the Old Testament* (Leiden: Brill, 1995).

28. Peels in *Vengeance of God*, for instance, does not believe that the covenants entail retribution, while Hans Barstad does in his essay "Deuteronomists, Persians, Greeks," in *Did Moses Speak Attic? Jewish Historiography and Scripture in the Hellenistic Period*, ed. Lester L. Grabbe (Sheffield: Sheffield Academic, 2001), 67.

but it also fails to explain the instances we discussed previously when God repents of actions God has done. There would be no need for God to do this if God had acted dispassionately and in proper proportion.

In chapter 5 of his book, the prophet Micah conveys a pretty grim message from God. It was intended as something joyous. God was working to throw off the enemies that surrounded Israel and Judah and remove from the land things that had the potential to lead the people astray. The means of accomplishing this, however, involved destruction and death. For just a sampling of this, consider these three verses framed by the prophet as the very words of God: "I will cut off the cities of your land and throw down all your strongholds; and I will cut off sorceries from your hand, and you shall have no more soothsayers; . . . and I will uproot your sacred poles from among you and destroy your towns" (Mic. 5:11–12, 14 [10–11, 13 Heb.]). Presumably, sorceries would end because all the people doing sorceries would be killed. Soothsayers would face the same fate. Religious objects like sacred poles would be destroyed along with entire towns. One could argue, and many biblical scholars do, that all this death and destruction was not vindictive on God's part but restorative.[29] God would cleanse the land of harmful people and objects so that God's people could follow divine instruction more easily and deeply. This was heavy punishment, to be sure, but it flowed from the demands of objective justice.

This claim is hard to sustain once the reader arrives at the final verse of Micah 5: "And in anger [$\bar{\jmath}ap$] and wrath [$\d{h}\bar{e}m\hat{a}$] I will execute vengeance [$n\bar{a}q\bar{a}m$] on the nations that did not obey" (5:15 [14 Heb.]). In the previous chapter we looked at some of the ways biblical authors talked about God's emotions relating to anger. In Micah 5:15 the prophet, supposedly speaking God's very words, says that God's motivation for destroying people and property was to "execute vengeance." The nations did not obey and this made God angry and wrathful. It is out of that emotional state that God inflicts pain upon those who brought displeasure upon God. The same scholars who argue that the punishment God dispenses in this account was merely justice are the same scholars who argue that the word for vengeance does not mean vengeance in this context but merely the application of a covenant obligation.[30] It is true that in Deuteronomistic covenants there are punishments listed for failure to follow the covenant's stipulations. However, in Micah God specifically says that God acted out of an aggravated emotional state. In any other situation we would say that a person inflicting punishment because they are angry is at least partially engaging in vengeance and not acting with pure dispassionate justice.

---

29. Francis I. Andersen and David Noel Freedman, *Micah* (Anchor Bible 24E; New York: Doubleday, 2000), 492.

30. See, for instance, Andersen and Freedman, *Micah*, 492, and Peels, *Vengeance of God*.

Furthermore, and it is rather odd that this needs explanation, Micah 5:15 (14 Heb.) explicitly says that God acted in vengeance. The difficulty is, again, that some scholars, because of their theological or philosophical assumptions, rule out the possibility that God could ever act this way. When they come to occurrences of the verb *nqm* used with God as the subject, they say it means something other than vengeance. They are perfectly happy to say that this word does signal vengeance when a human is the subject, yet when it is used with God all of a sudden the standard meaning of the word is changed.[31] The authoritative Hebrew dictionaries and lexicons define *nqm* as "to take revenge/avenge oneself."[32] They offer no other definitions. Neither should theologians.

Judges 15 provides a very clear example of what *nqm* means. The strong man Samson, after being away for some time, goes to visit his wife during the wheat harvest. The woman's father does not let Samson see her. He tells Samson that he has given Samson's wife to another man. Samson is understandably displeased. Samson rounds up three hundred foxes and ties them into pairs by their tails. He puts a burning torch between each pair. Samson releases the foxes into the grain fields surrounding his father-in-law. The people whose fields are ruined are, in turn, understandably displeased. Things escalate quickly and horrifically. The people who own the fields capture Samson's wife, along with her father, and burn them alive. When Samson finds out, he tells the people who had killed his wife, "If this is what you do, I swear I will not stop until I have taken revenge [*niqqamtî*] on you" (Judg. 15:7). Samson slaughters them all.

The use of the verb *nqm* in the Samson story includes both elements I mentioned above that reflect vengeance. One element is implied—retaliatory action is motivated by intense emotions. We can imagine that Samson was highly emotional when he discovered that his father-in-law's countrymen burned up his wife. I can only guess at the intensity of anger and hatred he must have felt. Out of this emotional state Samson killed every person he could find. This fulfills the second criteria of vengeance—a response that is oftentimes out of proportion to the offense. Certainly, burning Samson's wife and his father-in-law was horrific, but killing every single person Samson came across was an atrocity also. It goes against a biblical stipulation that was intended to put a limit on retribution so that violence would not spiral out of control as it did in this story:

---

31. I have discussed this phenomenon with a different phrase in a different biblical passage but the method is the same and happens quite often. Charles Halton, "An Indecent Proposal: The Theological Core of the Book of Ruth," *Scandinavian Journal of the Old Testament* 26:1 (2012): 30–43.

32. Ludwig Koehler and Walter Baumgartner, *The Hebrew and Aramaic Lexicon of the Old Testament*, trans. M. J. E. Richardson (Leiden: Brill, 2001), 721, and David J. A. Clines, ed., *The Concise Dictionary of Classical Hebrew* (Sheffield: Sheffield Phoenix, 2009), 283.

"If any harm follows, then you shall give life for life, eye for eye, tooth for tooth, hand for hand, foot for foot, burn for burn, wound for wound, stripe for stripe" (Exod. 21:23–25).[33] Slaughtering an entire community is not proportional to the killing of two people. Nor is it designed to be restorative in any way. How can someone be restored to right behavior when they are dead? Samson's act of *nqm* was a vengeful reprisal if there ever was one. If this is what the word means in the Samson story, without compelling evidence *in the accounts themselves* (as opposed to a priori theological assumptions), this is what the word means in texts that attribute acts of *nqm* to God.

We have seen that in Micah 5 God acts out of an emotional state of anger and wrath.[34] This satisfies the first criteria I offered to determine if an act is vengeful. The other criteria we need to discuss is whether God's reprisals are ever out of proportion to the wrongs that were done. I mentioned previously that the mere fact that God regrets acts of punishment implies this. There is also at least one passage that explicitly says people suffered more than the harm they caused. Remember that the prophet of Isaiah 40:2 reported that God said this to him: "Speak tenderly to Jerusalem, and cry to her that she has served her term, that her penalty is paid, that she has received from the Lord's hand double for all her sins." The Judeans had seen the temple destroyed, Jerusalem sacked, and a good number of people forcibly removed from their land. God admits that these disasters came from the divine hand and that they were double the people's sins.

Some scholars argue that the double penalty the Judeans endured from God was not excessive punishment at all but in line with judicial compensation.[35] For instance, Exodus 22:7 (6 Heb.) outlines a situation in which a thief is required to pay back not only the original amount of money they stole but an additional payment to the victim that is equal to what they took. Presumably, this "double payment" was a form of restitution. It compensated the victim not only for the loss but also for the time and money they expended in recovering what was stolen. Restitution also functions as a deterrent. If a criminal only has to repay what they steal, they might be more motivated to attempt a theft. If we accept that the double penalty mentioned in Isaiah 40 includes restitution instead of reprisal—and we should note that this explanation is an assumption that is not made clear in the text itself—we still should

---

33. "This kind of ordered and proportionate response to injury was designed to limit the reaction to the kind of incidents that, if not dealt with adequately, can escalate into feuds that endure for generations. One of the most outrageous things that Jesus [in Matt. 5] ever attempted was to replace this sane and carefully calibrated response to injustice with a system of non-resistance" Richard Holloway, *On Forgiveness* (Edinburgh: Canongate, 2015), 69.

34. Among other passages, see also Jer. 5:7–18 for examples of God acting out of a heightened emotional state.

35. John L. McKenzie, *Second Isaiah* (Anchor Bible; Garden City, NY: Doubleday, 1968), 17.

ask why a god would need restitution, particularly given the nature of the punishment referred to in Isaiah 40.

What kind of compensation would God receive by punishing humans for disobedience? Even more, what kind of compensation would God receive by punishing humans twice as much as their infractions deserved? Does seeing people suffer bring God happiness? And if so, does God inflict an amount of harm so that God's happiness at human suffering exceeds the pain God felt at human disobedience? Restitution is normally paid back in monetary units. If a person experiences a loss of property, restitution allows them to replace the property and then some. When God punishes humanity, people do not return money to God. They do not give God services in kind. They suffer. So again, if the divine punishment described in Isaiah 40 is interpreted as restitution, what does God receive from it and how does God benefit?

Now, to the other half of restitution—its role in deterring wayward behavior. Why would a double portion of punishment need to be applied to the residents of Judah to deter them in the future from violating the terms of the Deuteronomistic covenants when *the covenant itself lists in detail a series of punishments if the covenant is broken*? In other words, the curses within the covenant are the deterrent. In our parlance, it would be cruel and unusual to double the harm that is already established as sufficient to deter bad behavior. Maybe someone would argue: Well, the Judeans violated the covenant in spite of its listed consequences, so God had to ratchet up the intensity in order to keep these offenses from continuing. This would mean that God is fueling an escalating cycle of increasing violence. God is like Samson in the story above. Each time someone does something contrary to what God intends, God's reprisal becomes more and more severe, more and more disproportional to the harm that was committed. It's not a good look. Neither is the idea that God was angry and out of this anger God struck an outsized blow against the people he loved. But at least this fits with the other portraits of God we have discussed. It also has the advantage of taking the passage in Isaiah 40 at face value.

JEALOUS

Jealousy encompasses several things, but at root it signals someone who is "upset and angry because someone that you love seems interested in another person" and who out of this apprehension becomes "extremely careful in protecting someone or something."[36] In other words, jealousy occurs when someone believes they might lose something or someone they value and so they work

36. *Cambridge Dictionary Online*, s.v. "jealous," https://dictionary.cambridge.org/us/dictionary/english/jealous 2021.

to preserve their hold on it. The most common situation that provokes jealousy in the Bible, and likely outside of it as well, is when a person fears that a friend or lover will leave them to go off with someone else. Jealousy arises when someone has a fear of being left out, whether this refers to romantic, platonic, or religious relationships.[37] The prospect of losing a friend or lover often creates a combination of anxiety and anger. This combination creates jealousy.

The Hebrew root *qn'* is usually translated as jealousy / to be jealous. I say usually because when biblical authors use this word in connection to God, some translators render it as *zealous* to avoid a perceived negative connotation surrounding the word *jealous*. There is no linguistic reason to do this, however. Like almost all Hebrew words, *qn'* has a fairly large semantic range, but jealousy is very clearly in the center of it. And if the word means jealousy when it refers to a human, the meaning of the word should not fundamentally change when it refers to God. If God feels and acts in a very different way than humans do, the biblical authors, if they were competent, would have selected a different word to represent that. If they used the same word to convey vastly different meanings, they were very bad communicators indeed.

Another thing we should note is that when the authors of the Hebrew Bible attribute jealousy to God, they do not convey a pejorative connotation with it. Contemporary readers might find the word to be objectionable, but these authors didn't. For instance, the Decalogues of Exodus and Deuteronomy explicitly describe God as "a jealous God" (*'ēl qannā'*).[38] Even though biblical scholars have spent a good deal of effort trying to understand what this descriptive means (because, again, they want to avoid attributing negative connotations to God), the meaning of *qn'* is quite clear from the context of the passage itself. Before we look at that, though, we should examine the use of *qn'* in Proverbs 6:34.

Some scholars see Proverbs 6:20–35 as an interpretive expansion on the idea underneath the statements in the Decalogues that mention God's jealousy.[39] Both Proverbs and the Decalogues tell their audiences to give weight to the instruction of their parents, forbid theft and adultery, and tell a man not to desire another man's wife. The difference between the passages is the subject of jealousy.[40] In the Decalogues, God is jealous, while Proverbs refers

---

37. Ronald E. Long, "Heavenly Sex: The Moral Authority of an Impossible Dream," *Theology and Sexuality* 11:3 (2005): 31–46.

38. Exod. 20:5 and Deut. 5:9.

39. Michael Fishbane, "Torah and Tradition," in *Tradition and Theology in the Old Testament*, ed. Douglas A. Knight (Philadelphia: Fortress, 1977), 275–300, and Bernd U. Schipper, "'Teach Them Diligently to Your Son!' The Book of Proverbs and Deuteronomy," in *Reading Proverbs Intertextually*, ed. Katharine J. Dell and Will Kynes (London: T&T Clark, 2019), 21–34.

40. For instance, David M. Carr, *The Formation of the Hebrew Bible: A New Reconstruction* (Oxford: Oxford University Press, 2011), 420.

to a husband: "For jealousy [*qinʾâ*] arouses a husband's fury, and he shows no restraint when he takes revenge" (6:34). Proverbs provides a good test case for the meaning of the word *qinʾâ*.

In Proverbs 6:34, the use of *qnʾ* fits the standard definition of jealousy. This proverb describes a husband who believes his wife has committed adultery. The husband is angry and acts out of this anger to take revenge on the people involved. Instead of settling for the normal protocol of accepting restitution when something of value is taken from a person—even accepting a restitution payment of up to seven times the worth of what was stolen—the jealous husband will not abide by any prescribed response. This is quite harrowing since the husband is not required to show mercy or restraint of any kind to a wife or other person he suspects is involved in the adultery.[41] The same lack of restraint seems to apply to God when this "jealous God" is angry at humans who follow after another deity.

The Decalogues say that if the Hebrew people worship other deities, God will punish not only the specific people who did this but their children too. "You shall not bow down to [idols of other gods] or worship them; for I the LORD your God am a jealous God, punishing children for the iniquity of parents, to the third and fourth generation of those who reject me" (Deut. 5:9//Exod. 20:5). Uninvolved parties suffer at the hand of God if a person close to them does not follow God rightly. These suffering parties include children who are yet to be born. It seems extreme and also unfair to punish yet-to-be-born children for something they did not do. This seems unfair not only to my innate sense of conscience, but also to the prophet Ezekiel.[42]

Ezekiel presented his contemporaries with a message he believed came from God. He begins chapter 18 with these words:

> The word of the LORD came to me: What do you mean by repeating this proverb concerning the land of Israel, "The parents have eaten sour grapes, and the children's teeth are set on edge"? As I live, says the LORD God, this proverb shall no more be used by you in Israel. Know that all lives are mine; the life of the parent as well as the life of the child is mine: it is only the person who sins that shall die. (18:1–4)

The rest of the chapter unpacks this radical idea: God will punish offenders for their sins but not innocent bystanders.[43] These innocent bystanders

---

41. Eve Levavi Feinstein, *Sexual Pollution in the Hebrew Bible* (Oxford: Oxford University Press, 2014), 48.

42. I am not in any way lessening the influence of human moral consensus or conscience when forming moral and ethical judgment. The biblical prophets often appealed to human moral consensus and not divine law when they preached to the people. John Barton, *Ethics and the Old Testament* (London: SCM, 1998), 61.

43. A form of this idea also appears in Deut. 24:16.

include children. This contradicts the self-description God gives within the Decalogues in which God says, "You shall not bow down to [idols of other gods] or worship them; for I the LORD your God am a jealous God [*ʾēl qannāʾ*], punishing children for the iniquity of parents, to the third and the fourth generation of those who reject me" (Exod. 20:5). The God of Sinai says that God is jealous. This jealousy is further defined in a very concrete way. When God becomes angry at the Hebrews' waywardness, God will punish not only the offenders but even people three and four steps removed. According to Ezekiel, this kind of thinking is patently unfair. Toward the end of chapter 18 of Ezekiel's book, the prophet issues a broadside attack against God's promise of jealous retribution laid out in the Decalogues:[44]

> Yet you say, "Why should not the son suffer for the iniquity of the father?" When the son has done what is lawful and right, and has been careful to observe all my statutes, he shall surely live. The person who sins shall die. A child shall not suffer for the iniquity of a parent, nor a parent suffer for the iniquity of a child; the righteousness of the righteous shall be his own, and the wickedness of the wicked shall be his own. (18:19–20)

Even in antiquity, the writers of the Talmud said that Ezekiel "annulled" divine teaching given in the Decalogues.[45] The jealousy that once motivated God to act with barely or completely unrestrained retribution is now bounded and restricted to only the individual offenders. Yet God continues to act jealously in the latter half of the Old Testament.

In the book of Zechariah a divine messenger tells the prophet: "Thus says the LORD of hosts; I am very jealous [*qinnēʾtî*] for Jerusalem and for Zion" (1:14). God is jealous because foreign peoples are making life difficult for the city's inhabitants while the offenders go about life just fine and no justice is in sight. God tells the people of Jerusalem that that is about to change. In the next breath God says, "And I am extremely angry with the nations that are at ease; for while I was only a little angry, they made the disaster worse" (1:15). These verses link jealousy with the emotion of anger. We will return to the link of jealousy and anger in the conclusion of this chapter.

Anger is not the only linkage biblical authors create with jealousy. Isaiah 59:17 uses jealousy as a synonym for vengeance: "He put on righteousness like a breastplate, and a helmet of salvation on his head; he put on garments of

---

44. Some commentators believe that Ezekiel is interacting with Deut. 24:16 instead of the Decalogues. Moshe Greenberg, *Ezekiel 1–20* (Anchor Bible 22; New York: Doubleday, 1983), 332–33. This certainly may be the case, but even if it is, Ezekiel is undercutting the moral rationale of the Decalogue passages if not the specific verse itself.

45. Jon D. Levenson, *Sinai and Zion: An Entry into the Jewish Bible* (Minneapolis: Winston, 1985), 63.

vengeance [nāqām] for clothing, and wrapped himself in jealousy [qinʾâ] as in a mantle."[46] Isaiah 59 is a recitation of injustices the enemies of God have committed. This list culminates in God's promise of requital. It seems as if God has a storehouse of pent-up anger that is waiting to be unleashed. When the time for this arrives, God's jealousy and vengeance flow through the divine being unchecked. From this position, God unleashes incredible destruction upon the objects of God's wrath. Again, this is similar to the jealousy of a cuckolded spouse who rejects standard metrics of compensation in favor of wide-eyed bloodlust.

Zephaniah 1 is the last passage relating to jealousy that we will examine. It is, perhaps, the most disturbing of all. Zephaniah wastes absolutely no time in getting to the heart of his message. He relays an oracle from God that describes a coming day of judgment in which the Lord says, "I will utterly sweep away everything from the face of the earth" (1:2). The prophet continues, quoting God, and elaborates precisely what God intends to do. God will sweep away every living thing: humans, animals, birds, and fish (1:3). At face value this statement seems to violate the promise God made to Noah to never again lash out against the earth in total destruction. The prophet seems to walk back this rash threat somewhat, though.

Further down the oracle, certain types of people who will be destroyed are marked out: every idolatrous priest will be killed (1:4–6), political leaders will be punished (1:8), greedy merchants will be disposed of (1:11), and the wealthy will be plundered (1:13). This seems to imply that divine punishment will be specific and not comprehensive. Yet at the very end of the chapter God reiterates that the destruction will be total, "In the fire of his jealousy [ʾēš qinʾātô] the whole earth shall be consumed; for a full, a terrible end he will make of all the inhabitants of the earth" (1:18).[47] Of course, it didn't turn out this way. God did not destroy the entire planet, because you are here reading this book. Nonetheless, God's expressed desire to do so cuts against God's previously stated desire to never repeat the devastation of the flood. It seems that once again God's emotions carried God farther than what the divine mind thought was good and right. God's fit of jealousy caused God to want what God knows God should never wish—the complete destruction of animal life. This potential to lead God to desire to commit barbarous acts is not the only troubling aspect of divine jealousy.

Traditionally, and still to this day, many theologians justify God's jealousy. They say it is totally fine for God to be jealous. In fact, some biblical scholars

---

46. This translation corrects the NRSV. For some reason, likely due to the theological assumptions we discussed above, the NRSV translates qinʾâ as "fury."
47. This translation corrects the NRSV. For some reason, likely due to the theological assumptions we discussed above, the NRSV translates qinʾātô as "his passion."

go beyond an assertion that divine jealousy is merely benign. They say it is a positive good. For instance, one scholar says this about God's jealousy:

> Jealousy guards God's actions from ever being influenced by an impure motive (Ex 20:5; 34:14). It guarantees that God will always be true to his holy character, will keep his promises and will nourish his established relationships.... Jealousy is the energy that keeps vital covenant love (ḥesed) and leads God to bless his people as promised in the covenant.[48]

This is not an uncommon perspective. Yet several things about it are problematic. I am not sure how jealousy is able to guard God's actions from being influenced by an impure motive. As we will see below, jealousy itself can be an impure motive. But even if it is not, how does emotional pique make a sentient actor pure? We see from several of the biblical passages we examined that God's emotions, including jealousy, cause God to act in ways that are not good and that God later regrets.

Furthermore, the account in Zephaniah seems to undercut the assertion that God's jealousy guarantees that God will always keep divine promises. In Zephaniah 1, God's jealousy causes God to want to violate God's promise to never repeat an act of categorical destruction. The fact that God did not follow through with this desire did not come about because of God's jealousy. God's jealousy was *the very character trait that caused God* to want to break God's promise. Jealousy does not always cause God to act badly, but sometimes it does.

More fundamentally, though, the very nature of jealousy as it was understood in the biblical period (and also, in many quarters, to this day) is troubling. Susannah Cornwall identifies the primary reason why biblical authors and contemporary theologians believe it is perfectly acceptable for God to be jealous: they understand "jealousy [as] a legitimate and understandable quality in a man protective of his property."[49] A man becomes jealous of his wife when she unites with another man because the woman *is his property*. Keep in mind that jealousy is different from sadness, loss, or betrayal—some of the other emotions one could feel when a loved one leaves for someone else. Jealousy is a mixture of fear and anger that stems from the threat that what belongs to a person may be taken away from them. The theological justification of jealousy goes like this: just as a man keeps a woman (or in the biblical period, women) as his property, so also God keeps humans as God's property. God is rightly jealous when humans become enamored of different gods, because

---

48. John E. Hartley, "Holy and Holiness, Clean and Unclean," in *Dictionary of the Old Testament: Pentateuch*, ed. T. Desmond Alexander and David W. Baker (Downers Grove, IL: InterVarsity, 2003), 430.

49. Susannah Cornwall, *Un/familiar Theology: Reconceiving Sex Reproduction and Generativity* (London: T&T Clark, 2017), 55.

the humans God created belong to God just as a husband's wife belongs to the man. Most people today would find this rationale distasteful. Like Ezekiel looking back on God's self-description in the Decalogues as a jealous God and finding it deficient, we also should see jealousy as, for the most part, an unproductive emotion that has the potential to produce great harm.

FORGIVING

Thankfully, God's response to human waywardness is not only jealousy but also forgiveness. In many ways, forgiveness works to mitigate jealousy and its retributive sense of justice. Forgiveness marks a transition from one relational position to another, from a stance of animosity to a place where peace is possible.[50] It makes a break with the past and creates space for a new future. Forgiveness allows a person to move beyond vindictiveness and anger to embrace a refreshed emotional stance toward a person. Forgiveness does not regard past wrongs as trivial, nor does it sweep them aside and act like the hurts they caused do not matter.[51]

Evil is evil and always will be. There is no forgiveness for a terrible *act*. Yet the *person* who commits an evil act can certainly be forgiven. This kind of thinking depends upon a distinction between act and agent.[52] If we do not recognize the reality that destructive acts are always wrong and never excusable, and if the past is not adequately dealt with, previous wrongs will continue to cause harm.[53] When a person forgives, they recall what another *person* did to them. The harm is not papered over nor minimized in any way. They accept the reality of the harm that was caused, but they release the negative desire for retribution they have against the offender. This makes it possible, but not inevitable, for the relationship to return to, more or less, the way it was before the offense took place.[54] There are times when we forgive someone else not

---

50. Aaron T. Looney, *Vladimir Jankélévitch: The Time of Forgiveness* (New York: Fordham University Press, 2015), 1–2.
51. Charles L. Griswold, *Forgiveness: A Philosophical Exploration* (Cambridge: Cambridge University Press, 2007), 53.
52. Holloway, *On Forgiveness*, xii–xiii. It may seem tautological that there is a distinction between act and agent; however, not every religious tradition thinks this way. For instance, Buddhist teacher Thich Nhat Hanh writes, "We are what we feel and perceive. If we are angry, we are the anger. If we are in love, we are love." *Peace Is Every Step: The Path of Mindfulness in Everyday Life* (New York: Bantam, 1991), 13. There are also nonreligious philosophers who disagree with the distinction between act and agent, at least in terms of identity and culpability; for instance, Alain Badiou, "The Subject Supposed to Be a Christian," in *The Adventure of French Philosophy*, ed. and trans. Bruno Bosteels (London: Verso, 2012), 330–36.
53. Desmond Tutu, *No Future without Forgiveness* (New York: Doubleday, 1999), 28.
54. This is not to say that boundaries are not set or precautions put into place to protect against future harm.

for their benefit but for our own well-being, so that we can seek healing from internal bitterness and anger.[55] Both of these motivations—for the self and for the offender—are appropriate.

One key to forgiveness is an awareness that humans act within particular contexts.[56] Sometimes these contexts cause us to behave in ways we wouldn't normally wish to. When I am hungry I can become irritable. My loved ones forgive me when I say hurtful things when I am hungry, in part, because they realize I would not have acted that way if my belly was full. They understand that I am a product of my situation and that my physical condition produced emotions within me that were unproductive. In other words, one of the reasons they forgive me is because they do not hold me fully responsible for my speech in that moment.

There are times, however, when I am in perfectly fine physical shape. I am rested, satiated, and unstressed. And yet, I still do something that causes harm. If people forgive me for these things, they still do so understanding that I am a contextual being. Hopefully, I will learn from the situation and not repeat the wrongs I did. In any case, every human being is in a constant state of change. I am not identical to the person I was a few minutes ago. Refusing to let go of grievances against a person who no longer exists is rather pointless. We all commit wrongs and hurt other people. If we refuse to forgive others, how can we in good conscience expect others to forgive us?

Sometimes we forgive people for noble reasons—Nelson Mandela and Desmond Tutu's work with the Truth and Reconciliation Commission in South Africa is an example. Mandela and Tutu understood that for their country to avoid the civil wars and bloody cycles of revenge that other nations experienced after cataclysmic political reversals, they had to seek a path of restorative forgiveness rather than retributive punishment.[57] At other times, forgiveness is given grudgingly and under threat or coercion. Think of a tired parent telling a child they must accept their sibling's apology after their favorite toy was smashed in front of their eyes. The forgiveness the child gives in that moment will not be pristine. Or think about a politician who sits for an interview with a nationally syndicated television show and magnanimously forgives an opponent for taunting them with vulgar insults. Perhaps this act of forgiveness is extended with less than ideal motives.

The authors of the Hebrew Bible often describe divine forgiveness in ways that reflect some of these very human dynamics. The author of Psalm 25

---

55. Anthony G. Reddie, *Working against the Grain: Re-Imagining Black Theology in the 21st Century* (Sheffield: Equinox, 2008), 238 n. 41.
56. Terry Eagleton, *Radical Sacrifice* (New Haven: Yale University Press, 2018), 125.
57. Tutu, *No Future without Forgiveness*, 15–32.

describes being anxious and in distress (25:16–18). The precise nature of the suffering is not known. This ambiguity concerning the source of suffering is probably purposeful in order to allow this psalm to be applied to any situation of personal or communal calamity. The petitioner believes that committing a sin caused God to respond by bringing this misfortune (25:11). Psalm 25 assumes an idea that was common in the ancient world—if a person is suffering, it is a sign that God is punishing them for some offense. The psalmist asks for relief from the distress but says that relief will only come when God forgives the sinner. The psalmist directs the petition to God and says, "forgive my vices, for they are many" (25:11b, my trans.). Immediately before this statement there is a very curious phrase.

The psalmist introduces the plea by saying, "For the sake of your reputation [šimkâ], forgive my vices" (25:11a, my trans.). A slightly uncharitable reader might regard this statement as a form of extortion. It's almost as if the psalmist is saying: If you don't forgive me, God, word of your stingy and unforgiving character is going to travel and folks are not going to think well of you. A more generous interpretation is that the psalmist pointed out that by forgiving the psalmist, God would remind other people of God's benevolent and forgiving ways and therefore people would think highly of the god of Israel. Either way we understand it, the psalmist highlights the benefits and pitfalls associated with God's choice of whether to release the petitioner from suffering. The author of Psalm 25 does not believe that God's response is predetermined. The psalmist believes that divine forgiveness is not certain. One factor God considers when weighing whether to forgive someone is the impact forgiveness will have on the divine reputation.

Another aspect of divine forgiveness is linked to one of the positive attributes of God that the psalmist references in another song—God's incredible memory. In Psalm 105:7–11, God is described as a being who remembers the promises God made to people in the past—to Abraham and Isaac and Jacob. Theologian Lauren Winner concludes from this that "God does not generically remember."[58] God does not have a vague and hazy recollection of the commitments God has made. God remembers the precise nature of the agreements God enters as well as the specific people to whom divine promises are made. God does not merely remember agreements, though. God keeps individual people in the front of God's mind. In Isaiah 49 the prophet reports God as saying, "Can a woman forget her nursing child, or show no compassion for the child of her womb? Even these may forget, yet I

---

58. Lauren F. Winner, *The Dangers of Christian Practice: On Wayward Gifts, Characteristic Damage, and Sin* (New Haven: Yale University Press, 2018), 52.

will not forget you" (49:15).[59] The writers of the Hebrew Bible often frame God's memory as something that is comforting. Since God will not forget people, they can know that deliverance will ultimately arrive. Yet God's memory cuts both ways. God also remembers, in detail, the failings of God's creatures.

For instance, the prophet Jeremiah, speaking for God, specifies the sins the Israelites committed and then goes into detail documenting them. The book of Jeremiah opens with Jeremiah's call to be a mouthpiece for God. God tells Jeremiah that he must bring to the people a message of impending judgment. Israel will be invaded because they have violated the agreement they made with God. God specifies to the prophet the particular sins they committed—"they have made offerings to other gods, and worshiped the works of their own hands" (1:16). Jeremiah, again speaking for God, repeats and expands this accusation in 2:1–3:5.[60] This section documents specific grievances, which include their ancestors worshiping Baal and complaining about God while the current generation made alliances with foreign powers instead of trusting in God. These are not vague notions. Specific actions from the past and present remained in the divine mind for generations. And yet, the prophet says that God will forgive them. There are several statements to this effect within the book of Jeremiah, but the most dramatic may be in chapter 31. God says that the people will be forgiven and they will enter into a new covenant (31:31–34). God promises to restore everything that the people lost when Israel was invaded and a good many people were forcibly deported. God says that forgiveness will include the reconstitution and rebuilding of the nation. We will discuss Jeremiah 31 further in a moment; for now it is enough for us to note that in this instance God forgave the people and promised to restore them.

It is not always like this with God. There are times when God does forgive people but the relationship, at least with some individuals, does not go back to normal. In Numbers 14:20–25 God forgives the Hebrews for their lack of trust after Moses led them out of Egypt. Once they experienced hardships, the people began to doubt whether God had the desire or even the ability to help them. Even though God forgives them, God says that the people who distrusted God will not be allowed to enter the land God intended for them. Furthermore, God's forgiveness seems rather reluctant. Moses pleads with God to forgive the people, and this is how God responds:

---

59. For a very insightful discussion of this passage and others like it, see Kosuke Koyama, "The God of the Bible and the Peoples of the Earth," in *The People's Companion to the Bible*, ed. Curtiss Paul DeYoung et al. (Minneapolis: Fortress, 2010), 71.

60. Jack R. Lundbom, *Jeremiah 1–20* (Anchor Bible 21A; New York: Doubleday, 1999), 262.

> I do forgive, just as you have asked; nevertheless—as I live, and as all the earth shall be filled with the glory of the Lord—none of the people who have seen my glory and the signs that I did in Egypt and in the wilderness, and yet have tested me these ten times and have not obeyed my voice, shall see the land that I swore to give to their ancestors; none of those who despised me shall see it. (14:20–23)

Even though God tells Moses that the people are forgiven, it doesn't seem as though they are. God's response is grudging. You can almost hear the exasperation in the divine voice as God says: I do forgive, *just as you have asked*. . . . One can imagine that God was tired of hearing Moses plead his case and so he forgave the people just to make Moses shut up. The next word out of God's mouth is *nevertheless*. This "nevertheless" qualifies and bounds the forgiveness God offers. The people are forgiven and yet their relationship with God is not fully restored. The Hebrews who did not trust God will not experience the blessing of entering the land. So what exactly does God's forgiveness accomplish here? Possibly, God no longer harbors ill will toward the people. Yet some of the rhetoric in God's statement signals that this may not be the case. The "nevertheless," the almost imprecatory exclamation "as I live," the specific enumeration of the times the people tested God, God's statement that the people "despised me," and God's preventing these people from seeing the land all point to God still being angry and not fully forgiving them.

That God seems to grant quasi forgiveness and refuses to fully restore the people is not the most interesting feature of this passage, though. The way that Moses persuades God to forgive the people is not what pious readers of the Bible might normally expect. Moses does not base his request on the people's repentance. Instead, Moses bases it on God's character. He reminds God that God is a loving god and therefore should forgive the people so that God would be consistent with the divine character.[61] Moses in effect says, "Hey, you say you are God, so you better act like it by forgiving these people." In response, God forgives but not completely. God holds something back and continues to refuse to fully release the people from their past wrongs and let them enter into the land. The people as a whole endure as a result of this forgiveness—Israel continues to be a cohesive entity and God's relationship with the nation goes back to normal in the grand scale of time—but the individuals who sinned against God do not have their relationship restored.[62] Forgiveness happens, but it takes place on a bigger plane than particular individuals.

---

61. Samuel E. Balentine, *Prayer in the Hebrew Bible: The Drama of Divine-Human Dialogue* (Minneapolis: Fortress, 1993), 134.
62. My dear friend and an excellent biblical scholar, Angela Roskop Erisman, pointed out this individual vs. communal dynamic to me.

Israelite individuals experience forgiveness as partial while the nation experiences it more fully.

If Numbers 14 records an instance of partial divine forgiveness, other passages recall times when God was not willing to forgive at all—2 Kings 24, for instance. This passage critiques Jehoiakim, king of Judah, and his relationship to his Babylonian overlords.[63] Jehoiakim rebels against the king of Babylonia, which causes Babylonian and assorted forces to descend upon Judah. The writer of the books of Kings says that while Jehoiakim's rebellion was the proximate cause of Judah's suffering, the ultimate reason for it was that God was punishing the nation for the sins of a previous king, Manasseh.[64] The narrator specifies that Manasseh's shedding of "innocent blood" was particularly troubling to God. It is this latter offense which 2 Kings 24:4 says "Yahweh was not willing to forgive."[65] God was sending destruction whether the Judeans repented or not.

The Chronicler must have been troubled by this passage, because when he discusses Jehoiakim he deletes any reference to the past sins of Manasseh as well as any hint that God would be unwilling to forgive. According to 2 Chronicles 36:5, the sole reason for Jehoiakim's trouble with Babylon was his own disobedience. If the Chronicler were to read the book of Lamentations he would likely be even more troubled. Lamentations 3:42–44 expresses an astonishing claim. The God whom other biblical writers describe as eternally forgiving and endlessly benevolent has had enough. God will not even let a prayer enter the divine ear. The poet looks at the situation the people are in and says to God, "We have transgressed and rebelled, and you have not forgiven. You have wrapped yourself with anger and pursued us, killing without pity; you have wrapped yourself with a cloud so that no prayer can pass through."[66] The poet of Lamentations is certain that God will offer no forgiveness.

It is understandable that God would punish wrongdoing. As Old Testament scholar John Rogerson observes, "If YHWH did not punish his people for these wrongdoings, it would be an immoral world in which they were living.... The mercies without the judgement would amount to cheap grace,

---

63. Mordechai Cogan and Hayim Tadmor, *II Kings* (Anchor Bible 11; New York: Doubleday, 1988), 307.

64. For a list of these sins see 2 Kgs. 21.

65. The NRSV translates this phrase as "the LORD was not willing to pardon," but the same verb is used here that is elsewhere translated as "to forgive," so I have harmonized these translations for better clarity.

66. The imagery of God hiding from a praying people inside a cloud that does not let a single petition penetrate it recalls many of the anthropomorphic dynamics we discussed in previous chapters. As Robert Carroll notes, "The metaphor of divine hiding combines all the anthropomorphic language of the Bible. It represents a god who has face and eyes and whose social mores reflect an emperor or king's gestures of averting or turning the face to the petitioner." *Wolf in the Sheepfold* (London: SCM, 1997), 55.

and would yield a view of God for whom respect could quickly evaporate."[67] While I do not agree with Rogerson's analysis—for instance, why is forgiving people and withholding punishment immoral?—I do think his point is theologically valid. A conception of a god who dispenses appropriate judgment is a very reasonable and traditional way of imagining the divine. However, the god of Lamentations 3 is not this. That god is on a Lamech-like killing spree, devoid of compassion and pity, refusing to forgive and unwilling to entertain any prayer. Remember what the Babylonian invasion entailed: armies breaking down city walls, razing homes, raping women and killing men, flaying people alive, kidnapping children, looting sanctuaries, and so on. According to Kings and Lamentations, God brought this to Judah because God was unwilling to forgive. It sounds like a god overcome by emotions. God is often forgiving, to be sure. But there are times when even God's patience has worn thin and vengeance is the only thing in view.

FORGETTING

It is time we return to Jeremiah 31. This is an especially intriguing passage because it not only deals with divine forgiveness but it also states how this forgiveness, at least in a certain case, will be accomplished. God tells the prophet, "I will forgive their iniquity, and remember their sin no more" (31:34). God approaches forgiveness by pulling apart history, memory, and person.[68] Normally, these three are fused together. When we think of a person we have a memory of what that person has done. We believe our memory is a reliable account that represents an adequate summation of the person's character. Our understanding of a person *is* our historical memory of them. However, when God says in Jeremiah 31 that God will forgive the people, instead of viewing the people in light of God's memory of what that nation has done, God deletes the offenses from the divine memory. The offenses are culled from the historical record. Ever after, when God recalls the memory of that group, their transgression no longer exists.[69]

After this happens, God relates to a different people. With only a selected record of what the nation has done, the identity of the group as it relates to God is now changed. Think of it this way: How would we understand George

---

67. John W. Rogerson, *A Theology of the Old Testament: Cultural Memory, Communication, and Being Human* (Minneapolis: Fortress, 2010), 163.
68. Paul Ricoeur, *La mémoire, l'histoire, l'oubli* (Paris: Seuil, 2000); translated by K. Blamey and D. Pellauer as *Memory, History, Forgetting* (Chicago: University of Chicago Press, 2004).
69. We normally think of forgetfulness as something bad, but Lewis Hyde provides many examples of its benefits. *A Primer for Forgetting: Getting Past the Past* (New York: Farrar, Straus & Giroux, 2019).

Washington if every memory of him being the president of the United States were washed away? Who would he be to us then? A ruthless slave owner?[70] A military general? Washington's identity would fundamentally shift. Our relationship to Washington would change along with it. His face would not be printed on money, his name would not appear in history books, and people would not visit his home. In all likelihood, he would be forgotten, as almost all businessmen are.

But how, exactly, is divine forgetting accomplished? It seems as if forgetting would be impossible for a being with superhuman capacities in all things, including memory. Even if God *wanted* to forget, how could God prevent the divine mind from recalling information about a person whom God knows? Søren Kierkegaard thought divine forgetting was a form of uncreating. He admitted the idea was absurd, a paradox humans cannot possibly understand. He outlined it anyway: "It is the Deity's joy to forgive sins; just as God is almighty in creating out of nothing, so he is almighty in—uncreating something, for to forget, almightily to forget, is indeed to uncreate something."[71] I can see how someone could uncreate *something*. Buildings can be torn down, trees can be burned up, and meals can be eaten. That is to say, things can be made to no longer exist. But are memories *things*? They certainly are not tangible. To make a memory go away, we would have to alter the brain that housed it. The most extreme alteration would be to cause the brain, and concomitantly the person animated by that brain, to die. If a brain dies, its memories cease to exist.

Carl Jung believed that there were times when God's memory failed not because of a conscious choice by the divine to expunge God's memory of certain events but because God, like us, merely forgets things. Jung pointed to the story of Job to prove his point.[72] There was no need for Job to undergo all the sufferings he did, Jung says. When the Satan confronted God about Job, God should have consulted God's own omniscient mind and immediately discovered what Job would do in any hypothetical test. Yet God momentarily forgot that God knows everything. And so, God suggested the Satan put Job to the test. On one hand, Jung's interpretation seems absurd. How could God forget to do something as trivial as consult God's own understanding? This is like a person forgetting their own name. And furthermore, I can imagine someone responding, God doesn't forget anything, much less a central aspect

---

70. For a historical account of the Washington family's merciless enslaving, see the excellent book by Erica Armstrong Dunbar, *Never Caught: The Washingtons' Relentless Pursuit of Their Runaway Slave Ona Judge* (New York: 37 Ink, 2017).

71. This quote appears in David J. Gouwens, *Kierkegaard as Religious Thinker* (Cambridge: Cambridge University Press, 1996), 136.

72. *Answer to Job* (Princeton: Princeton University Press, 2010).

of God's own character. That rejoinder makes perfect sense. Until you read the story of Noah in the book of Genesis.

After the floodwaters receded and the ark rested on dry ground, the animals along with Noah's family disembarked. One of the first things Noah did after exiting the boat was build an altar and make sacrifices on it. God saw the sacrifice and committed to never again do something as destructive as the flood (Gen. 8:21). In Genesis 9, God makes a new covenant with Noah and his family. God then tells Noah a very curious thing. God says that rainbows will be a sign of this new covenant between God and sentient life on earth. "This is the sign of the covenant that I make between me and you and every living creature that is with you, for all future generations: I have set my bow in the clouds, and it shall be a sign of the covenant between me and the earth" (9:12–13). This passage relays a beautiful expression of peace. God is no longer at war. The bow is set down and peace reigns in its place.[73] We might expect the sign of the rainbow to be a reminder to humanity that God will never again lash out in categorical annihilation. Every time a person might fear that God's vengeance is on the way, the sight of a rainbow would melt the terror in their heart as they remember God's promise of peace. That interpretation of the rainbow makes a lot of sense, but it is not the interpretation God gives it.

The next two phrases in Genesis 9 upend a natural expectation. God says that the rainbow will be a sign *for God*, to remind the divine mind of the covenant God swore to uphold:

> When I bring clouds over the earth and the bow is seen in the clouds, I will remember my covenant that is between me and you and every living creature of all flesh; and the waters shall never again become a flood to destroy all flesh. When the bow is in the clouds, I will see it and remember the everlasting covenant between God and every living creature of all flesh that is on the earth. (9:14–16)

The rainbow is not for humanity. It is intended to jog God's memory so that God never again sends a great flood. This raises a significant theological question: why would God need a memory crutch? The only honest answer is because God is prone to forget things. Perhaps this forgetfulness is absent-mindedness where the divine mind is momentarily unaware of certain facts that are stored in God's brain. Maybe this is a good interpretation, but I doubt it. The forgetfulness lying behind this passage and others like it is a forgetfulness that comes about when one's emotions run hot. In the heat of rage God focuses on ways to slake God's vengeful thirst. The obligations God makes to

---

73. Walter Brueggemann, *Genesis* (Interpretation; Atlanta: John Knox, 1982), 84.

patience and love in various covenants are not at the top of the divine mind in times of pique. The rainbow functions as a sign for God to pause and deescalate God's emotional state instead of ramping it up to culminate in a giant conflagration.

Theologians have made a mistake by thinking of God's character as static properties that yield mathematical results. Divine character produces tendencies of behavior, but these are exactly that—tendencies. Just like human persons, there are moments when God acts contrary to God's ideals. God becomes angry and dispenses punishment that is greater than what God would want to give out in a normal state of mind. God then regrets actions God committed in the past. God creates situations that inflict great pain upon others so that God can receive applause, as Job painfully learned. God creates signs like rainbows intended to put the brakes on God's emotional outbursts and remind God of the ways God desires to act when God is in a good frame of mind. These are not descriptions of a static god.

Walter Brueggemann notes that God's character changes over the course of biblical witness. It moves, albeit very slowly, away from "the common theology of sanctions, to a fidelity that is generative."[74] Brueggemann is saying that God's essential character gradually shifts from being focused on making and enforcing binary judgments to a stance of radical solidarity and faithfulness to creation. I think this is generally true but we must add more caveats to this than I have space to enumerate here. Let me mention of few cautions and then reflect on what I see as the central and extremely valuable aspect of Brueggemann's observation.

As for the caveats, we must not think that this movement of God's character means that the earlier writers of the Bible thought of God in anthropomorphic terms and later ones did not.[75] The humanlike pictures of God are not confined to the older texts within the Old Testament, as if an anthropomorphic understanding of God was an archaic idea that the Israelites eventually grew out of. There are humanlike portrayals of God in Second Isaiah, and 2 Chronicles 6:40 repeats a section of the older parallel text in 1 Kings 8:52 that mentions God's ear.[76] The book of Deuteronomy, whose origin is typically regarded as fairly late, pictures God dispensing parent-like discipline and care (Deut. 8:5 and 1:31, respectively).[77] This is only a sampling of the

---

74. *God, Neighbor, Empire: The Excess of Divine Fidelity and the Command of Common Good* (Waco, TX: Baylor University Press, 2016), 115.

75. This is one of James L. Kugel's arguments in *The God of Old: Inside the Lost World of the Bible* (New York: Free Press, 2003).

76. Horst Dietrich Preuss, *Old Testament Theology*, vol. 1, trans. Leo G. Perdue (Old Testament Library; Louisville: Westminster John Knox, 1995), 245.

77. Deanna A. Thompson, *Deuteronomy* (Belief: A Theological Commentary on the Bible; Louisville: Westminster John Knox, 2014), 93.

many humanlike pictures of God that appear in texts that are assumed to be of later origin. Furthermore, to say that there is a gradual shift in the Hebrew Bible's understanding of God's character does not mean that the shift is uniform and all authors adhere to it. At almost every point in time, differences of perspective coexist. The picture of God as a binary judge never goes away completely; it continues in various iterations into the New Testament.

One of the insightful contributions of Brueggemann's observation is that it further underscores the idea that the divine-human relationship is a genuine one. Our relationship is not a one-way street in which humanity alone is in a state of change while God remains static and unmoved.[78] Some philosophers and theologians have argued that God changes over time, but Brueggemann's notation of this precise shift in God's character opens up a potentially revolutionary pathway for theological imagination. God, like humans, is in a process of understanding how to deal with God's emotions more productively and interact with other conscious beings more beneficially.

As we have seen, many of the authors of the Hebrew Bible understand God to be a being who has emotions, and these emotions profoundly shape God's behavior in good ways and bad. Interaction with humanity helps God come to understand the divine self more deeply. God lashes out in catastrophic violence and then regrets what God did in a fit of rage. God learns from experiences of regret and puts into place a sign to remind God of who God wants to become. Like a human who practices mindfulness or goes on retreat to refine a spiritual discipline, God also works on becoming God's "best self." This is not as crazy as it may sound. This understanding of God that is embedded in the Hebrew Bible is very similar to the idea in the Gospels that Jesus's understanding of himself and this world grew and developed.

One of the most intriguing passages in the New Testament is Hebrews 5:5–10. Verse 8 says that Jesus "learned obedience through what he suffered." That is to say, one of Jesus's central character traits was not fully learned until Jesus experienced intense suffering. Suffering is an emotional state as well as a physical one.[79] Jesus's psychological and emotional life expanded when he underwent extreme pain. Possibly, this deepened Jesus's empathy and compassion for those who are wrongly accused or suffer in any way? Maybe this deepened Jesus's desire to be obedient to God's intentions? Regardless of the specific ways in which Jesus learned obedience, it was something he had to learn. If this was true for Jesus in the New Testament, why would it be any different for the God of the Hebrew Bible?

---

78. Balentine, *Prayer in the Hebrew Bible*, 36.
79. Luke Timothy Johnson, *Hebrews: A Commentary* (New Testament Library; Louisville: Westminster John Knox, 2006), 149–52.

The typical answer is that Jesus was a fusion of the divine and human. Jesus's human nature learned but the divine parts of him did not.[80] This does not seem to square with the passages from the Hebrew Bible that we have examined. Instead of seeing a radical discontinuity between humanity and the divine, the writers of the Old Testament often pictured God as a being who has incredible knowledge but also forgets things, who is patient yet vengeful, and who is just but also capable of jealousy. And, with experience, God can change. Undesirable or unproductive parts of God's character can be mitigated. We will discuss this further in the next chapter, but perhaps one thing we should conclude from the portraits of God's character in the Hebrew Bible is that instead of seeing Jesus's humanlike experience as a temporary add-on to the Christ's divine nature, we should interpret Jesus's humanlike nature as a natural manifestation of the way God has always been.

---

80. Kierkegaard, for example, believed it was only Christ's human nature that learned obedience, not the divine. David R. Law, *Kierkegaard's Kenotic Christology* (Oxford: Oxford University Press, 2013), 73. This discussion of whether Christ's divine nature suffered has been going on for quite some time. Arguments raged already in the fifth century. John O'Keefe, "Impassible Suffering? Divine Passion and Fifth-Century Christology," *Theological Studies* 58 (1997): 39–60.

7

Embracing a Humanlike God

To be any good, theology must start with imagination.[1] Theology is an act that seeks to join together people, planet, and God. It envisions ultimate meaning, finds connections between seemingly disparate things, makes peace where there is animosity, provides a framework for love and acceptance to flourish, and propels people outward from self-focus to care for others. All of this depends upon imagination.[2] It takes creative storytelling to forgive someone who has wronged us. We must move past their most recent acts of harm and imagine that person in the light of love and compassion. Conceptualizing an invisible God requires artistic effort, too—especially so as we live in a capitalistic culture that reduces everything to economic utility. And to make peace we must refuse to accept the status quo of transactionally based relationships and societal hierarchies and courageously forge a new way of interacting with one another. All of these acts depend on our imagination. And our imaginations, like the rest of our thought life, begin with our experience.

It could be no other way. We are not able to imagine things that we have absolutely no connection with. As far out as creativity can reach, there always remains a touchpoint to our particular human experience. Our human experience is the starting point for our imaginations about God. Elizabeth Mburu points out that some of the most important early Christian theologians were based in Africa and that currently a huge percentage of the world's Christians live in sub-Saharan Africa. African hermeneutical tradition has always seen

---

1. "It is at the level of the imagination that any full engagement with life takes place." Amos Niven Wilder, *Theopoetics: Theology and the Religious Imagination* (Philadelphia: Fortress, 1976), 2. This observation is particularly true with theological life.

2. For a more detailed treatment of this, see Willie James Jennings's incredible book, *The Christian Imagination: Theology and the Origins of Race* (New Haven: Yale University Press, 2010).

contextualization—or the human experience of individuals and communities—as a foundational aspect of biblical interpretation.[3]

This idea has far-reaching implications for our thoughts about God. One of the most brilliant theologians of our time, James Cone, captures an idea that has long been a part of Black religious communities but that many Eurocentric theologians have forgotten:

> Whether theologians acknowledge it or not, all theologies begin with experience. Theologians from the Western theological tradition often regard their theology as universal, something that everyone must study. But no theology is universal. . . . We are all particular human beings, finite creatures, and we create our understanding of God out of our experience. Hopefully, our own experience points to the universal, but it is never identical with it. For when we mistake our own talk about God with ultimate reality, we turn it into ideology.[4]

Our interpretations are accurate to a greater or lesser degree. But we do not know whether their accuracy is greater or lesser. Nor do we know which of our interpretations or theological speculations are flat-out wrong. We know that some of them must be. I don't think any reader of this book is egotistical enough to believe that 100 percent of their beliefs about God are totally correct. As James Cone said, our theologies, since they are based upon our experience, are never identical to ultimate reality. Theological ideas, even those we think are based on scriptural passages, are not ultimately based on these texts because we necessarily interpret them out of our experience.[5] As I discussed in chapter 1, there is a degree of slippage between our theological ideas—our understandings of God—and reality. There may be, we hope, overlap between the two, but we are never able to understand God exactly as God is.

This does not mean that we can never speak of God with any confidence at all.[6] Our knowledge of God is partial and flawed, yes, but as long as we

---

3. *African Hermeneutics* (Bukuru, Nigeria: Hippo Books, 2019), 4–5.
4. *Said I Wasn't Gonna Tell Nobody* (Maryknoll, NY: Orbis, 2018), 112. For discussions of the long history of these ideas within Black communities, see Noel Leo Erskine, *Plantation Church: How African American Religion Was Born in Caribbean Slavery* (Oxford: Oxford University Press, 2014); Diana L. Hayes, *No Crystal Stair: Womanist Spirituality* (Maryknoll, NY: Orbis, 2016); and Barbara A. Holmes, *Joy Unspeakable: Contemplative Practices of the Black Church*, 2nd ed. (Minneapolis: Fortress, 2017).
5. Here we should note Umberto Eco's fabulous definition of text as "a machine conceived in order to elicit interpretations." *Interpretation and Overinterpretation*, ed. Stefan Collini (Cambridge: Cambridge University Press, 1982), 85. For a succinct explanation of interpretive complexities of classical texts, see Sandra Marie Schneiders, *The Revelatory Text: Interpreting the New Testament as Sacred Scripture*, 2nd ed. (Collegeville, MN: Liturgical Press, 1999), 151–66.
6. Rubén Rosario Rodríguez, *Dogmatics after Babel: Beyond the Theologies of Word and Culture* (Louisville: Westminster John Knox, 2018), 123.

acknowledge that there are no monopoly interpretations, including our own, we are on safe ground.[7] In fact, every single person on the planet has a degree of confidence in their theological imagination. It could be no other way. It is true that there is no understanding of sacred text and world which can explain everything accurately. Every act of imaging God is contingent and open to correction. Nonetheless, we must live our lives. And we live our lives out of our perception of what is around us, whether that perception is vocalized or not. Our picture of God becomes *functionally real* for us even though it is not entirely true in reality. That is, our ideas of God will always be wrong in various ways. The God we picture in our minds does not exist in reality. It is our own, unique creation that, again, may approximate God more or less. Yet because it is not completely true, our understanding of God is fiction. It does not represent God as God is. However, our understanding of God *becomes real* for us as we use it to guide our lives. There is a confidence that necessarily underlies this legal fiction. We base the decisions of our lives on our foundational beliefs, after all. Our idea of God may change in the next moment, but for now we act on the understanding of God we have in the present.

This means, I believe, that it would be beneficial for us to form our theologies backward, to reverse engineer them with the aim of constructing an image of God that will help us become more compassionate and loving people. If we know that a portion of what we imagine God to be is wrong—and yet we do not know which part is wrong—and therefore our theologies will always and only be *functionally real* and never *absolutely real*, then why shouldn't we use our theological imagination to create a functionally real picture of God that will enable us to become better people? Hoping to arrive at an entirely accurate understanding of God is a fool's errand. It will never happen. Instead of being concerned to get our theology *correct*, we should put more effort into creating a theology that is *beneficial*.

What if we understood the act of theologizing along the lines of Augustine's analogy of interpreting Scripture? Augustine said that interpreting Scripture is like a person walking to another village. The point is to arrive there; whether you accidentally walk through a field or stick to the road the entire way, it makes no difference. And Augustine said that love and charity is the village that people travel to when interpreting the Bible. The same should be true when forming ideas about God. The goal of our theologies is

---

7. There are some explanations that put themselves forward as monopoly interpretations, but these are clearly flawed and on the wane. Wolfgang Iser, *The Range of Interpretation* (New York: Columbia University Press, 2000), 2–5. Two of the more recent monopolistic contenders are the ideologies of white supremacy and capitalism. Both of these interpretations are threadbare, as devastatingly shown by, respectively, Claudia Rankine, *The White Card: A Play* (Minneapolis: Graywolf, 2019), and Arundhati Roy, *Capitalism: A Ghost Story* (Chicago: Haymarket, 2014).

to make us more loving people and to deepen our capacity for charity. Again, this is not to say that efforts to better understand who God is in reality are unimportant, only that what is more important is that we create a functionally real theology that encourages love and compassion which tangibly lessen the suffering of other people. And, I would argue, when we do *that* we actually get closer to an accurate understanding of who God is in reality.[8]

The humanlike portraits of God within the Hebrew Scriptures are helpful in this effort to reverse engineer our theology in at least a couple of ways. One of the challenges for those who wish to consciously practice a religiously informed life is that since God is invisible, it often takes work to make God feel real. Psychological anthropologist Tanya Luhrmann describes this effort as creating a paracosm. A paracosm is an alternate world that exists alongside the reality we humans inhabit. In theological language, the paracosm goes by names such as heaven or the divine realm. As we have seen, the writers of the Bible went to great lengths to describe this paracosm in detail. Furthermore, they imagined that the divine paracosm often intersects with the material world we live in. The humanlike portraits of God give us detailed stories in which the editors of the Bible build out this paracosm and the literary characters of the Bible live in relation to God. Anthropological research has shown that the more detailed the stories that make up a religious tradition and the more the stories relate to our previously experienced events as humans, the more real the paracosm and God seem to be.[9]

In other words, we cannot build a paracosm out of an abstraction. It is very hard to have a relational connection with an analytic description. It is very hard for an analytic description to transform us into more compassionate and loving people. If our understanding of God remains on a propositional level, God will not feel real to us. The humanlike portrayals of God give us detailed stories from which we can imagine a divine paracosm. They also provide experiential touchpoints to our human experience which help make our paracosms feel more real.

The humanlike pictures of God in the Hebrew Scriptures also present underappreciated stories of God that can help us consider our theology from new perspectives. These accounts can help us understand more deeply what it means to be human and, concomitantly, what it means to be God, since

---

8. Jesus seems to imply this on at least two occasions. In Matt. 7:15–20 Jesus says that theological messages, like fruit trees, can be judged on the quality of what they produce. If a tree produces bad fruit, the tree must be diseased. If a theology tends to produce fratricide, division, and hatred, that picture of God must be diseased as well. In John 13:34–35 Jesus gives his disciples a "new command," that they love one another. He goes on to say that outsiders will know whether they genuinely follow Jesus by observing whether the disciples practice love.

9. T. M. Luhrmann, *How God Becomes Real: Kindling the Presence of Invisible Others* (Princeton: Princeton University Press, 2020), 25–57.

humans are created in God's image. Anthropomorphic representations of God can also expose and interrogate unhelpful theologies. They can then suggest new, more beneficial ways to think about God, because they provide material for theological reflection that is often overlooked. And perhaps most valuable of all, the humanlike stories of God in the Old Testament are downright fun.[10] They can be, if we let them, sandboxes of religious imagination.

A THEOLOGY OF HERMENEUTIC ACTIVITY

The only way our religious imaginations will work productively is if many of us shift the way we understand the act of doing theology. Even in the verbs I used, this shift is evident. Theology is not something timeless and static. It is not a repository of truth that modern people carve from the Bible as if we were digging into a deposit of Carrara marble. *Theology is something we do.*[11] It is something we perform.[12] It is something we construct. It is something we act out and embody.[13] It is the set of stories we live by, a process in which we engage with these stories using the mind and the sensory systems of our bodies to form a beneficial vision that guides us as we move through this world. As we experience more of the world, we return to our foundational stories with new eyes, expanded contexts, and a different set of preconceptions. Theology is a circular process that continues to spin at every moment of life.

Our interpretations of our stories and sacred texts change as we bring new experiences and assumptions to the act of reading. These new interpretations will then shift the ways we move through the world. Our engagement with text, world, and God is in a constant state of change because we, as human beings, are constantly changing. Based on the humanlike portrayals of God in the Old Testament, I would argue that God is constantly changing too. God is learning how to control divine emotions more productively, relate better to God's creation, and understand more deeply the divine self. Theology is not something to be laid down and then picked up sometime

---

10. For an entire book on the topic of how play is an integral part of spiritual life and practice, see Ian Edgar, *The God Who Plays: A Playful Approach to Theology and Spirituality* (Eugene, OR: Cascade, 2017).

11. Terry Veling defines "practical theology" along these lines (*Practical Theology: "One Earth as It Is in Heaven"* [Maryknoll, NY: Orbis, 2005], 4–5), but I would argue that all theologies are practiced.

12. Natalie Wigg-Stevenson, *Transgressive Devotion: Theology as Performance Art* (London: SCM, 2021).

13. Like David Dark, I see religion and theology as something everyone does, theist and atheist alike. Dark, *Life's Too Short to Pretend You're Not Religious* (Downers Grove, IL: InterVarsity, 2016).

later, even for God. It is an ongoing act that occurs even when we are not consciously thinking about it.

Just as our definitions of what theology is must change, we must expand our understanding of what biblical interpretation entails. As I discussed in chapter 2, there are contradictory texts in the Hebrew Bible. Some clearly demonstrate that God is very human; others strongly refute this. I have spent most of this book discussing biblical accounts that depict God in anthropomorphic ways. I could have explored verses that speak of God as utterly nonhuman. I do not mean to discount one way of speaking of God in favor of another. Rather, I have tried to highlight an underappreciated view of God that is present in the Bible but absent from much of Eurocentric theology. Instead of choosing one set of biblical accounts over against another, we should instead practice a nonlinear form of reading the Bible.[14]

Instead of harmonizing the many different pictures of God that are contained in the anthology of writings that make up the Bible, we should do what the editors of the Bible did—respect the outlook and integrity of each piece and hold them in coequal tension with each other, appreciating the conflicting understandings of God. Scripture's authors pick up metaphors of God, take from them what is helpful, and discard them later in favor of different patterns of meaning.[15] Very rarely do the editors of the Bible try to make the metaphors they use cohere around the same portrait of God that other authors posit. They understand that the stories they tell of God create their own miniworlds. Stories do not often deliver a full system of beliefs.[16] Rather, stories create emotional associations and vivid mental images, and they construct powerful commitments within those who hear them.[17] Stories do not create theologies, though. People can use them to do this, but the theologian is the one *making* philosophical propositions out of stories. This is all the more true when we create theologies from the Bible, since the Bible is a collection of many, many stories. As David Aaron observes, "A potpourri of texts from the entire corpus will ultimately produce whatever theological construct the interpreter wishes to find. Selecting texts means ultimately creating theology, not describing the ideological world that dominated in the past."[18]

---

14. David H. Aaron, "Shedding Light on God's Body in Rabbinic Midrashim: Reflections on the Theory of a Luminous Adam," *Harvard Theological Review* 90:3 (1997): 313.

15. "Whereas theology wishes to create a god of philosophy, capable of being described in a systematic and coherent manner, the biblical writers pick up and discard metaphors of God, loosely modeling their character on an Oriental potentate." Mary E. Mills, *Images of God in the Old Testament* (Collegeville, MN: Liturgical Press, 1998), 146.

16. P. R. Davies, *Whose Bible Is It Anyway?* (Sheffield: Sheffield Academic, 1995), 82.

17. Patrick D. Miller, *Stewards of the Mysteries of God: Preaching the Old Testament—and the New* (Eugene, OR: Cascade, 2013), 160.

18. Aaron, "Shedding Light on God's Body," 313.

In this book, I have done what Aaron criticizes. I have brought together a selected group of texts to form a theology of divine humanness. However, I have done this not to build a definitive picture of who God is, but to offer an alternative understanding of God that has potential to generate other and more deeply developed portraits of God, which will enable us to better create our paracosms, which will help us more compassionately live in this world. I do think that the theology I have outlined builds upon ideas that are behind many biblical stories. But Aaron is right. By selecting the texts I have examined in this book, I have constructed a theology of God. The act of making theology should neither surprise nor bother us. The real questions we should ask are, Does this theology help us produce a beneficial idea of God? Will this idea of God help us become better and more loving people? I think it can.

FROM MONSTER TO MYSTERY

One of the oldest and most difficult of all theological questions concerns God and the existence of evil. To some degree, this difficulty is manufactured by theologians. In saying this I do not mean that the emotions that go along with suffering are manufactured, but that the extreme philosophical efforts that are required to explain how God is not culpable for calamity, yet at the same time is the cause of it, shouldn't be needed at all.[19] Traditional Eurocentric theologies that attribute a list of *omni*s to God—God knows everything, including future choices; God is all-powerful and can do absolutely anything; God is everywhere, and nothing escapes God's notice or is outside God's power—have a very hard time dealing with the existence of evil. Of course, there are ways theologians try to address this situation, but none are very satisfying. Theologians come up with elaborate and mind-twisting schemes that purportedly demonstrate that God knows everything, causes everything to be, and yet is not responsible for the evil that is done.[20] Instead of expending so much energy formulating a web of abstract propositions, these theologians could have opted for a short play in the sandbox of anthropomorphic reflection. Doing so would not have solved every aspect of the problem of evil, but it could have expanded the breadth of their interactions with it and also saved

---

19. In this discussion I am specifically talking about *calamity*, evil and sufferings that are not punishment but hardships we experience but do not deserve. To be sure, the Deuteronomist attributes certain hardships to breaches in the covenant the Hebrews made with God. This is a separate issue and not what I am presently discussing.

20. One of the most elaborate was the theory of "middle knowledge" put forward by the sixteenth-century Spanish Jesuit Luis de Molina in *On Divine Foreknowledge, Part IV of the Concordia*, trans. Alfred J. Freddoso (Ithaca, NY: Cornell University Press, 1988). I won't even try to explain it here.

many people a lot of unnecessary anguish and mental effort as they came to terms with suffering.

The Hebrew Bible rarely addresses the philosophical roots of the problem of evil.[21] Instead, its authors stress that God is with people as they suffer. Suffering happens, we all know, and rather than spend a lot of time analyzing its source, biblical authors focus their attention on ways of thought that can help us endure it.[22] Hardship is a given, in their minds, an ever-present companion. God is too, though. God hears the Hebrews' cry when they are enslaved in Egypt, and God leaves heaven to come to Egypt and to their aid. God journeys *in the midst* of the people as they travel through the wilderness of Sinai. God's presence is crucial. God is not looking at their difficulties from afar and pulling a string here and there to alleviate them. God enters the time and place of particular people and puts God's body in the middle of their struggles. It is from this position that God promises to guide and protect the Hebrews.[23]

Notice what the idea of an embodied God has done. It entirely changes our relation to God and even God's own perspective. Instead of the divine functioning as a distant, abstract, and transcendent god who has no specific and physical connection to a suffering people, God becomes entrenched in trial as a cosufferer. As the Hebrews wander through the dust, so also does God. This does not address the philosophical questions surrounding the existence of suffering, but it does address them emotionally.

The idea of an embodied God has been very helpful to many folks as they process some of the most extreme acts of evil humanity has experienced. For instance, philosopher Richard Kearney asks, "So where was God in Dachau and Treblinka?" His answer: "Suffering with his people. . . . The only Messiah still credible after the death camps would be one who wanted to come but could not because humans failed to invite the sacred stranger into existence."[24] This is a profoundly anthropomorphic answer that I will unpack further in a moment. We should appreciate that it pictures a God who is, in a humanlike

---

21. Certainly, as James L. Crenshaw has shown, theologians formed theologies based on what they thought was implied in texts within the Hebrew Bible to address the topic of theodicy, but this is an interpretive move that the biblical authors may or may not have endorsed. *Defending God: Biblical Responses to the Problem of Evil* (Oxford: Oxford University Press, 2005).

22. As James Carroll puts it, "God changes the meaning of suffering by joining us in it." *The Truth at the Heart of the Lie: How the Catholic Church Lost Its Soul: A Memoir of Faith* (New York: Random House, 104.

23. "The God of the Old Testament is not an abstract deity ruling everything by immutable decree, but lives alongside his people." John Barton, "The Dark Side of the God in the Old Testament," in *Ethical and Unethical in the Old Testament: God and Humans in Dialogue*, ed. Katherine Dell (New York: T&T Clark, 2010), 130.

24. Richard Kearney, *Anatheism: Returning to God after God* (New York: Columbia University Press, 2011), 61.

way, very limited. And curiously, God's *limitation* is a comfort in this instance because it takes blame for evil away from God. Furthermore, since God is limited, God must travel to the camps to suffer alongside prisoners. This God is not distant or even omnipresent. It is a God who, out of all the places on earth, chose to go to the camps.

According to Kearney's framing, God did not prevent Dachau because God couldn't. God needed an invitation to act, a people whose imagination called God into being in that place. God does not act in unilateral fashion, but as an influencing and persuasive force.[25] More like a benevolent parent than a pluripotent dictator. Some people might find this idea of God lacking. Perhaps they are comforted by imagining a God who is unlimited and universally powerful. A common response to a changing and chaotic world is to imagine a stable and all-powerful god. God's stability gives us a sense of peace and firmness. But this also leaves us with a God who is all-powerful and sovereign over everything, and so on some level Dachau must have received God's blessing. This understanding of God turns God into a moral monster who is, in fact, worse than the human mastermind of the Holocaust. A god who actively causes the world's evil from afar is certainly worth fearing, but worth loving and worshiping? Not at all.

There is much about God that remains mysterious in Kearney's formulation. It does not *explain* the existence of evil as much as it *consoles* people going through it. It is mysterious how the God who (according to confession) created the universe is then particularized as a cosufferer in a concentration camp. Yet a mysterious God is far more preferable, in my opinion, to a monstrous one.

Some people desire a more thorough explanation. Maybe consolation is not all they need. They want a system of thought that can bring philosophical clarity to the problem of evil. For those who want this, more traditional theological discourse is available. My point in this book is that we do not have to choose between the biblical portraits of a humanlike God and the traditional, analytic descriptions of God that theologians offer. Both have their role.

To a large extent, Christians don't know how to deal with this. Jonathan Sacks, the former chief rabbi of the United Kingdom, provides an analogy of how to join together two contradictory approaches to understanding God:

> Monotheism is not an easy faith. Recall the verse from Isaiah: "I form the light, and create darkness: I make peace, and create evil." How can God who is all-good, create evil? . . . The simplest answer is that the bad God does is a response to the bad we do. It is justice, punishment, retribution. This is how Jews coped with the crisis of defeat and exile: "Because of our sins we were exiled from our land." . . . But it is

---

25. Robert Karl Gnuse, *The Old Testament and Process Theology* (Atlanta: Chalice, 2000), 67.

not easy to see God as the source of bad as well as good, judgement as well as forgiveness, justice as well as love. The rabbis did this by understanding the two primary names of God in the Bible, *Elokim* (E) and *Hashem* (J), as referring respectively to God-as-Justice and God-as-Compassion. Niels Bohr, the Nobel Prize–winning physicist, said that he came to his Theory of Complementarity when his son stole something from a local shop. He found himself thinking of his son as a father would do, then as a judge would do, and realized that while he had to think both ways, he could not do so simultaneously. He had to "switch" from one to the other. That is what monotheism asks of its followers: to think of God as both a father and a judge. A judge punishes, a parent forgives. A judge enforces the law, a parent embodies love. God is both, but it is hard to think of both at the same time.[26]

To Sacks's very helpful discussion we should add that the God who is the transcendent creator of the universe is also the embodied prisoner of Treblinka and the homeless wanderer in the book of Numbers. God is both creator and sufferer, but it is hard to think of both realities at the same time. As biblical scholar David Penchansky observes, "There can be no one image of God that works in all circumstances."[27] Sometimes it is helpful to imagine a God of unlimited creative power; at other times a limited and cosuffering God is more beneficial. Unless we embrace the idea that God is multiform, we are in danger of creating a divine monster.

There is another important way of understanding God that we must embrace to avoid creating a divine monster in God and human monsters of us. The humanlike pictures of God represent God as changing and learning over time. God becomes more compassionate and forgiving in the way God relates to the world. This causes God to change God's way of thinking and acting. In chapter 4 we saw that the divine mind changed when God discovered new information. God regretted making Saul king when Saul did not obey what God told Saul to do. So God removed Saul from the throne and appointed David in his place. In the story of Noah, God realized that emotional pique caused God to overreact, and we saw in chapter 6 that God committed to not destroying the earth again. To aid in this commitment, God set up the rainbow as a sign to remind the divine mind of the promise God made. I would like to bring these portraits of God into conversation with the discoveries we made concerning God's gender in chapter 3.

In chapter 3 we examined one of the stipulations in a section of Deuteronomy that translations commonly title "Those Excluded from the Assembly."

---

26. *Not in God's Name: Confronting Religious Violence* (New York: Schocken, 2015), 52–53.
27. David Penchansky, *What Rough Beast? Images of God in the Hebrew Bible* (Louisville: Westminster John Knox, 1999), 94.

This section, Deuteronomy 23:1–8, lists the types of people God prohibited from worshiping with the Hebrews. We looked at the first category on this list, those whose genitalia did not conform to a binary view of sex and gender. Other people were excluded from worship, too. Deuteronomy 23:3–6 prohibits Amonites and Moabites, and 23:7–8 excludes Edomites. We learn from subsequent biblical authors that these folks were later included within the religious community. Inclusion of Moabites is the clearest example. An entire book of the Bible, Ruth, demonstrates this. The protagonist of the story, Ruth the Moabite, becomes part of the Hebrew people. King David himself is descended from her. It is hard to imagine being more included within a people than for the royal line to flow from your body. Such it is with Ruth. And yet this goes against the divine commands in Deuteronomy 23. According to Deuteronomy, Ruth should never have been permitted to join the assembly.

Theologians address this in various ways. Perhaps the most common is to say that the author of Deuteronomy misunderstood God, and the book of Ruth was included in the canon to correct this. Notice what this response does. It says that the human authors of Scripture changed—they corrected a theological mistake—while God remained the same. God always loved nonbinary people and Moabites even though some of the authors of the Bible did not. These human authors of the Bible inserted exclusionary language into God's mouth. Exclusion was never God's intended message. I don't have a bone to pick with this approach on a philosophical or historical level. Yet this interpretive strategy cuts against the grain of the biblical text. This explanation is not how the Bible itself frames the story.

Instead of thinking that humans got the divine message wrong, what if we imagined God's approach is the variable that changed? What if God came to learn that the exclusionary stipulations God gave in Deuteronomy should be done away with? What if, like the instance we examined with Saul, God received new information that caused God's mind to change? The commands in Deuteronomy are framed as coming from God. There is no hedging on the part of the author. The exclusionary stipulations are portrayed as originating from the divine. They are categorical imperatives. There is no hint anywhere in Deuteronomy that these commands are temporary. And yet, God later allows a Moabite to build the Davidic line and nonbinary folks to enter the worshiping community. One way to understand this is to imagine God as evolving into a more compassionate being, changing the divine mind away from exclusion. I don't know which experiences caused this shift in God. Maybe it was when God repeatedly witnessed many Moabites acting with greater love and fidelity than most Hebrews. Ruth was a tipping point. When she came along and showed extreme loyalty and care for her mother-in-law, God finally discarded the command to exclude Moabites. I'm having fun in the theological sandbox, but there is an important theological principle here we should not overlook.

Whatever interpretive paths we choose to take, these examples show that divine commands are not static. It does not matter *in function* whether we understand these commands to have been misunderstood by human authors or assume there were changes within the divine mind. Either way, a handful of biblical commands were done away with. The entire way the people of God operated changed. Instead of composing a list of people to exclude, the people of God are called to embrace and include the people who were once ostracized. This shows us something important about God and about how we as humans should move through the world. We cannot approach Scripture with a goal to strictly enforce the static commands it contains. Instead, we must interact with the Bible in a way that increases our love for others and our inclusion of them within our community.[28] We should not merely adhere to the imperatives we find in Scripture (some of which God might not believe anymore!). The goal of theology construction should be to transform us into an inclusive community that welcomes all into it and makes people feel as though they belong.[29]

I want to push us farther than this, though. The Jewish and Christian Scriptures contain story lines in which God explicitly commands the community God saved to exclude particular groups of people. As the story unfolds, each of these categories of exclusion is walked back. One by one, the people whom God forbade to enter the assembly are welcomed in. The story line of the Bible implies that God changed. Experience, reflection, emotional trajectories, and new information caused God to move to a deeper and more expansive realization of love and compassion. If humans are called to imitate God, then we must view our lives as opportunities to change and more deeply live into love and compassion as well.[30] We are not called to blindly and strictly adhere to abstract laws.[31] We are to interact with particular situations in lov-

---

28. For example, Richard B. Hays, *Echoes of Scripture in the Letters of Paul* (New Haven: Yale University Press, 1989), 191.

29. Willie James Jennings, *After Whiteness: An Education in Belonging* (Grand Rapids: Eerdmans, 2020).

30. The call to act the way God acts is a feature of almost every religion. They may use different vocabulary to explain it, but most religions believe we imitate God (Thomas à Kempis, *The Imitation of Christ*, trans. Robert Jeffery [London: Penguin, 2013]), emulate God (Samer Akkach, *Cosmology and Architecture in Premodern Islam: An Architectural Reading of Mystical Ideas* [Albany: State University of New York Press, 2005], 50), or become attuned to the divine (Michael Fishbane, *Sacred Attunement: A Jewish Theology* [Chicago: University of Chicago Press, 2008]).

31. As Massimo Recalcati notes, Judas was only able to view the world in light of abstract, universal laws. He was unable to understand it when Jesus elevated the particular needs of a person or situation above the supposedly universal laws prevalent in their society. This is one of the main things that led Judas to betray Jesus. *La Notte del Getsemani* (Turin: Einaudi, 2019), chap. 6, "Il tradimento di Giuda," EBL.

ing ways with the goals of reducing suffering and including the other. This commitment opens us to an evolution of consciousness. We are, like God, to move from a place of exclusion and anger-fueled violence to a life of inclusion, radical forgiveness, and compassion. This is the path God is on. If we are not on it too, we are not imitating God.

A BASIS FOR RELATIONSHIP

Not only do humanlike portraits of God help us avoid a monstrous conception of God and become more compassionate people, but they also form generative bases for a relationship with God. At root, anthropomorphic pictures of God describe the divine as a conscious being who is similar to us. This provides a touchpoint on which a relationship can be built. In most cases, the more contact there is between forms of being, the more potential there is for a deep and mutual emotional connection. We are able to have relationships with dogs and cats because, for one reason, they are sentient beings who have emotional lives and innate senses of fairness. We can have a significant relationship with a tree or patch of ground, but the nature of the relationship will be different and more symbolic.[32] Landscapes may recall feelings of one's upbringing and trees may convey a sense of protection. But a person does not have the same kind of encounter with them as with a conscious mind.

Analytic theologies facilitate a relationship with God that is like the one a person has with a tree or landscape. God is conceived in terms of abstract ideas. Omniscient. Transcendent. Triune. One can study this kind of god with the use of logic. One can also feel comforted while resting on the cosmic protection this god provides. But a god of abstract ideas largely remains an object. God is a mental idea one assents to, not a person to know.[33]

Ideas create allegiance, but stories make relationships and define who we are.[34] Psychologist Robert Sternberg studied the way people fall in love and noticed that "we tend to fall in love with people whose stories are the same as ours or similar to our own, but whose roles in these stories are complementary to ours."[35] This is precisely what we have in the biblical stories that present

---

32. For a discussion of the relational dynamics between people and trees, see Owain Jones and Paul Cloke, *Tree Cultures: The Place of Trees and Trees in Their Place* (Oxford: Berg, 2002). For a meditation on relationships with landscapes, see John O'Donohue, *Walking in Wonder: Eternal Wisdom for a Modern World* (New York: Convergent, 2018), 43–66.

33. Thomas Merton, *New Seeds of Contemplation* (New York: New Directions, 1961), 8.

34. Thomas King, *The Truth about Stories: A Native Narrative* (Minneapolis: University of Minnesota Press, 2008), 1–30.

35. *Love Is a Story: A New Theory of Relationships* (Oxford: Oxford University Press, 1998), x.

God as a humanlike figure. We identify with God because we notice that God struggles like we do. God loves, forgives, has regret, gets angry, has remorse, apologizes, swears to never do a ghastly act again and then does it. This connects us to the divine. And yet, God's role in the stories is different from ours in a way that dovetails with us. When humans are unruly, God corrects them. When humans are lonely, God gives them the divine presence. When people need help, God rescues them. And, yes, there are times when God overreacts, and we identify with this, too.

There is mystery and ambiguity in all of this. Just as in Jacob's encounter with the man-god in Genesis 32, it is often difficult to determine the shape of God in the Bible and in the world. Is God able to help in a particular situation or is God's cosuffering presence all that is available? Is God acting in a way that is consistent with divine character or have God's emotions caused rash behavior? How can God be divine and yet humanlike, too? Even these unanswered questions, and myriads of others, have the potential to draw us closer to God. Only clunky stories tie up every loose end. Mystery invites imaginative exploration. It draws us closer and prompts deeper examination.[36] A God who is thoroughly explained and comprehended is boring. A humanlike God is paradoxical and intriguing.

Not only do the biblical pictures of God as a humanlike figure draw us closer to God, but they can also create connections between people of differing religious traditions. Rabbi Irving Greenberg describes how the stories of Jesus helped him understand his Jewish faith more deeply. Jesus provided him a lens through which he could process God's relationship to the Holocaust. As Rabbi Greenberg came to see God in a more human light he gained a greater appreciation for the Christian religion:

> This God had not stopped the Holocaust maybe because this God was suffering and wanted me to stop the Holocaust. As a Jew, I had hesitated to use language of God suffering, because it seems to be a Christian patent. But it's not so. I came to see this has been a central belief of the Jewish people—that God shares our pain. Indeed Christianity was never more Jewish than when it expressed it in those terms—that God suffers with humans.[37]

---

36. "Without ambiguity there are no stories, and without stories, as [Thomas] King notes, there is no truth. Which means that truth, in truth, is multiple." Laurel C. Schneider, "The Gravity of Love: Theopoetics and Ontological Imagination," in *Theopoetic Folds: Philosophizing Multifariousness*, ed. Roland Faber and Jeremy Fackenthal (Perspectives in Continental Philosophy; New York: Fordham University Press, 2013), 121.

37. Rabbi Irving Greenberg, "Easing the Divine Suffering," in *The Life of Meaning: Reflections on Faith, Doubt, and Repairing the World*, ed. Bob Abernethy and William Bole (New York: Seven Stories, 2002), 60.

The notion that God suffers—an anthropomorphic idea if there ever was one—was the entryway for Rabbi Greenberg to a deepened understanding of the central tenets of Judaism. It gave him a context in which he could better wrestle with the existence of evil. The picture of a suffering God also cultivated a heightened affinity with people of other religions. A humanlike understanding of God connected Rabbi Greenberg more deeply to his God, his anguish about evil, his own religion, and Christians.[38]

I will talk more about how Christians can practice something similar to Rabbi Greenberg's approach and deepen their sense of dependence and familial connection to Jewish people, but anyone can picture God in humanlike ways to enhance their relationship with God and others. If we believe that humans are made in God's image, this implies that we will understand God and other people better the more deeply we imagine God in human terms. Let me put that a different way. Regardless of our religious affiliation, if we see a foundational connection between humanity and ultimate consciousness, we must necessarily see ourselves connected to every human person. This is all the more true for those whose outlook is informed by the Jewish and Christian Scriptures. If we are called, as Deuteronomy 6:5 says, to love God with all of our heart, mind, and strength, then at the same time we must love other humans in the same way. There are no exceptions. To love God means to love the primordial human image. Every derivative of this image has an organic connection to the divine. So, *to love other humans is to love God*. To hate other humans is to hate God. God is not merely a distant creator. God is similar to every single human in very basic ways.

In fact, we could say that God's similarity to humanity is greater than God's difference. God displays the same embodied presence, mind, emotions, and character traits that we typically associate with humans. To be sure, God displays these features on a bigger scale than we do, but the divine features are essentially the same. If we are more similar to God than we are different, our imagined human differences—biological sex, nationality, skin color, love preferences, and so on—are so correspondingly small. Each human being is wonderfully unique, but our similarities transcend our differences and bind us to one another. Anthropomorphic understandings of God are some of the most powerful ecumenical bridges there are.

---

38. There is a danger, though, in developing a connection with people formerly regarded as strangers. As Toni Morrison points out, "The danger of sympathizing with the stranger is the possibility of becoming a stranger." *The Origin of Others* (Cambridge: Harvard University Press, 2017), 30. Perhaps this is why many resist embracing the humanlike portrayals of God. Yet there is a vibrant idea common to the Eastern Church of *theosis*, or "being made God." This concept is also prominent in Chinese forms of Christianity. See Alexander Chow, *Theosis, Sino-Christian Theology and the Second Chinese Enlightenment: Heaven and Humanity in Unity* (New York: Palgrave Macmillan, 2013).

A HUMANLIKE GOD AND THE INCARNATION

Theologian Kelly Brown Douglas shows us how an understanding of an incarnate God, a god who has a body and inhabits a particular space, can help us endure some of the most trying times of suffering. Her approach is similar to the one Rabbi Greenberg takes for the Holocaust, but Douglas is a Christian addressing injustices that Black and Latinx people endure in America. She addresses the central questions in Matthew 25:31–46, "But, Lord, where did we see you dying and on the cross?," and reframes Jesus's answer for today's world:

> And Jesus would answer: "On a Florida sidewalk with Trayvon, or at the U.S./Mexican border with an immigrant refused asylum, or in the detention center with a brown child separated from his or her parents, or in a juvenile court with the black child trapped in the poverty-to-prison pipeline. As you did to one of the least of these, you did it to me."[39]

Brown, following the Gospel passage, does not picture Jesus as merely present alongside the marginalized and oppressed person. Jesus is identified *as* that very person. The suffering which that individual experiences, Jesus says, was done to him too. In a mysterious and unexplained way, Jesus is present in the bodies of those who are the targets of injustice. God is present with them, inside their skin, it seems.

This idea should not surprise us. This understanding of God is present in the many passages of the Hebrew Bible that we have studied. God journeys with the Israelites as they plod through the wilderness. God is there, in a tent, in the middle of the camp. God is a pillar of fire by night and a cloud by day. God resides in the ark and is ready to jump out and protect the people of Israel when they are threatened. God lives in the Jerusalem temple, and the people travel there so they can pray. In all of these situations, and many more, the writers of the Old Testament imply that God occupies a particular space and acts in human ways. There is a very small shift in the way that early Christians understood that Jesus was God, but for the most part they merely continue to develop the same line of thought that had its origin in the Hebrew Bible—God is an embodied god.[40] Jesus was, to them, merely the fullest manifestation to date of the humanlike God they read about in the Hebrew Bible.

---

39. This appears in the introduction to Kelly Brown Douglas, *The Black Christ*, 25th anniv. ed. (Maryknoll, NY: Orbis, 2019).

40. Benjamin D. Sommer, *The Bodies of God and the World of Ancient Israel* (Cambridge: Cambridge University Press, 2009), 136.

In this chapter, I explored only a few implications of adding a human-shaped imagination of God into our theological vocabulary. There are many more. Humanlike perspectives of the divine give us new words we can use as we rethink and reformulate our understandings of God as we move forward into an age of profound change and new discoveries.[41] Our theologies will not be relevant, nor should we expect them to be true, if they do not develop as human understandings become more precise and far-reaching. The more we learn about ourselves and the world around us, the more our ideas of God will shift. We should welcome this theological movement as much as we welcome advances in medicine, science, and technology. Stale ideas of the divine are of no help to anyone except, perhaps, to those who benefit from the current structures of power remaining the same.

Imagining God as embodied does something more for us, too. In addition to adding new words to our dictionaries, a human-shaped God provides a helpful counterbalance to theologies that stress God's transcendence. Terry A. Veling's poem "Incarnation" expresses this idea very well:

> For every lofty idea
> You need a lowly idea.
> For every hope and aspiration
> You need a circumstance and situation.
> For every spirit that rises
> You need a spirit made flesh.[42]

The Hebrew Scriptures are a wellspring of lowly ideas, circumstances, and situations, and spirits made flesh. They provide folks who desire it the raw material to think about God anew, to imagine God in different ways, to recover a second naiveté that is informed by contemporary discoveries.[43] The humanlike portraits of God in the Bible can help us remove the expired cans from religion's cupboard and cook with fresh ingredients.[44]

The embodied God of the Hebrew Bible shows us an image of the divine that many people in postindustrial economies have forgotten. As we reread these stories, we discover new ways of imagining ultimate meaning and our place within it. But we shouldn't read the Hebrew Scriptures merely to retrieve a lexicon of the past. Codified and institutionalized religions often

---

41. As I see it, this act of reformulating our understandings of God is two-pronged. It should address the two questions Katherine Sonderegger highlights in her magnificent *Systematic Theology: The Doctrine of God*, vol. 1 (Minneapolis: Fortress, 2015): Who is God? And what is God?

42. This poem appears in Terry Veling's foreword to L. Callid Keefe-Perry, *Way to Water: A Theopoetics Primer* (Eugene, OR: Cascade, 2014), xv. Reprinted with permission.

43. Paul Ricoeur, *The Symbolism of Evil*, trans. Emerson Buchanan (Boston: Beacon, 1967), 349–51.

44. Recalcati, *La Notte del Getsemani*.

mistake their role as conservatories of pristine theologies instead of places where tradition is kept so it may be reconceived and reconfigured for the present. When this ossification takes hold, religions become enforcers of power instead of incubators of love.[45]

We should be inspired by the writers of the Bible to courageously go forward and create new pictures of who God is, discover new ways of imagining the divine that expand our theological dictionaries. Then we can use these new ideas, in concert with the old ones we have inherited, to construct theologies that will help us become more loving and compassionate people. We will be better equipped to join with God in the transformative movement from exclusion to inclusion. We will refuse to distance ourselves from those who are suffering and instead be present with them, seeking for them restorative justice instead of vengeance. In short, we will be doing theology, enacting and embodying it with our entire selves.

---

45. Theology itself should be an act of liberating love, as eloquently demonstrated by Robyn Henderson-Espinoza, *Activist Theology* (Minneapolis: Fortress, 2019), and Ada María Isasi-Díaz, *Mujerista Theology: A Theology for the Twenty-First Century* (Maryknoll, NY: Orbis, 1996).

Index of Biblical References

OLD TESTAMENT

Genesis
1:1–2:4a	33
1:6–7	58
1:27	78–79, 85, 86–87
1:28	107
1–2	35, 37
2:7	54
2:18–19	33–34
3:8	28, 28n2, 112
3:9–13	113
3:19	32n17
4:1	84
4:1–16	114
5:1–3	79
5:2	86
6:1–4	115n68, 147
6:6	29–32, 38, 43
7:11	58n11
8:2	58n11
8:21	116–17, 149–50, 185
9	132
9:12–16	185
9:15	161
10:32	107–8
11	107–8, 112
11:4	108
11:5	59, 108
12–17	132
18:23–25	163
18:28	164
22	106
22:1	104
32	202
32:24 (25 Heb.)	76
32:30	77
35:7	67
35:14	68

Exodus
3	56, 72
3:7–9	112
12:8–9	32
17:7	105
19–24	132
19:18	56
20:5	172–74, 176
21:23–25	170
22:7 (6 Heb.)	170
24:15–18	56
25	58n12
25:10–22	64
26:20	87
28:30	112
32:12–14	115
32:14	28n2
33	63n23
33:23	111
34:5	162
34:14	176

Leviticus
8:8	112
21:20	88
24:19–20	141

Numbers
2	63
4:15	151
9:15–23	64
10:33–36	64–65
10:35	65n30
12:5–10	62–63, 64
13–14	140n52
14:20–25	180–82
23	28
23:19	30, 32, 38, 43, 115, 118

Deuteronomy
1:26–27	140
1:31	186
5:9	172–73
6:4–9	128
6:5	203
7:9	128
8:2	106
8:5	186
10:14	58
10:14–15	134
10:17–19	134–35
16:7	32
23:1	88
23:1–8	199
23:12–14	109–10
24:16	173
32:11–12	81
32:18	81, 84
33:16	72
33:26	71

Joshua
24:26–7	68

Judges
6:11	68
15:7	169

1 Samuel
1:3	73
14	129
15	115
15:11	119–20
15:29	115n66, 118–20
15:35	119–20
18:1	129
18:3	129
20:16–23	131
28:13–14	55

2 Samuel
1:26	130
6:6–7	150–53
6:7	153
15:8	73
22:11	71
24:10–17	58n12

1 Kings
3:9	97
8:52	186
12:28	69
22:19	58n12
22:23	119n73

2 Kings
5:12–19	60–62
7:2	58n11
10	69
13:6	69–70
19:35	58n12
21	182 n64
24:4	182

2 Chronicles
6:40	186
34:7	158
35:13	32, 32n15

Job
1–2	103, 139, 160
1:6	58n12
1:6–12	58n12
2:1	58n12
16:9	140
26:11	58
42:10	160

Psalms
5:5	143
11:5	143
18	111
18:11	71
21:2 (3 Heb.)	99
25:11	179
25:16–18	179
33:13–15	58
50	71
51:10 (12 Heb.)	99–100
68:1	65, 65n30
68:7	65
68:29	66
76:65	50
103:8	158
104:15	97–98
105:7–11	179
110:4	115
115:16–17	57
130	xvii
139:21–22	141
145:8–9	133

Proverbs
6:16–19	143
6:20–35	172–73
6:32	99
6:34	172
15:3	28
16:23	99
26:4–5	34

Song of Songs
1–8	84

Isaiah
1:14	163
1:29–30	68
5:25	146
6:1	74–76
6:2	58n12
6:1–5	74n52
19:1	71
24:18	58n11
40:2	162, 170–71
42:13–14	91
42:14	81
49:15	81, 179–80
54:7–9	148–50
55:6	60
56:3–5	88–89
59:17	174–75
66:1	76
66:13	81

Jeremiah
1:16	180
2:1–3:5	180
4:28	115
5:7–18	170n34
8:18–9:1	137–38
9:3 (2 Heb.)	138
17:9–10	114
31:3–4	135
31:20	136
31:31–34	180, 183–84

Lamentations
3:42–44	182–83

Ezekiel
1:26	74
1:26–28	74n52
10	58n12
18:1–4	173
18:19–20	174

Daniel
7	74n52
7:9	74
8:16	58n12
9:21	58n12
12:1	58n12

Hosea
1–14	84
4:13	68
12:4 (5 Heb.)	77–78
12:11	69n38
13:8	81

Amos
9:1	54, 56

Jonah
3:10	115, 116n66

Micah
5:11–14	168–69

Zephaniah
1:1–18	175–76

Zechariah
1:7–17	109, 112
1:14–15	174

Malachi
1:2–5	141–42

NEW TESTAMENT

Matthew
6:13 — 104n34
25:31–46 — 204

Luke
11:4 — 104n34

Acts
8 — 89–90
17:28 — 44–45

Romans
1:18 — 145

1 Corinthians
13:2 — 20
13:4–7 — 20
13:12 — 9

Hebrews
5:5–10 — 187

James
2:19 — 19

1 John
3:7–10 — 20

Revelation
7:9 — 90

RABBINIC LITERATURE

MISHNAH

Avot
1:1 — xviii
5:4 — 103n29

BABYLONIAN TALMUD

Sanhedrin
89b — 103n31

MIDRASH

Genesis Rabbah
8:1 — 86–87

MESOPOTAMIAN SOURCES

Enmerkar and the Lord of Aratta
1 — 12

Enuma Elish
1–2 — 54, 71

Laws of Hammurabi
xlvii 79–xlviii 2 — 59n13

Sumerian Temple Hymns
1–2 — 35

OTHER ANCIENT SOURCES

Kutamuwa — 96–97
Odyssey — 103n31
Euthyphro — 158–59

Index of Subjects

Aaron, 62–63, 151–52
Aaron, David, 37, 48–50, 194–95
Abana (modern-day Barada River), 61
Abel, 80n70, 114
Abraham, 120
  descendants of, 134
  God's covenant with/promises to, 132, 179
  and Isaac, 103–4, 112–13
  as prophet, 164–65
  and Sodom, 163–65
Absalom, 73
abundance, 71, 167
accommodation, 30–31, 43, 149
actions/God's actions, 150, 158–59, 161, 166–68, 176
  call to act the way God acts, 200–201
  See also specific topics, e.g., regret/divine regret
Adam, xivn11, 28, 33–34, 80, 86–87, 113, 117
adultery, 99
affect. *See* emotion/emotions
Africa, 139
  African hermeneutical tradition, 189–90
  sub-Saharan, 189–90
African Americans, 204
  Black religious communities, 190
agape, 20
agency, 100
Ahab, 69
altar, 54, 56, 67–68, 117–18, 149, 185
Alter, Robert, 107n40
Althaus-Reid, Marcella, xiiin8
ambiguity, 39, 85, 131n24, 179, 202

America, 204. *See also* Latin America; North America; *specific topics*
Amonites, 199
Amorites, 140
Amos, 54, 56
analytic theologies, 201
androgyny, 86–87
angels, 58n12, 75, 77, 87
  fallen, 147
  male, mating with human women, 116n67, 117n68, 147
  punishment for, 116
anger/divine anger, 28, 143–53
  jealousy and, 174–76
  See also regret/divine regret; wrath, divine
animals, 12–13, 33, 79, 201
  and perceiving God, 8
  as perceiving numbers, 13n29
anthropomorphisms, 46–48
anxiety, 14. *See also* fear
apology, 146, 160, 178, 202
Aquinas, Thomas. *See* Thomas Aquinas
Aram, 60–61
arguments, 15–16
Aristotle, 5, 41, 106n39, 124, 157
ark, Noah's, 116, 149, 185
ark of the covenant, 62, 64–66, 150–52, 164, 204
Asherah, 70n39, 71
asherah pole, 70–72
Assyrians, 99, 136
atheism, 193n13
attributes, actions vs., 166
Atum, 54
Auerbach, Erich, 103n31

Index of Subjects

Augustine of Hippo, xvii, 19–20, 24, 46, 108, 191
Auld, A. Graeme, 131n24
authority, 60, 78–79

Baal, 69–71, 81n73, 180
Babel, tower of, 107–8, 114
Babylon, 59
Babylonia, 71, 182–83
Babylonian exile, 148–49
Babylonian invasion, 148–49, 183
Baggio, Giosuè, 10–11
Balaam, 118–19
Balak, 118
Baldwin, James, 18n39
Balthasar, Hans Urs von, 46n55
baptism, 89, 132n26
Barr, James, 48n60, 74n52
Barstad, Hans, 167n28
Barth, Karl, 53n1, 87–88, 132n27
beauty, xii, 38, 40, 121n1, 125, 127, 144n60, 153
ben Eleazar, Jeremiah, Rabbi, 86–87
Beowulf, 145
Berger, John, xii, 50n67
Bergmann, Claudia, 91n113
"best self," God as becoming, 164, 187
Bethel, 69–70, 72
Bible
    human authors of, 199
    metaphors for, 29n5
    study, point/goal of, 18–19
    translators, 29
    witness, biblical, xv, 10, 186
    See also hermeneutics/ hermeneutic activity; New Testament; Old Testament
birth/birthing terminology, 81, 91
Black Americans, 204
Black religious communities, 190
blood, 95–96
body/bodies, 54–57
    and change of ideas, 18
    mind-body connection, 100–102
    rḥm-love and, 133
    See also embodiment; lower body
body of God, 53–92
    embodiment, 74–81
    gender and sex, 81–92

    localized presence, 57–60
    temporary theophanies, 72–74
Bohr, Niels, 198
bowels, 93, 98, 136
brain, 124–26. *See also* mind/minds
breath/breathing, 96, 102
Breed, Brennan, 36
Brettler, Marc, 47n59
Brindled Moor (Outer Hebrides, Scotland), xi, xiii, xvii, 14
Brown Douglas, Kelly, 92n116, 204
Brueggemann, Walter, 37n25, 104n34, 148, 186–87
Buddhism, 177n52
buttocks, 111

Cain, 80n70, 114
calamity, 137, 195n19
calves, golden, 69–70, 72
Calvin, John, 30–33, 36, 104, 115
Cambodia, 139
Canaan, 67, 71–72, 132, 146
    Canaanite religion, 71–72
capitalism, 189, 191n7
Carroll, James, 196n22
Carroll, Robert, 182n66
Cassuto, Umberto, 34n18
castration, 88
Celtic tradition, 94n4
Chalmers, David, 9n19
change, 17–18
    "best self," God as becoming, 164, 187
    God as constantly changing, 115–20, 186, 193, 198
    healing, 89–90
    of mind/of God's mind, 30, 115–20
    See also transformation
character/divine character, 157–88
Character of Consciousness, The (Chalmers), 9n19
charity, 19–22, 25, 191–92
    as goal of biblical study, 19
    as radical love, 21
    See also love
Chinese Christianity, 203n38
Chirimuuta, Mazviita, 9–10
choices, 102–6. *See also* free will
Chretien, Jean-Louis, 108
Christ. *See* Jesus Christ

Christianity, xvi–xviii, 81–82, 84, 128, 132n26, 200, 203
  Abraham as prophet, 164–65
  Christian community, 89–90
  a Christian way of moving through the world, 9
  Eastern Church/Chinese forms of, 203n38
  in sub-Saharan Africa, 189–90
  Western, 19, 46
Christology, 115n63, 188n80
Chronicles, books of/the Chronicler, 32–36, 158, 182
climate change, 44
cloud/clouds, 71–72, 74, 185
  God in/God shielded by, 63–65, 162, 182, 204
  of smoke, 56
  of unknowing, 5n10
colonial theology, xiiin8, 89
colonization, 11n26
colors, 4–5, 8–9, 123
community, Christian, 89–90
compassion, 116, 123, 127, 133–35, 148, 179, 183, 187, 189, 191–92, 195, 198–201, 206
  rḥm, 133
  See also forgiveness; love; mercy, divine
Complementarity, Theory of (Niels Bohr), 198
concentration camps, 196–97. See also Holocaust
Cone, James H., xviin19, 190
confirmation bias, 14
conscience, 78, 99, 173
consciousness, 79–80
contemplative Christians, 19n41
contemplative prayer, 5
contradiction, 28, 31, 34–39, 197–98
Conzelman, Hans, 132n27
Cooper, John W., 94n8
Cornwall, Susannah, 90–91, 176
Cornwall, UK, xiii
courage, 189
covenants/divine covenants, 128–35, 142
  with Abraham, 132
  Deuteronomistic, 171
  with the Hebrews, 135, 195n19
  with Moses/Sinaitic, 64, 132, 134
  with Noah, 133, 161, 175, 185, 198

creation, 33, 80, 186, 193
  God as creator, 198, 203
  God's love for, 132–34
  reason for, 127, 154–55
  See also earth; universe
creation accounts, 33, 54
  Enuma Elish, 54, 71
Creel, Richard E., 31n10
Crenshaw, James L., 196n21
crime, 16–17
Crockett, Clayton, xvi
curse/curses, 87, 103, 117–18, 141, 149, 167, 171

Dahood, Mitchell, 98n18
Damascus, 61
Dan, 69–70, 72
Daniel, 74
Dark, David, 193n13
darkness, 197
Darwin, Charles, 80n70, 121–23, 145, 153
David, 70, 99, 199
  and Jonathan, 129–32
  as King, 198–99
Davis, Angela, 24
Davis, Ellen, 160–61
death, 57, 87, 90–91, 96–97, 124, 168
death camps, 196–97. See also Holocaust
Deborah, 67–68
Decalogues, 65–66, 162, 172–74, 177
deception, 11n26, 119
defecation, 110
De La Torre, Miguel A., 104n33
Democritus, 2
Descartes, René, 94, 96, 115
desire, 100, 133n29
  affective, 153–55
  See also erotic passion
Deuteronomistic covenants, 171
Deuteronomy, book of, 64, 72, 81, 128, 134, 140–41, 167–68, 186, 195n19, 198–99
diaspora people of God, 148
Diaz, Hernan, 3n4
discernment, 81
divorce, 130
Douglas, Kelly Brown, 92n116, 204
Dubus, Andre, xv
Dulin, John, 93n1
Dunbar, Erica Armstrong, 184n70

Index of Subjects

Eagleton, Terry, 20–21
earth, 80n70, 107–10
  as good, 155
  See also creation
Eastern Christianity, 203n38
Eastern Orthodox theologians, xviin21
Eco, Umberto, 41, 190n5
ecumenism, 203
Eden, garden of, xivn11, 28, 112–13, 117, 128
  the new Eden, 128, 132n26
Edomites, 142, 199
Egypt, 54, 105–6, 112, 132, 134, 140–41, 180–81, 196
Eichrodt, Walther, 95–96
Einstein, Albert, 27–28, 37
ejaculation, 93
El, 71, 146n64
election, divine, 142
Elisha, 61–62
ʾĕlōhîm, 55–56, 62, 77, 82
Elohim tradition, 84
embodiment, 39, 74–81
  embodying theology/theology as embodied practice, 38, 206
Emlyn-Jones, Chris, 158n4
emotion/emotions, 122–28
  animals and, 79n68
  of God, 28, 121–55, 193
  reason and, 153–55
  See also specific emotions, e.g., sadness
Endlösung in Nazi Germany, 17
enemies, 21, 65, 81, 109, 111, 131, 137–38, 140–43, 168, 175
English language, 12, 144
Enheduanna, 34–35
Enlil temple, 35
Enmerkar (Mesopotamian king), 12
Enuma Elish, 54, 71
environment, 44–45
Ephraim, 136
Epimenides, 45
Epirus, 66
Eridu, 35
Erisman, Angela Roskop, 181n62
erotic passion. *See* sexual/erotic love
Esau, 142
Eslinger, Lyle, 75

Ethiopian eunuch, 89–90
eunuchs, 88–90
Eurocentric theologies, 113, 115, 190, 194–95
Euthyphro, 158–59, 161
Evagrius, 145
Eve, 28, 33, 84n88, 86–87, 113, 117
evil, 28, 116, 137, 143, 147, 149, 177
  existence of, 195–97, 203
  good and bad, source of, 198
  See also specific topics, e.g., free will; Holocaust
exclusion/exclusionary language, 199
excrement, 110
Exodus, book of/the exodus story, 106–7, 158
eyes/eyesight, 4–5, 8–10, 108, 111
Ezekiel, 74, 136, 173–74, 177

faces/face of God, 77–78, 111
faith
  of Abraham, 103–4, 112–13
  See also Christianity
fear, 14n32, 122–24, 176
  of God (fearing God), 197
  kua, 123–24
feelings. *See* emotion/emotions
Feldmeier, Reinhard, 145–46
feminist theology, 81–82
fire theophany, 72, 204
firmament, 58
flood, the great, 116–17, 132, 147–50, 161, 175, 185
  rainbow after, 161, 185
flourishing, 15, 23, 189
foreigners, 88–89, 135. *See also* immigrants; strangers
forgetting/divine forgetting, 183–88
forgiveness, 202
  divine, 177–84, 198
  forgiving others, 178, 189
freedom, 42, 53n1
free will, 23–25, 103–6
Fretheim, Terence E., 55n6, 104n35, 105n38, 108n45, 138n47
friendship, 38, 130
  of David and Jonathan, 129–32

garden of Eden. *See* Eden, garden of
Geeraerts, Dirk, 161

Index of Subjects

gender
　and exclusion from worship, 199
　God and, 28, 81–92
　intersex, 85–87, 89–90, 92, 102
Genesis, book of, 28, 33, 86–88, 116.
　See also individual names, e.g., Noah;
　specific topics and events
Genesis Rabbah, 86
genitals, 75, 81n73, 84, 88, 93, 136
genocide, 17, 139, 149. *See also* flood, the
　great; Holocaust
Gersonides, 106n39
Gerstenberger, Erhard, 28n4
Ghana, 93n1
giants, 116n68, 147
Gideon, 68
global warming, 44
God
　as becoming "best self," 164, 187
　character of, 157–88
　as constantly changing, 115–20, 186,
　　193, 198
　as creator, 198, 203
　emotions of, 121–55, 193
　face of, 77–78
　as father, 82, 198
　full-orbed, 23–25
　home of, 66
　humanlike and not, 27–51, 202
　as hyperobject, 44–46
　imitation of, 200–201
　the Incarnation, 21, 204–6
　knowing/our knowledge of, 18–22, 38,
　　190–91
　as learning/the way God learns,
　　110–15, 198
　limitation of, 197
　as multiform, 198
　as parent, 186, 198
　presence of, 6, 56–60, 64, 108
　real vs. the God of our imagination,
　　2–11
　See also body of God; image of God;
　　mind of God; Trinity/Trinitarian
　　thought; Yahweh; *specific attributes,*
　　e.g., transcendence; *specific topics,*
　　e.g., forgiveness; love; mercy, divine
golden calves, 69–70, 72
Goldingay, John, 105n38
Goliath, 129

good/goodness
　and bad, source of, 198
　and justice, 159–61
　the world as, 155
Gospels, 37, 187
grace, 83
　cheap, 182
Greece, ancient, 66–67, 158–59. *See also*
　Plato; Socrates
Greenberg, Rabbi Irving, 202–4
Gregory of Nyssa, 28n3, 46, 87
grief. *See* sadness
groupthink, 14
guilt, 23
Guthrie, Stewart Elliot, 46n56

Habakkuk, 140n50
Hall, Douglas John, 79n68
Halton, Charles, 169n31
Hammurabi's Laws, 59n13
Hamori, Esther J., 76n57
Hanh, Thich Nhat, 177n52
Hartshorne, Charles, 8
Hasel, Gerhard F., 29n6
hate/hatred, 139–43, 169, 203
healing, 89–90
Heaney, Seamus, 145
heart, 97–100, 108
　"My heart is sick," 138
heaven, 28, 35, 47, 53–54, 56–60, 62–64,
　　66–68, 71, 76–77, 82, 90–91, 108–9,
　　111–14, 134, 192, 196
　home of God, 66
　See also throne, divine
Hebrew Bible. *See* Old Testament
Hebrew language, 41n39, 144
Hebrews (people), 84, 105–6, 109, 120,
　　128, 134–35, 140–41, 173–74, 196,
　　199
　God's covenant with, 135, 195n19
　See also Israelites; Moses
Hebron, 73–74
Hegel, Georg Wilhelm Friedrich,
　133n29
Heidegger, Martin, xiv
heresy, xiiin8
hermeneutics/hermeneutic activity,
　37–38, 43, 115, 189–90
　a theology of, 193–95
Heschel, Abraham Joshua, 59–60

Index of Subjects 215

ḥesed, 133
hierarchies, 78–79, 82, 107, 115n62, 189
holiness, 136
Holloway, Richard, 22, 23, 170n33, 177n52
Holocaust, 17, 21, 139–40, 196–98, 202, 204
Holy of Holies, 62, 64
Holy Spirit, 45
home of God, 66
homosexuality, 130
Hopi people, 12
Hosea, 77–78, 81
human beings/humanity, 107n43
   the human experience, 13, 45, 47, 55n7, 91, 94, 122, 144, 189–90, 192
   overestimating themselves (ourselves), 107n43
   See also creation; image of God; *specific topics and attributes, e.g.*, emotion/emotions
Hume, David, 47
humiliation, 11n26
Hunter, Trent, 29n5
Hyde, Lewis, 183n69
hyperobjects, 44–46

ideas, 17–18, 201
   change in, 17–18
identity, human, 91. *See also* gender
ideology, 15, 190
idolatry
   golden calves, 69–70, 72
   See also Baal; paganism/pagan worship
image of God, 47–48, 55–56, 78–82, 85, 87–88, 91, 154, 191, 198, 202
imagination, 38, 42, 45, 122, 125, 189, 202
   imagining God/theological, xiii, xv–xvi, 2–11, 38, 125, 134, 158, 181, 187, 189, 191, 193, 197, 205
Imagining God: Dominion as Stewardship (Hall), 79n68
imitation of God, 200–201
immanence, divine, xvii
immigrants, 21, 204. *See also* foreigners; strangers
immutability, divine, 115, 196n23
impassibility, divine, 31
impassible, God as, 31

imprisonment, 204. *See also* concentration camps
Incarnation, the, 21, 204–6
"Incarnation" (Veling), 205
"An Indecent Proposal: The Theological Core of the Book of Ruth" (Halton), 169n31
indigenous people, 12, 80n70
infinite God, idea of, 46
information, 3n4. *See also* knowledge
injustice, 145, 166, 170n33, 175, 204
intelligence
   human, 3n4
   plant, 79n66
   See also knowledge; mind/minds
intersex, 85–87, 89–90, 92, 102
In the Distance (Diaz), 3n4
Isaac, 103–4, 112–13, 179
Isaiah/book of Isaiah, 60, 68, 74–76, 88–89, 91, 99, 146, 148–50, 162–63, 170–71, 174–75, 179, 186, 197
Isidore of Seville, 40
Islam, 164–65
Israel
   God's love for, 84
   the name, story behind, 76
   as new Eden, 128
   tribes of, 63
Israelites, 47–48, 50, 53–54, 56–57, 64, 67, 81, 95, 102, 111–12, 134–36, 142–44, 180, 186, 204
   God's relationship with, 81, 128, 181
   See also Hebrews (people)

Jacob, 63, 67–68, 86, 179
   encounter with the man-God, 76–78, 202
   and Esau, 142
   and Rachel, 129n19
James, book of, 19–20
jealousy, 171–77
Jehoahaz, king of Israel, 69
Jehoiakim, king of Judah, 182
Jehu, 69–70, 72
Jennings, Willie James, 89–90, 189n2
Jeremiah ben Eleazar, Rabbi, 86–87
Jeremiah/book of Jeremiah, xviii, 114, 135–38, 180, 183
Jeroboam, 69–70
Jerome, 19n44

Index of Subjects

Jerusalem, 138–39, 162–63, 170, 174. *See also* temple, Jerusalem
Jesus Christ, 91, 115n63, 202
   human/divine nature of, 187–88
   the Incarnation, 21, 204–6
   "new command" to love, 192n8
Jews. *See* Israelites; Judaism
Jezebel, 69
Job/book of Job, 103, 139–42, 160–61, 184, 186
Johnson, Elizabeth, xvin17, 7, 83–84
Johnson, Mark, 16
Jonathan, 129–32
Jordan River, 61, 132n26
joy, 124, 184
Judah (son of Jacob and Leah), 63
Judah, kingdom of, 70, 73, 99, 119n73, 130, 137, 163, 168, 171, 182–83
   Babylonian exile (or templeless period), 148–49
Judah, Rabbi, 164
Judaism, xvii–xviii, 81–82, 84, 128, 132n26, 200, 203
   Abraham as prophet, 164–65
   and book of Deuteronomy, 128
   diaspora people of God, 148
   exodus story, 106–7
   the Holocaust, 17, 21, 139–40, 196–98, 202, 204
   Maimonides, xivn11
   See also Hebrews (people); Israelites
Judas, 200n31
judgment, divine, 145nt63, 149, 166, 198
Julian of Norwich, 83
Jung, Carl, 184
Jung, Patricia Beattie, 91n112
justice, 158–66
   Abraham's sense of, 163–65
   divine, 158–62, 166, 168
   objective, 168
   restorative, 146, 150, 167, 206

Kalimi, Isaac, 32–33
Kant, Immanuel, 3
Käsemann, Ernst, xvi
Katumuwa, 96–97
Kearney, Richard, 134n33, 196–97
Kessler, John, 29n5
Keynes, John Maynard, 166
Kierkegaard, Søren, 184, 188n80

Kim, Grace Ji-Sun, 115n62
King, Thomas, 202n36
Kings, books of, 72, 182–83
Knausgaard, Karl Ove, 10n23
Knierim, Rolf, 97–100
knowledge, 47, 111
   God's, 110–15, 188, 198
   knowing God, 38, 190–91
   learning/the way God learns, 110–15, 198
   "middle knowledge," 195n20
   things God doesn't know, 102–7
   See also mind of God; *specific topics, e.g.*, hermeneutics/hermeneutic activity
Kohathites, 151
Koyama, Kosuke, 180n59
Kraus, Hans-Joachim, 98n19
kua, 123–24
!Kung culture, 124
Kwok, Pui-lan, 38

Lakoff, George, 16
Lamentations, book of, 182–83
language/languages, 11–18, 28, 99, 144–45
   Babel, tower of, 107–8, 114
   after death, 90
   influence of, 15–17
   purpose of, 11–15
   source of, 99
   translation of, 148
   See also metaphor/metaphors; *specific languages/descriptions*
Lapsley, Jacqueline E., 135n36
Latin America, 139
Latinx Americans, 204
law, divine, 173n42. *See also* Decalogues
laws, 123, 200
Leah, 63
legs, God's, 76
Leopardi, Giacamo, 42
Levites, 63
Libet, Benjamin, 100–101
lies/lying, 118–19
light, 5, 27–28, 197
loneliness, 155, 202
longing, 100. *See also* desire
Lord's Prayer, 104n34
Lourdes, 73–74

Index of Subjects

love, 128–35, 202, 206
  and doing theology, 206
  and forgiving others, 189
  for God, 197, 203
  God's, for creation, 132–35, 200–202
  and hate, 142
  and imitating God, 200–201
  "new command" to, 192n8
  New Testament paradigm of, 21
  for others, 203
  rhm, 133
  sexual/erotic, 84, 129–31, 135
  and similar stories, 201
  for strangers/foreigners, 134–35
  See also charity; compassion; friendship
lower body, 93, 98, 109–11, 136
  nakedness, 5n10, 110, 113
  sexual organs, 75, 81n73, 84, 88, 93, 136
Luhrmann, Tanya, 192
Luz, 67–68
lying/lies, 119

Maimonides, xivn11
Malachi, 143
Manasseh, 182
Mandela, Nelson, 178
Marduk, 54, 68, 71
marginalized/oppressed persons, 204
marriage, 129–30
Martin, Trayvon, 204
Mary, 22, 74
Masoretic Text, 72n48, 138
matter, 3n4
Maudlin, Tim, 14
Mburu, Elizabeth, 189
McCabe, Herbert, 127
McCarraher, Eugene, 66n32
McGilchrist, Iain, 13, 40n34
memory/God's memory, 179–80
  forgetting/divine forgetting, 183–88
  of plants, 79n66
men, 82
mercy, divine, 116, 133, 136, 152, 158, 162, 173, 182. *See also* compassion
Merton, Thomas, xvi
Mesopotamia, 4, 12, 35, 58–59, 68, 71, 112–13, 129n19, 138
metaphor/metaphors, 39–43, 47–51, 194
metaphysics, 19, 67

metonymy, 95
Micah, 168–70
Micaiah, 119n73
Michels, Barry, 24n56
Middlemas, Jill, 148n70
midwife, God imagined as, 81
Miller, Patrick D., 145n63
Mills, Mary E., 194n15
mind/minds, 94–100
  change of, 117–19
  mind-body connection, 100–102
mind of God, 93–120
  changes in, 28, 30, 115–20
  and goings-on of earth, 107–10
  things God doesn't know, 102–7
  the way God learns, 110–15, 198
  See also specific topics, e.g., emotion/emotions; memory/God's memory; regret/divine regret
miracles, 74
Miriam, 62–63
misogyny, 82n81
Moabites, 199
modesty of God, 76
Molina, Luis de, 195n20
monastic Christians, 19n41
monotheism, 197–98
monster, attributes of, 195–201, 198
Morrison, Toni, 21, 203n38
Morton, Timothy, 45
Moses, 56, 62–65, 72, 77, 111–12, 140, 162, 180–81
  God's covenant with, 64, 132, 134
mother, God as, 83
motivation, 155
Mount Sinai. *See* Sinai, Mount
Mount Zion *See* Zion/Mount Zion
Muslims (Islam), 164–65
mystery, 195–202
mystical presence of God, 6, 108
mysticism, xvi, 5n10
mythology, 2, 159

Naaman, 60–62
Nacon, 150
nakedness, 5n10, 110, 113
nationality, 90
Native Americans, 12, 80n70
nature/the natural world, 66–67. *See also* creation

Nazi Germany, 17. *See also* Holocaust
Nemet-Nejat, Karen, 129n19
Nephilim, 116n68, 147
New Testament, xv, 21, 89, 132n27, 187.
    See also Gospels
nḥm (change of mind), 117–19
Nicene Creed, 82n83
Niceno–Constantinopolitan Creed, 87
Nippur, 35
Noah, 116–17, 132–33, 147–50, 164–65
    ark of. *See* ark, Noah
    God's covenant with, 133, 161, 175, 185, 198
non-resistance, 170n33
North America, 93, 123
nose
    becoming hot, 146–47, 153
    "long of nose," 162–63
Not in God's Name: Confronting Religious Violence (Sacks), 134n31
nqm ("to avenge"), 167, 169–70
numbers, animals' ability to perceive, 13n29
Numbers, book of, 30–31, 65, 118, 198

obedience, 134, 167, 187
    of Abraham, 103–4, 112–13
O'Connor, Kathleen M., 137
Old Testament, 41, 47–48, 53–62, 66–67, 72–75, 81–82, 88, 94–98, 100, 102, 110–13, 135–36, 142–48, 159–67, 172–88
    humanlike presentations of God of, xii–xviii, 2, 28–30, 35–38, 51, 54, 76, 78, 117, 138, 165, 186–87, 192–94, 196–98, 204–6
    Pentateuch, 128
    theology, 28–30, 50–51, 81, 85, 95, 97, 128
    See also prophets; *specific books, names, topics, and events*
omniscience, divine, 38, 59, 184, 201
oppression, 83, 112, 204
oracle, 54, 118, 163, 175
Origen, 166
Ó Tuama, Pádraig, 21–22
Our Lady of Lourdes, 73–74

paganism/pagan worship, 68–71, 173–75, 180. *See also* idolatry
pain. *See* suffering

paracosm, 192
Parallax View, The (Žižek), 6
particles, 27
Passover sacrifice, 32–33
patience/patience of God, 162–65
patriarchy, 82
Paul, 9, 20, 40–45
Pauw, Amy Plantinga, 99
peace, 60, 155, 166–67, 177, 185, 189, 197
Peels, H. G. L., 167nn27–28
Pelikan, Jaroslav, 115n63
Penchansky, David, 198
Peniel, 77–78
Pentateuch, 128
personality, 157
Pharisees, 97
Pharpar (el Awaj River), 61
philia, 20
Philip, 89–90
physics, 3n4
pigeons, 12–13
Pinn, Anthony B., 92n116
plants
    intelligence of, 79n66
    trees, 66–67, 201
Plato, 46, 122–23, 158–59
posture, 102
poverty, 23, 204
power, 107
    divine, 198
    dynamics of, xiiin8
    structures of, 205–6
praise, 57
prayer, 5, 70, 128, 182–83
    Lord's Prayer, 104n34
Preddy, William, 158n4
presence of God, 6, 56–60, 64, 108
prison, 204. *See also* concentration camps
prophets, 48, 60, 70, 74, 76, 119, 173n42
    Abraham as, 164–65
    See also individual names
Proverbs, book of, 81, 143
Psalms/the psalmist, xvii, 133, 141, 143, 158, 178–79
punishment, divine, 158, 165–75.
    See also flood, great; vengeance/vengefulness

Quinton, Anthony, 157–58

Index of Subjects 219

Rachel, 129n19
racism, 17, 204
Radcliffe, Timothy, xiiin9
Radner, Ephraim, 15n35
rage. *See* anger/divine anger; wrath, divine
rainbow, 161, 185
Rashi, 103
rationality, 145, 153–55
readiness potential, 100
reason and emotion, 153–55
Recalcati, Massimo, 200n31
redemption, 132n27, 161
Red Sea, 132n26
regret/divine regret, xvii, 117, 119–20, 150, 155, 161, 164, 170, 176, 186–87, 198, 202
  anger and, 146–47, 202
relationships, 45, 155, 201
  basis for, 201–3
  See also specific relationships, e.g., friendship
religion, 193n13, 200n30, 206
  animals and, 79n68
  monotheism, 197–98
  and violence, 134n31
  See also specific religions
remorse. *See* regret/divine regret
repentance, 99, 116, 137, 149, 168, 181–82
restitution, 170
restorative justice, 146, 150, 167, 206
retribution, 167. *See also* punishment, divine; vengeance/vengefulness
Reuben, 63
revelation, 64, 91
Revelation, book of, 90
revenge. *See* vengeance/vengefulness
rḥm, 133
righteousness, 143, 145n63, 163–64, 174
ritual/rituals, 6, 65, 68, 123–24, 151
  kua, 123–24
Roberts, J. Deotis, 92n116
rocks, 79
  God in stone, 66–72
Rogerson, John, 28n4, 55n5, 182–83
Rowley, H. H., xivn11
Russell, Bertrand, 1, 3–6, 8
Ruth/book of Ruth, 169n31, 199
Rwanda, 139

Sacks, Jonathan, 134n31, 197–98
Sacks, Oliver, 94n6
sacred objects (tabernacle/temple objects), 151
sacred poles, 69–70, 168
sacred spaces, 66, 68, 71
sacred stranger, 168
sacred texts, xiv, 5, 37, 83, 191, 193
sacrifice
  to God, 60, 73, 103, 112, 117–18, 149, 185
  pagan, 68
  Passover, 32–33
Sadducees, 97
sadness, 102, 124, 135–39, 148
salvation, 132, 174
Sam'al (ancient town), 96
Samaria, 69–70, 72–73
Samson, 169–71
Samuel/book of Samuel, 55–56, 72–73, 119–20
Samuel bar Nahman, Rabbi, 87
Satan, 103–4, 160–61, 184
Saul, 55–56, 113, 118–20, 129–31, 198–99
Sayers, Dorothy, 85
Schaefer, Donovan O., 79n68, 153
Scripture, Sacred. *See* Bible
Scruton, Roger, 79n69
Seibert, Eric A., 116n66
semen, 93
Seth, 80
sex (gender). *See* gender
sexual/erotic love, 84, 129–31, 135
sexual organs, 75, 81n73, 84, 88, 93, 136
Shamash, 58–59, 71
shame, 23
Sharp, Carolyn, xviii
Shaw, Susan M., 115n62
Shechem, 67–68
Shiloh, 73–74
sight, physical and theological, 8, 111. *See also* eyes/eyesight
sin, 87, 150
  after the flood, 117
  sin nature, 24n56
  See also forgiveness, divine; judgment, divine; punishment, divine
Sinai, Mount
  the God of, 174
  God's appearance at, 56
Sinaitic covenant, 64, 132, 134

Sinai Peninsula, 62
Sinai wilderness, 72, 196
slavery, 21, 106, 184, 196
sleep, 102
Smith, Mark, 35n20
Socrates, 158–59, 161, 163
Sodom, 163–64
solidarity, 186
Solomon, 97
Sommer, Benjamin D., ix, xv, 57, 70, 204
Sonderegger, Katherine, 205n41
Song of Songs, 84
sorcery, 168
sorrow. *See* regret/divine regret; sadness
Soskice, Janet, 48, 50
soul/souls, 96
South Africa, 18, 178
space, language and, 13
speech markers, 138
sperm, 93
Spieckermann, Hermann, 145–46
Spinoza, Baruch, 47
"spiritual unions," 130–31
status quo, 189
Sternberg, Robert, 201
stone, God in, 66–72
stories, 24, 47, 159, 189, 194, 201
strangers, 203n38
    love for, 134–35
    the sacred stranger, 168
Stump, Eleonore, 164
Stutz, Phil, 24n56
Sudan, 139
suffering, 136–37, 187
    calamity, 137, 195n19
    God as cosufferer, 196–98
    that humanity brings God, 155
    of Jesus, 187
    source of, 178–79
Suriano, Matthew J., 95n10
Systematic Theology: The Doctrine of God (Sonderegger), 205n41

tabernacle, 62–66, 81–82, 87
    handling of sacred objects, 151
Talmud, 103n31, 174
Tanakh. *See* Old Testament
Taylor, Charles, 66
tears. *See* sadness
temperament, 157

temple, Jerusalem, 62, 66–72, 148, 204
    "templeless period," 148–49
    temple objects, handling of, 151
    See also tabernacle
temple in Shiloh, 73n49
temptation, 104n34
Ten Commandments. *See* Decalogues
Terrien, Samuel, 65n28
tests, 103–7, 112–13
Tetragrammaton (YHWH), 82. *See also* Yahweh
texts, 95n10, 190n5
    sacred texts, xiv, 5, 37, 83, 191, 193
theism, 193n13
theology/theologies, 17–18, 24–25, 37–38, 128, 189–95, 205–6
    analytic, 201
    Deuteronomy and, 128
    doing theology, 206
    embodying/as embodied practice, 38, 206
    goal of, 191–92, 200
    of hermeneutic activity, 193–95
    and imagination, 189
    and knowing God, 190–91
    traditional, xiv–xvi, 38, 197
    See also specific descriptions, e.g., Eurocentric theologies
theophanies, temporary, 72–74
theosis, 203n38
Thich Nhat Hanh. *See* Hanh, Thich Nhat
Thomas Aquinas, 5
Thomas, Keith, 130
throne, divine, 58–59, 74–76, 90, 119
Thummim, 112–13
Tiamat, 54
time, language and, 13
transcendence, xvii, 50–51, 83–85, 196, 198, 201, 205
transformation, xviii, 160, 206. *See also* change
treaties, 129
trees, 66–67, 201
tribalism/tribal affiliation, 15, 90
Trible, Phyllis, 133
Trinity/Trinitarian thought, 31–32, 87, 92n114, 155n79, 201
trust (of Abraham), 103–4, 112–13
truth, 18–19, 202n36

Index of Subjects

Truth and Reconciliation Commission of South Africa, 18, 178
Tuan, Yi-Fu, xi
Tugwell, Simon, 5n10
Turkey, 96
Tutu, Desmond, 139, 178

Ugaritic literature, 35n20, 71, 81n73, 146n64
Ullendorff, Edward, 109n49
United States, 204. *See also* North America
universe, 3n4, 44–45, 127. *See also* creation
Ur, 35, 132
Urim, 112–13
Uzzah, 150–53, 164

Veldhuis, Niek, 35n20
Veling, Terry A., 205
vengeance/vengefulness, 76, 135, 165–71, 174–75, 178, 183, 185, 206
  nqm, 167, 169–70
violence, 15n35, 41, 123, 134n31, 143, 165, 169–71, 187, 201
vitality, 95–97, 99
Vriezen, Theodorus, 81

wager, 135n33, 160–61
Waltke, Bruce K., 117n70
Ward, Keith, 127
wars, 139
Washington, George, 183–84
Weil, Simone, 133n29
Weinandy, Thomas, 115–16
Weinfeld, Moshe, 132n25, 141n52

Wellum, Stephen, 29n5
Wheeler, John Archibald, 3n4
white supremacy, 191n7
Wilder, Amos Niven, 189n1
will, 100
  free, 23–25, 106
Williams, Delores S., 81n74
Williams, Rowan, 14, 116n67
Winner, Lauren, 39n31, 179–80
wisdom/divine wisdom, 81, 97. *See also* knowledge; mind of God
wisdom literature, 34
witness, biblical, xv, 10, 186
women, 81–83, 85
wood, God in, 66–72
Woolf, Virginia, 160
world
  as good, 155
  See also creation; earth
World Wars, 139
worship, 60–61, 65–66, 70–71, 73, 88, 164, 197
  those excluded from, 199
  See also idolatry; paganism/pagan worship
wrath, divine, 135–36, 140, 166, 168, 170, 175. *See also* anger/divine anger

Xenophanes, 47

Yahweh, xviii, 59–62, 65–76, 82, 116, 118, 138, 140, 146, 150, 182

Zechariah, book of, 174
Zeus, 66–67, 159
Zion/Mount Zion, 65, 174
Žižek, Slavoj, 6

www.ingramcontent.com/pod-product-compliance
Lightning Source LLC
Chambersburg PA
CBHW030254010526
44107CB00053B/1704